# Motorcycle Journeys Through
# Western Europe

## by Toby Ballentine

**Whitehorse Press**
Center Conway, New Hampshire

Photo credits: John Ashley Hall (p 26, 166), Toby Ballentine (p 122, front cover), Joseph Nonno (p 204), Ron Ayres (back cover), and photo p 272 courtesy Tourist Office of Spain in New York. All other photo credits are listed in the captions. The photos on the following pages are in the Wikimedia Commons—in the public domain: 53, 57, 284, 287; listed under the Creative Commons Attribution Share-Alike license: 55, 63, 69, 111, 197, 201, 216, 263, 265, 275, 277, 285, 288, 289, 291, 292, 293, 341; listed under GNU Free Document License: 42, 67, 68, 77, 89, 198, 255, 279, 313, 315, 317, 329, 332.

We recognize that some words, model names, and designations mentioned herein are the property of the trademark holder. We use them for identification purposes only.

Whitehorse Press books are also available at discounts in bulk quantity for sales and promotional use. For details about special sales or for a catalog of motorcycling books and videos, write to the publisher:
    Whitehorse Press
    107 East Conway Road
    Center Conway, New Hampshire 03813-4012
    Phone: 603-356-6556 or 800-531-1133
    E-mail: CustomerService@WhitehorsePress.com
    Internet: www.WhitehorsePress.com

ISBN-10: 1-884313-82-5
ISBN-13: 978-1-884313-82-0

5  4  3  2

Printed in China

# Acknowledgments

Europe is like a second home to me. I have met many wonderful people during my travels to that great continent and have fallen in love with its people, history, customs, and . . . .food! Even though I've visited Europe more times than I can count (the airlines should name a plane after me!), I always look forward with anticipation to my next trip. My thanks go to my many wonderful friends and family who live there and the hospitality shown me over the years. Thanks also to Whitehorse Press for their help (and patience) as we took this project from infancy to fruition. Your support has been invaluable. I would like to thank all my fellow travelers who had the foresight to take some photos of Europe while I just enjoyed the ride and only took "mental shots" (never do that again!). Thanks for coming to the rescue! In particular, I would like to thank Patsy Scott for her suggestions and help with the manuscript and in contributing/selecting the photos for each of the chapters. *Merci beacoup!*

And, Mom, thanks for instilling in me a desire not only to travel, but also to learn and grow and, hopefully, become a more tolerant and better person because of the many journeys we took together. This book is dedicated to you. I miss you.

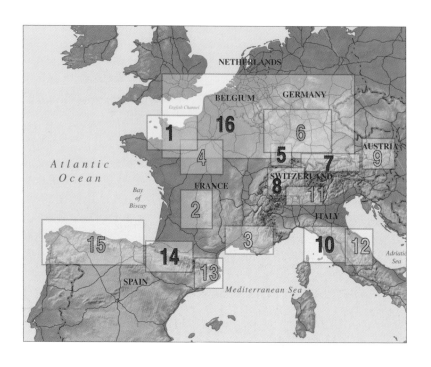

# Contents

# Introduction

Just after WWII my father spent two years in Nuremburg, Germany as part of the U. S. Army Occupation Forces. Since he was an officer, my mom and oldest brother got to accompany him. They lived in a typical German home (not on base) and had a typical German landlady named Frau Mann. During their stay in Germany, my parents fell in love with Europe and created many long lasting relationships. When my dad came back to the states at the end of his tour, he used the GI Bill to attend UC Berkley and became a 6th grade school teacher. My mom did odd jobs to earn some extra income

*Looking down from a hillside vineyard, the quaint town of Cochem, Germany, adorns the Mosel River Valley. Photo by Toby Ballentine.*

and between the two of them saved enough money for our family to visit Europe many times while I was growing up (I'm the youngest). We had a grand time exploring the continent with both my parents being our own personal escorts and history guides. Another thing I learned was how to do it inexpensively—you can't afford much on a teacher's salary!

In the summer of 1979, between my freshman and sophomore year in college, I took two months off and headed to Europe on my own. My parents were living in Holland so I made that my home base and traveled from Amsterdam to Sicily and Spain to Germany. My Eurail pass and backpack became my best friends as the European countryside glided by and I once again became enthralled with the history and culture of this great continent. Over the past 30 years, I've been back at least 30 times visiting friends and relatives . . . and renting motorcycles. Now the real fun began! Traveling across Europe on a motorcycle is one of life's purist joys. Rediscovering the continent on two wheels has been a dream come true for me. The journeys

*The northern coast of Spain with its blue waters and red-tiled roofed villages is a favorite vacation spot for Europeans. Photo courtesy of the Tourist Office of Spain in New York.*

*Castles like the Neuschwanstein, located in Füssen, Germany, can be found along many of the rivers in southern Germany. Photo by Cherise Ballentine.*

in this book are a result of all these travels over the past quarter century plus (I don't feel that old!). Many thanks to my parents and children for keeping the dream alive and well!

Crisscrossing Europe as both a traveler and motorcyclist has taught me many valuable lessons—lessons that I am going to share with you that will make your trip to Europe easier, less expensive, and a lot more enjoyable. As a motorcyclist, the first lesson I learned was that most travel guides are what I call "destination" travel guides. These books are very thorough in the "what to see and where to visit" department for a particular city, but don't elaborate much on how to get there. Many tourists spend a hectic summer taking trains, autobahns, and airplanes to London, Paris, Amsterdam, or Munich and neglect the small cities and backcountry roads because they are too anxious to arrive at the next destination. This book will focus on what I consider are some of the most scenic motorcycle routes in Europe as you travel to your destination. As a motorcyclist I have always agreed with the mantra "it's the journey, not the destination" that truly makes a trip worthwhile.

*Old timbered structures are commonplace in northern France. The family store is typically located on the bottom level and the living quarters are above.*
*Photo by John Ashley Hall.*

The second lesson I learned was that Europe *can* be done a whole lot cheaper than you ever imagined. You can rent a bike in Europe for about the same price as a rental in the U. S. (even at the current exchange rate). You can find very comfortable accommodations for $50 to $80 per night for two. You can camp in very stylish well-maintained campsites for $15 to $30 per night for two. All it takes is a little planning, a little courage, a positive attitude, and some help from this book. I will guide you through the process in this introductory section and then share about 17 motorcycle routes through central Europe in the remaining chapters of this book. You decide what trip you prefer, combine it with a few others if you like, line up your bike rental, and then take that European motorcycle trip you've always dreamed of.

This book complements John Hermann's masterful *Motorcycle Journeys Through the Alps & Beyond* in the Whitehorse Press Motorcycle Journeys series and I'd like you to think of the two books as companions. Though both books are about motorcycling in Europe, Hermann's book is an excellent comprehensive coverage of the motorcycling roads in Europe's alpine areas (the Swiss Alps, the Pyrénées on the French-Spanish border, the Picos de Europa in Spain, and on the island of Corsica). This book explores a much broader area of western Europe and places as much emphasis on experiencing the history and culture of the different countries in western Europe as on the ride. The trips described in this book are multi-day loops, each one organized around a different theme, such as the chateaux along the Loire River, World War II battlefields, or the hill towns of Italy. If the alpine areas visited in this book entice you to explore further, I heartily recommend Hermann's book as your guide.

*Pick up fresh vegetables from the central market to go with your bread and cheese, and you have the ingredients for a delicious (and inexpensive!) meal. Photo by Toby Ballentine.*

## HOW THIS BOOK IS ORGANIZED

Many of the routes included in this book are well known in Europe, but are less familiar to those living outside the continent. Have you heard of the Romantische Strasse, Loire Valley, La Route des Crêtes, or Strada Chiantigiana? If so, then let me ask you this, have you driven them on a motorcycle? Have you felt the cool summer breeze blowing through your open visor as fairy-tale-like chateaux appear on the horizon? Have you scraped your boots winding down the Mosel River Valley as a medieval castle looms ahead? Have you climbed the hills of Tuscany trying to keep your eyes on the road but are distracted by an ancient walled city clinging tenaciously to the cliffs overhead? If not, then this book is for you. I am going to lay out some of the best motorcycle routes and destinations in Europe that include all of the above, then wrap them together with some beautiful blacktopped asphalt.

This book will be organized into five separate regions—France, Germany, Austria/Switzerland, Italy, and Spain. Each region will have one or two airline accessible metropolitan hubs from which you can pick up your rental bike. Two to five detailed motorcycle routes and itineraries will be laid out from each hub. These trips are an average of one week in length and

*The chateaux in the Loire Valley are surrounded by beautifully kept gardens.*
*Photo by John Ashley Hall.*

*Many European towns like this one in northern Italy have narrow streets that are the right size for a motocycle. Photo by Toby Ballentine.*

cover several hundred miles. If you have longer than a week, the routes can be linked together to form a web of several week long journeys that are two, three, or four weeks in length (up to two months if you have the time). For example, let's say you fly into Munich, Germany, and want to start with the popular Alpine Road. You can link this trip with the Romantic Road or Neckar River Valley going north, or head south on the Blue Danube route in Austria and then west to Switzerland and the French Alps or farther south to the hill towns of Tuscany, Italy. Just so you know, these itineraries steer clear of the really large cities. The focus is on less populous, history- and

*A bird's eye view of the city of Brugge in Belgium. Photo by John Ashley Hall.*

culture-rich cities and towns like Pamplona (running of the bulls) in Spain, Avignon in France or Berchtesgaden in Germany. If you want to make detours into large cities like Vienna, Zürich, or Paris be my guest. Just don't get caught in a roundabout, you may spend the rest of your trip there!

One note about distances from the European perspective—in my opinion, if you want to enjoy and absorb these journeys, a week's trip should only be between 700 to 900 miles. That may not seem like much on a bike, but I firmly believe a more leisurely pace will be a lot more rewarding. Just remember, Europe is not like the U.S. where wide-open spaces are commonplace and the next town is 200 miles down the road. Remote villages, medieval fortresses, grand cathedrals, and picturesque castles are frequent and another one is often only 20 miles down the road. And each one has its own history and character. Back in medieval times, 20 miles was at least a day's journey and often separated totally different kingdoms. So slow it down, and spend an afternoon exploring Siena or an evening enjoying *tapas* in Logroño. The choice is yours.

I conclude the book with two final chapters on what I call the Band of Brothers Motorcycle Tour and the Grand Tour. The Band of Brothers Tour follows the journeys of the World War II veterans made famous by Stephen Ambrose's book and the HBO miniseries. This is a great trip because not only does it delve into some fascinating history, but takes you across several countries starting at the D-day beaches in France and then ending up in the beautiful Austrian alps of Zell am See. The final trip, the Grand Tour, links several trips together to give you a comprehensive adventure across all of central Europe. This trip of a lifetime takes at least six to eight weeks. After you finish reading this book you first will have to decide which area seems most appealing, then you will need to check with your boss to see how much time you can take off!

*Here we are in the birthplace of Belgian waffles. There is nothing like the real thing. Photo by Mark Allred.*

## GETTING THERE AND MOTORCYCLE RENTALS

Many of you may have already been to Europe. Nowadays, buying a ticket is as simple as a mouse click away. Just be sure to do your research ahead of time! Planning is the key ingredient when preparing for a motorcycle trip to Europe. The site I use most often to check flights is www.kayak.com, but there are dozens to choose from. Pick the one you feel most comfortable with, then begin the process. Remember that high season is July and August. At that time, it seems all of Europe is off on vacation! Ticket prices command the highest levels during the summer. If at all possible, try to go in September and October. These are great months to travel in Europe, especially in Italy, France, and Spain. Even early September can be perfect in the Swiss Alps. Not only is it less crowded, but also you have no problem finding a place to stay without reservations and many prices are discounted. Regardless, anytime is great from about April to October. Just be prepared for inclement weather and if it's too cold, then point the bike south and find that warmer weather. It's really not that far!

There are numerous motorcycle rental businesses in Europe. Just do an Internet search and numerous hits will pop up. I prefer starting in Germany, Holland, Spain, or Switzerland. Some of the rental outfits and websites are as follows:

*When you arrive at your day's destination go to Tourist Information and find a place in your price range to stay for the night. Photo by Toby Ballentine.*

*You come away from Versailles thinking that all the French royalty did in the 1500s was build chateaux, dress up, and party. What a life! Photo by John Ashley Hall.*

- Adventure Motorcycle Tours and Rentals offers bike rentals throughout Europe. See their website at www.rental-motorcycle.com.
- Bosenberg Motorcycle Excursions offer rentals in Germany, Italy, and Switzerland. See their website at www.bosenberg.com.
- Iberian Moto Tours rents bikes in Spain. Their website is www.bmwmotorental.com.
- Alps Tours by Moto-Charlie is based in Thun, Switzerland, and have some of the best rates in Europe. Their website is www.moto-charlie.com.

There are also several motorcycle touring companies that are all-inclusive i.e., motorcycle rental, tour guide, food, and accommodations in one package. A bit more expensive than I like, but they do a great job.

- Ayres Adventures offers tours throughout the world. It's a first class, great operation run by Ron Ayres. See www.ronayres.com.
- Edelweiss Bike Travel originally started in the Alps and now offers tours across the globe. See www.edelweissbike.com.
- Beach's Motorcycle Adventures also started in Europe and their website is www.bmca.com.

Depending on the type of motorcycle you prefer, the cost is about $100 to $200 per day (also fluctuates depending on the exchange rate) to rent a bike. Be sure to check your stateside insurance coverage before leaving, but most likely you will need to buy full coverage in Europe. This can be done when you rent the bike. All types of bikes are available, but often go by different names in Europe. Models not found in the U.S. are quite popular in Europe. Check the manufacturer's website for specifics on these different model types. The bikes I have rented in Europe include the BMW R1200RT, R1200GS, Kawasaki Concours, Honda ST Pan European and the Honda Varadero. I've never had a problem with any of them. Be sure the rental includes lockable bags as well.

You can also rent riding gear in Europe, but I would highly recommend taking your own. I remember once trying to save on packing and did not take my helmet. Big mistake! I rented one that didn't quite fit and ended up with a headache just about every day. It's like wearing a brand new pair of running shoes on that long anticipated marathon. Ouch! So if at all possible, take your own helmet and riding gear. Your own gear is already broken in and will make the ride that much more comfortable. And be sure, I

*While traveling through northern Spain you will find many small villages tucked into the valleys between the hills. Photo courtesy of the Tourist Office of Spain in New York.*

*The red wine produced in the Rioja region of Spain is the mainstay of its economy.*
*Photo courtesy of the Tourist Office of Spain in New York.*

*This is a typical campground in the Bavarian Alps. Not a bad view for 10 bucks a night! Photo by Rachelle Ballentine.*

repeat, be sure your gear is rainproof. Chaps will not cut it in my opinion. It rains frequently in Europe and you will get wet! Full riding gear is an absolute and remember, wearing a helmet is mandatory in Europe!

## ACCOMMODATIONS AND CAMPING IN EUROPE

When I travel though Europe I always take camping gear, but keep it to a minimum. All I usually take is a small tent, sleeping bag, air mattress, and a pillow (gotta have my pillow!). That's it—no cooking gear, no chair, no picnic table—no room for the extras! Other minor necessities like a towel, soap, and eating utensils are also taken but these are not cumbersome and can be stuffed in just about anywhere. There are usually small grocery stores and inexpensive restaurants at the campsites. Some of the best food I've eaten has been at these campground cafes. In Italy I remember buying some lasagna at the local cafe and it was to die for! So don't think you need to go to town and eat at an upscale restaurant to enjoy a good meal. Quite honestly, my favorite meal is finding a local bakery, buying a fresh baguette or dark rye bread, then dropping by the local grocery store for some fixins! Boursin cheese, brie, salami, fresh tomatoes, and a little *johanesbeersaft* (non-alcoholic red currant soft drink) and I'm one happy camper (especially after some dark Belgian chocolate!). Usually, I'll find a local park, sit on a bench, and do some people watching while enjoying my meal. I'm also a sucker for sitting outside at the local cafe for a drink and dessert. It's a great way to relax and a great way to meet the locals.

The camping areas in Europe are well kept and cost about $10 to $15 per night per person. There are more than 40,000 campgrounds throughout the continent and rarely do you need a reservation—motorcyclists can fit in just about anywhere. Usually the tent site is on a grassy field with no specific markings. If the campground is full, be prepared, your tent could be right next to your neighbors. The showers and facilities are clean and well serviced, although, sometimes you may need a token for hot water. Often laundry facilities and game rooms are also located on the premises. One of the best resources I've ever used to locate campsites in Europe is Mike and Terri Church's *Travelers Guide to European Camping*. The book is very comprehensive with evaluations and directions to hundreds of campsites. Their website is www.rollinghomes.com.

Although I camp a lot through Europe, sometimes staying in a clean room is a nice change and well worth the investment. My preference is the bed and breakfasts offered by the local populace. Often while driving my bike through a small village, I will see a sign posted out front advertising ZIMMER FREI or CHAMBRES D'HÔTES or just plain old BED & BREAKFAST. I'll stop and inquire, using my limited knowledge of the language (usually just some form of sign language) and end up staying the night or two or three. I love these places. Not only do I get a good night's rest, but the hosts are almost always very polite and helpful. The breakfasts are great and the prices are very reasonable. Depending on the country, bed & breakfasts cost around $30 to $50 per night (not bad!). If you want to stay in a particular town center, go to the local tourist info and ask them for a list of places to stay. Be sure to give them a price range, otherwise they will start with the most expensive hotels first. My advice is to mix it up . . . camp a few nights . . . stay in a bed & breakfast a few nights . . . splurge on that fancy hotel one night. It's amazing how much money you will save by doing it this way.

## MONEY/LANGUAGE/CUSTOMS

The euro is now Europe's comprehensive currency of exchange. This makes it a whole lot easier for travelers like us. Rather than exchange francs into marks or guilders into lire, there is now just one type of currency. So, no

*We are enjoying paella (rice casserole) in a typical Spanish square while a local entertainer sings and plays the accordian in the background. Photo by Toby Ballentine.*

more coming home with pockets full of change! Debit cards work very well in most European towns and cities. Be sure to carry a fair amount of cash on you since many stores and cafes do not take credit cards due to the fee charged. Credit card use is becoming more commonplace, but always have some reserve cash on you. Also one word of caution—bring an extra debit card just in case. And be sure the other card is tied to a different banking system, i.e., Cirrus vs. the Plus network. For the most part my card has worked without a hitch, but on an occasion or two it has not. Boy was I glad I had brought a substitute card! You may also want to ask the bank to raise the daily limit; $300 bucks may not cut it when you want to buy and ship that cuckoo clock home and the store doesn't take Visa or MasterCard.

Credit cards are accepted in most business establishments. Just remember that most credit card companies do charge a foreign transaction fee each time you use the card. Call them before you go and ask for a waiver (usually won't happen) and at the same time inform them of your travel plans. Don't want them canceling your card in Avignon, France because they think it has been stolen (not kidding, this has happened to me!)

One final note of caution—make copies of all of your pertinent documents, i.e., passport, credit cards and debit cards (front and back), and stash the copies someplace safe. Pick-pocketing is commonplace in Europe. If stolen or lost, immediately call the card company to let them know. They will work with you on how and where to pick up a new card. FYI, I also carry my wallet in my front pocket and have a money belt under my shirt for important documents. Better to be safe than sorry!

## DRIVING IN EUROPE

First things first—don't forget there are several different languages in Europe so be sure to learn the correct translation for unleaded gas. Don't be putting diesel in your bike. Can't tell you how close I've come to doing that . . . countless times! So double-check before topping off your tank. A couple other tidbits of advice—never pass on the right and don't turn right on red even after coming to a complete stop. The left lane is strictly for passing and is strictly enforced and a right turn is often not allowed on red. I wouldn't take the chance.

On a more positive note, drivers are usually more aware of motorcyclists in Europe than in the States. They will actually get out of your way when lane sharing and sometimes even smile and wave at you! Motorcyclists are also very friendly to each other. One custom I learned in France is what I call the "left leg wave." Rather than take your hand off the handlebars to acknowledge your fellow motorcyclist, merely lift your left leg off the peg and do a little wave. Definitely safer and easier than using your left hand!

Oh yes. Photo radar has invaded Europe. If you rent a bike, BEWARE! Can't tell you how many times I've come home after thinking the rental bill has been paid and on the next bill I get another surprise charge from a photo speed trap. Apparently, there is no such thing as a rental driver's Bill of Rights in Europe. They snap your mug; you pay the bill—no exceptions. Be careful and keep a look out for the photo traps!

## MAPS AND DIRECTIONS

Included in each chapter is a map outlining the route for that particular journey. Please be advised that even though the maps give fairly specific directions, they are primarily for orientation purposes. When my traveling buddies ask me for directions, I will usually circle an area of interest on a map then highlight the roads. That is basically what I have done in this book. This is not the GPS Bible to every single intersection and turn lane in Europe, rather, it provides a framework from which to tour Europe on your own. Maps are still needed and suggested as you plot out the finer details of your trip. So break down and buy that Michelin map and use it in conjunction with this book. Have a little faith in yourself, but remember if you do get lost, not to worry! Enjoy the ride anyway because even the bad roads on these trips are fantastic! Some of the best roads I've discovered in Europe are the ones I originally got lost on. So keep smiling, take a few deep breaths, ask a few questions, and before you know it you'll be on the right track again.

*Riding in the Swiss Alps is like a dream come true. Photo by Ron Ayres.*

*Don't worry! Between this book and your Michelin maps you'll know which way to go! Photo by Bradley Clark.*

## ONE FINAL NOTE

One final piece of advice—this book is only one source of information about traveling through Europe. Do your own research. There are many excellent books, just go to the travel section in your local bookstore. Books I use frequently, which contain in-depth resource material, are those in the Lonely Planet series and those by Rick Steves. And, if I were you, buy some maps. GPS is great, but in my opinion maps provide a better overview for the journey. Michelin has some of the best maps of Europe I know. I have been using them for years. Can't tell ya how many times I've scotch-taped them together. Maybe I'm just old fashioned, but there is nothing like the look and smell of an old map to get you motivated and excited about your next journey across Europe! *Bon voyage!*

# France

The thing I like most about France is its diversity. Most people go to Paris and that's it. France has so much more to offer and is one of the most visited countries in Europe by Europeans. That tells you something. If the locals vacation here, then there must be more than just one famous city in this huge country (relatively speaking). The chapters in this section explore the different parts of France and take you away from the large cities. You can visit coastlines, Alps, Roman ruins, medieval walled cities, vineyards, battlegrounds, and still only touch the surface. And the best part is France has thousands of campsites that make your journey convenient and inexpensive.

Motorcycles can be rented in most major metropolitan areas from Paris in the north to Marseilles and Nice in the south. The roads are well maintained and safe. Although toll roads are abundant, my journeys focus on the free "N" and "D" auto routes that crisscross the country. Rarely do I take you on a toll road—better twisties and a whole lot cheaper that way! Drivers for the most part are courteous in France, but speedy. And remember at the unmarked intersection, the vehicle on the right has the right of way.

The best place to buy gas is at the *hypermarches* or huge supermarkets. You can buy everything you need in these stores and the gas is definitely cheaper than buying along the auto routes. And, whatever you do, be sure to buy a fresh loaf of bread or baguette at the local *boulangeires* (bakery), then drop by the *boucherie* (butcher shop) for some fresh ham or salami, and finish it up with some dessert at the *patisseries* (pastry shop). I guarantee you will not go hungry in France. *Bon apetite* and *bon voyage!*

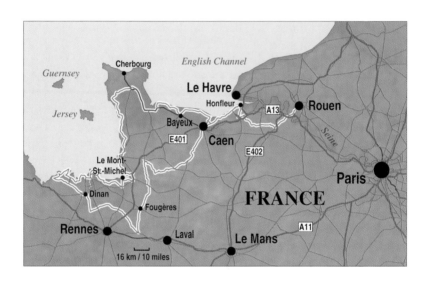

# D-Day and World War II Battleground Tour

**Distance:**   *1064 km/665 miles*
**Suggested Time Frame:**   *5–7 days*

Normandy and the D-Day Tour is one of my favorite rides. I have always been a history buff, and WWII has been an area of personal study for many years. The invasion of Normandy along the D-Day beaches was essential to the Allies in obtaining a foothold onto the European continent. The battles and memorials dedicated to the soldiers who fought along this crucial front are remarkable and well concentrated in a relatively small area making them easy to visit. Although this area was ravaged by WWII, many isolated towns and villages were not so devastated. Consequently, several medieval cities are still very well preserved providing an even deeper historical backdrop to Normandy and Brittany. The villages along the way have a unique ambiance—a mixture of both French and British influences. Best of all, the roads are well-maintained two-laners that wind across bounteous farmlands, coastal beaches, and wooded highlands.

This journey starts in Rouen, which is about 130km/80 miles from Paris or about 1.5 hours on the autobahn. The trip heads to Honfleur on the coast, winds by the D-Day beaches to Ste.-Mère-Église and to the fabulous abbey at Le Mont-St.-Michel before heading back through medieval Brittany and Normandy's forested hills to Caen. At Caen catch the autobahn back to Paris, which is about 232 km/145 miles or 2.5 hours away.

I would suggest about 5 to 7 days to complete this route, which is about 100–130 miles per day. I know that doesn't sound like much, but after wandering around the timbered streets of Rouen, eating seafood in Honfleur, spending some time at the WWII museum in Caen, visiting the beaches and Pointe du Hoc, then going back in time at Le Mont-St.-Michel, Dinan, and Fougères, you may think 5 to 7 days is not enough. And remember I'm taking you on the country roads, not the high-speed freeways.

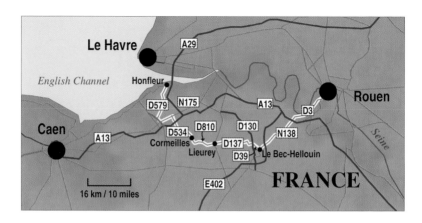

## Day 1  Rouen to Honfleur

All right, let's get started. First stop is Rouen. When you arrive at the outskirts of town follow the signs to CENTRE-VILLE or just keep an eye out for the tall gothic cathedral spires. Find a parking spot then begin a short walking tour of the city. Although ravaged by war, much was preserved and rebuilt in strict adherence to the original layout. This city ripples with history from William the Conqueror to Joan of Arc. For those who have seen *The Messenger* you can visit the old marketplace where Joan of Arc was burned at the stake. The most remarkable site is the Cathedral of Notre Dame. It is located in the very well restored old center. The Tourist Information (TI) is located just across from the Cathedral. Grab a walking tour map and enjoy the 2,000 years of history in Rouen. If you really like what you see, check out the *chambres d'hôtes* (bed and breakfasts) at the TI and spend the night!

Leaving Rouen can be a bit confusing, but I usually head out on the N138 then connect with the D3 and go through Grand-Couronne past Moulineaux and then after a few kilometers turn left on N138 again. Follow the N138 to the D39 and turn right to Le Bec-Hellouin. Total distance is about 56 km/35 miles.

Le Bec-Hellouin is an old monastic village set on the hillside of the Risle Valley. Noted as a theological center, several archbishops of Canterbury were educated here. The beautiful scenery and half-timbered houses make this a pleasant stop before heading on to Honfleur. If you have time, visit the abbey where monastic products are sold from the various workshops.

Continue on D39 through town and then join up with D130 for a quick left on D137 to Lieury. At Lieury the road changes to D810 to Cormeilles. At Cormeilles take D534 to N175. Turn left and then right at the A132/D579

*Night falls on the quaint harbor at Honfleur, France. Photo by John Ashley Hall.*

intersection. Follow D579 into Honfleur. These roads are for the most part gentle, winding country roads flowing across lush Normandy farmlands.

In Honfleur, make your first stop the Tourist Information, which is located by the public library on the Quai Lepaulmier. It is open until 6:30 and there is a long list of *chambres d'hôtes*. Many are outside of town, so find one that is best suited for you. Give them a price range to narrow the selection down if you are really on a tight budget. There is also a municipal campground just outside of town on the D34C toward the coast. It is conveniently located and only about 1 km from the harbor.

Honfleur is a picturesque town located right on the coast and is a great place to relax and unwind. Undamaged by WWII, the town carries its own charm and is a delight to visit. After finding a place to stay, wander around the old cobblestone streets and enjoy a fabulous seafood dinner at one of the many restaurants. You still may be suffering from jet lag, so get a good meal and a good night's rest before hitting the history-packed WWII beaches tomorrow.

### Day 1 – Rouen to Honfleur  112 km/70 miles

Start in Rouen.

Leave Rouen on the N138 south, connect with the D3, then get back on N138 and D39 to Le Bec-Hello,uin.

At Le Bec-Hellouin get on D39 to D130, then make a quick left on the D137 to Lieury.

At Lieury follow D810 to Cormeilles. Take D534 to N175 and turn left.

At the A132/D579 intersection turn right and then right again on D579 to Honfleur.

Arrive Honfleur on the Normandy Coast.

## DAY 2  Honfleur to Bayeux

Leave Honfleur on the D34C and then hook up with D513 to Caen. This coastal road winds beside beaches and through the resort communities of Trouville and Deauville. Stop for some breakfast pastries or go for a morning walk along one of the beaches. Continue past Cabourg to Caen.

Caen is about 82 km/50 miles from Honfleur and was a heavily contested battleground during the D-Day invasion. Originally one of the initial objectives of General Montgomery, the city wasn't captured for more than a month after the landings. Totally destroyed during WWII, Caen has been rebuilt and is now a thriving community of more than 100,000 people. I would suggest visiting the WWII museum, Le Memorial. It is well worth a visit and will definitely help you gain a better appreciation of the tragedies and sacrifices made during this horrific period. The museum is located off the ring road. Just follow the signs to LE MEMORIAL.

Our next stop will be Pegasus Bridge. Head back on the ring road to the D513 turnoff to Cabourg, then turn left on D37. Follow the signs to Pegasus Bridge. As you drive down D37 you will also see signs to the Airborne Museum. The actual bridge over the canal was replaced in 1994 and moved to this location in Ranville as a memorial to the soldiers who sacrificed their lives to capture this critical objective on D-Day. Visit the museum and get a feel for this daring attack. Continue on D37 to D514 and then cross the new bridge over the canal. The first bridge is the Horsa Bridge and the second is the new Pegasus Bridge. Both were objectives of the British Airborne forces. Originally called the Benouville Bridge, it was renamed "Pegasus" in honor of the British forces who attacked and captured it on D-Day. This remarkable feat was depicted in the classic movie, *The Longest Day*. The Café

*The seafood in Honfleur, France, is to die for, especially when eaten in an outdoor cafe next to the sea. Photo by John Ashley Hall.*

Gondrée, the first home to be liberated on D-day, is located on the western side of the Pegasus Bridge (second canal). Last time I visited, the daughter, who was a young child during the invasion, was still running the place.

**Day 2 – Honfleur to Bayeux  128 km/80 miles**

Leave Honfleur and take D34C and D513 to Trouville.
Arrive Trouville. Continue on D513 to Deauville.
Arrive Deauville. Continue to Caen on D513.
Arrive Caen. Go to the WWII Museum.
Leave Caen toward Cabourg on D513, turn left on D37.
Visit the Pegasus Bridge and Airborne Museum, then continue on D37.
Turn right on D514 to Ouistreham.
At Ouistreham turn left and continue on D514 along the coast to Arromanches.
Arrive Arromanches. Turn left on D516 to Bayeux.
Arrive Bayeux.

*The Bayeux Cathedral was built in the 11th century and is a classic example of Norman Gothic architecture. The building is a French national monument. Photo by John Ashley Hall.*

Continue north on D514 to Ouistreham and then turn left on the coast to Arromanches. This part of the trip will pass the Sword, Juno, and Gold beaches. These beaches were invaded by the British and Canadian Forces on D-Day. Utah and Omaha beaches are farther west of Arromanches. The ride along the coast winds through small villages with flowers blossoming along footpaths and under windowsills. Quite a different picture from what the area must have been experiencing on June 6, 1944.

When you arrive at Arromanches, take a breather and visit the small museum on the beach. Once the site of the world's largest artificial harbor during WWII, the town is now a small beach community with shops and restaurants lining the main street. Remains of the huge concrete blocks used to form the breakwater can still be seen. The town is charming and makes a great spot to grab a bite or something to drink.

Veer left at Arromanches on the D516 to Bayeux. Located on the Aure River, Bayeux dates back to Roman times. The city was not bombed during the war, so the timbered houses, cobblestone streets, and town center give Bayeux a warm, inviting ambiance. Check out the TI on the Pont St.-Jean for some *chambres d'hôtes* and pick up some excellent WWII guides. There is also a nice camping area about a 15-minute walk from the town center called Bayeux Camping Municipal. It's located just off the ring road Bd Périphérique d'Eindhoven. Fees are about six dollars per person. This city campsite is very clean with nice hot showers, municipal pool right next door, and a grocery store just across the street.

Bayeux makes a great base to tour the D-Day beaches/memorials and is also a very historic town itself. So spend some time in the city, visit the gothic cathedral, and the very famous Bayeux Tapestry depicting William the Conqueror's rise to power. But most importantly, treat yourself to some crepes at one of many *crêperies* lining the narrow cobblestone streets. I couldn't get enough of them. You may have to stay more than just one night!

# Day 3  Bayeux to Le Mont-St.-Michel

Now that you're over your jet lag, get up bright and early, as this is a big day. You will visit the American Cemetery at Coleville-St.-Laurent, Omaha Beach, Pointe du Hoc, Ste.-Mère-Église then swing around the peninsula along the Atlantic coast to Le Mont-St.-Michel. Total distance is about 276 km/173 miles.

Take the D6 out of Bayeux toward the coast and then turn left on D514 toward the cemetery. The American Cemetery is not on D514 per se, but on a loop road and bluff that overlooks Omaha Beach. There will be signs directing you to it.

A word of advice—be prepared. Since my father and two of my uncles served in the war, visiting this site was an emotional experience for me. Coming onto the immaculate grounds, you can feel the sacred majesty of this place. More than 9,400 spotless markers define the ultimate sacrifice made by these young men. Wander between the countless rows and view the diagrams/narrative at the center of this memorial. The enormity of the invasion was awe-inspiring. It was the largest amphibious assault in the

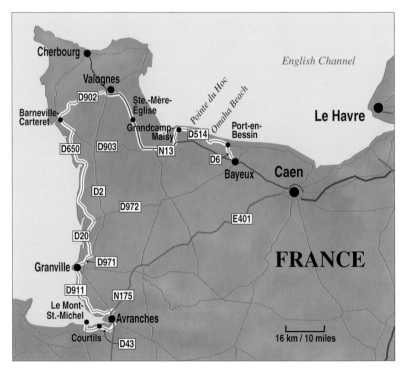

*The flags of Poland, Belgium, Canada, and the United States of America fly over Omaha Beach. Photo by John Ashley Hall.*

history of mankind. For those who saw *Saving Private Ryan*, the Niland brothers on whom the story is loosely based are found at Row 15 graves 11 and 12. Walk to the edge of the bluff and try to visualize the chaos and destruction that must have reigned on June 6, 1944. Honor their memory.

Continue down D514 and follow the signs to Omaha Beach. Drive slowly. Take a walk on the beach. Continue on to Pointe du Hoc where

### Day 3 – Bayeux to Le Mont-St.-Michel    276 km/173 miles

Leave Bayeux. Take D6 to Port-en-Bessin.

Arrive Port-en-Bessin. Turn left on D514 to Plage d'Omaha (Omaha Beach), American Cemetery and Point du Hoc. Continue on D514.

Arrive Grandcamp-Maisy, continue left on D514 to N13.

Turn right on N13 to Ste.-Mère-Église.

Continue on N13 to Valognes.

Arrive Valognes. Take the D902 to Barneville-Carteret.

Arrive Barneville-Carteret, go south on the D903, keep right on the D650, D20 and D971 to Granville.

Arrive Granville. Take the D911 to Avranches.

Arrive Avranches, take the D103/N175 to the D43 turnoff to Courtils/Bas-Courtils and then left on D75 to Le Mont-St.-Michel.

Arrive Le Mont-St.-Michel.

many bunkers still remain. The ground is still uneven from the heavy bombardment. Even though the guns were not at Pointe du Hoc but had been moved farther inland, the Rangers quickly responded and destroyed them before the Germans could put them into action. This saved countless lives. Of the 225 Rangers who scaled the cliffs only 90 survived.

One other WWII site along this route is Ste.-Mère-Église. Continue on D514 and turn right on N13. This town's claim to fame is two-fold. Firstly, it was the first town liberated by the Allies and, secondly, the paratrooper, John Steel, got his parachute caught in the church's steeple. For those of you interested in stained glass windows, inside the church is one of the Virgin Mary surrounded by paratroopers!

Continue on N13 to Valognes then swing around the ring road and take D902 to Barneville-Carteret. At this point you will be following the shoreline and the sandy beaches of the Atlantic. Take D903 south, then connect with D650, D20, and D971 to Granville. The D971 is also a very pleasant drive along the coast as you make your way to Granville. From Granville take the D911 to Avranches then the D103/N175 south to the D43

*The American Cemetery is on a grassy field next to Omaha Beach on the coast of Normandy. Photo by John Ashley Hall.*

*This memorial is dedicated to the troops who gave their lives on D-Day.*
*Photo by John Ashley Hall.*

intersection. Veer west back to the coast. The road changes to D75 at Courtils then D275 on to Le Mont-St.-Michel. You won't miss the abbey. The island appears on the horizon as if it's floating on top of the ocean.

You will probably be arriving late in the day at Le Mont-St.-Michel. As you get closer, keep your eyes open for *chambres d'hôtes* in the small towns approaching Le Mont-St.-Michel. The TI is located on the island and although it has a very comprehensive list, it can be swamped with tourists. Ardevon is a small town just a few kilometers from the abbey and is your best bet. The closer you get, the more difficult it is to find something. There is also a private campground just behind the Hotel Vert at the intersection of D27 and D976 (Camping du Mont-St.-Michel). It's grassy and only 2.5 km from the abbey.

Keep in mind that Le Mont-St.-Michel is extremely touristy, so the best time to visit is during the off season or at least during the weekdays. Coming at night is the best time as the floodlights create a magical kingdom (and I'm not talking about Disneyland). The abbey is open until midnight, so if you're not too tired, spend an enchanted evening at Le Mont-St.-Michel. Sleep in the next morning and continue your journey to Dinan after a good night's rest.

# Day 4 Le Mont-St.-Michel to Dinan

Today's ride will be a bit more leisurely. Start by sleeping late, then take the D976 toward Beauvoir and then west on the N176. Just a few kilometers down the road take D797 to St.-Broladre. At St.-Broladre take a left on D80 then right to Mont-Dol and follow the summit road to the top. This road is short but lets you lean in and out on some delightful curves before climbing to the summit. From here the views are spectacular. Panoramas of the Atlantic and Le Mont-St.-Michel unfold before you. There is a chapel and some windmills located at the top as well. Perfect place to snack on that chocolate bar you've been saving. Hopefully, it's not melted!

Wind back down the mountain and take D155 north to the coast. As the scenery changes from sandy beaches to rugged cliffs, the road also changes from D155 to D76 to D201 coming into St.-Malo. Follow the signs to Dinard on N137 and D168 over the bay. From Dinard take the D786 along the coast all the way to Port-à-la-Duc. After a few clicks head up the small peninsula on D16 to Cap Fréhel. Take a detour to the fortress at La Latte. Built in the 1300s (and used in several Hollywood movies), this castle sits

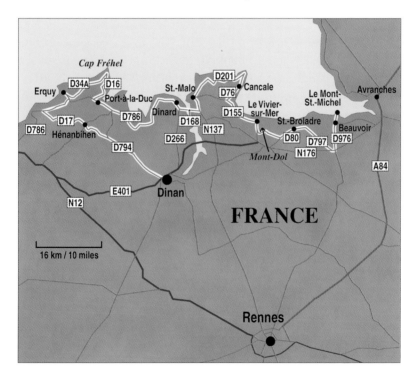

*Night falls over Le Mont-St.-Michel. Photo by John Ashley Hall.*

on a spit of land overlooking the ocean. It is a very impressive site and worth a visit if you have the time. After a visit to Cap Fréhel and the castle head back down the same way then take D34A and D786 toward Erquy. The road hugs the Atlantic with panoramic views opening up across the ocean. Stop along the way and enjoy a Magnum ice cream or just continue on as the sea breeze blows gently in your open visor.

### Day 4 – Le Mont-St.-Michel to Dinan  200 km/125 miles

Leave Le Mont-St.-Michel, go south to Beauvoir and connect with D976 to N176. Turn right and take the turnoff on D797 to St.-Broladre.

At St.-Broladre take a left on D80 then right to Mont-Dol. Take the summit road to the top. Come back down the mountain and reconnect with D155 to Le Vivier-sur-Mer and on to Cancale on D76. Take the D201 to St.-Malo.

Arrive St.-Malo. Take N137 and D168 to Dinard.

Arrive Dinard. Leave on the D786 to Port-à-la-Duc, turn right to Cap Fréhel on D16.

Arrive Cap Fréhel. Turn around and take D34A, D34 and D786 toward Erquy. Continue on D34 through La Couture then take a left on D17. This road takes you to Dinan but changes to D794 after Hénanbihen.

Arrive Dinan.

*The cliffs on the west side of the Cap Fréhel peninsula are rugged and steep.*
*Photo by Benh Lieu Song.*

Continue west on D786 then go south on D34 through La Couture. Hang a left on D17 toward Hénanbihen. The asphalt meanders gently through the farmlands then turns into D794 to Dinan. Once again follow the signs to *centre-ville* and visit the TI on Rue de l'Horlogne to check for *chambres*. The TI is open until 7 p.m. in the summer. Dinan has a great hostel, the Auberge Moulin du Méen, located on Vallee de la Fontaine des Eaux, phone #02-96-39-10-83. To get there turn left on Avenue de Aublette off the D794 and continue on Rue de Brest. This is an old converted windmill in a forested area about 2 km from the center of Dinan and 600 m from the port. Rooms for individuals, couples, and families are available and are reasonably priced. Dinan also has a very large municipal campground called Camping International de la Hallerais and is about 2 clicks from the city. This is a full-fledged KOA-like site with a swimming pool, mini-golf, etc. Take the N176 and the Taden exit. It's located right on the river.

Dinan is well worth an extended stay. Spend an afternoon and/or morning relaxing by the half-timbered homes and old medieval walls. Visit the basilica and Vieille Ville. Take a short walk or drive to the hillside village of Léhon for some crepes. Or just hang out at the old port and people watch at one of the cafes. This is what vacationing is all about!

*The perfect time to visit Le Mont-St.-Michel is at night after the crowds have disappeared. Photo by John Ashley Hall.*

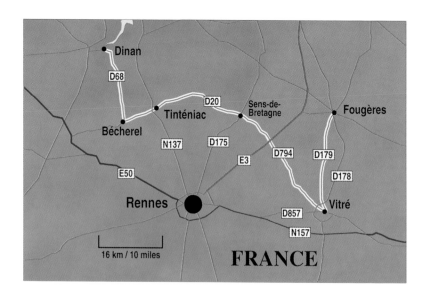

## Day 5  Dinan to Fougères

If you are into castles and medieval towns then take a day going from Dinan to Tinténiac to Vitré and finally to Fougères. This run is only 120 km/75 miles, but each town has its own character. Start by taking the D2 out of Dinan, which changes to D68. Turn left on D20 and head to Tinténiac. Tinténiac is a cute little town with an ornate church. The village is right next to a canal and is quite picturesque. Continue on D20 to Sens-de-Bretagne. Keep left as the road turns into D794 to Vitré. The blacktop winds through lush farmlands and small towns with church spires poking up over the horizon.

*A favorite snack while riding in France is frites, with mustard or mayonnaise. Photo by John Ashley Hall.*

*Time for a break. This cafe in northern France is the perfect place for lunch.
Photo by John Ashley Hall.*

Vitré is considered the gateway to Brittany and is another model medieval town. The castle is perched above the River Vilaine with great views of the surrounding area. Take a stroll around town and visit the elaborate gothic cathedral.

From Vitré, take the D179 to Fougères. This is another great drive though the French countryside and Fougères is another medieval town right out of a children's storybook. The city is located next to the Nancon River overlooking the valley. Half-timbered houses, a gothic cathedral, and mammoth fortress remind you of something out of Disneyworld (or is it the other way around). Find a *chambres* at the TI on 2 Rue National, pick up an information guide and enjoy your stay in fantasyland! If you want to camp, a small municipal campground is located on the east side of town. It's called Camping Municipal de Paron and is just off the D17.

## Day 5 - Dinan to Fougères  120 km/75 miles

Leave Dinan take the D2, D68 to Bécherel. Turn left on D20 to Tinténiac. Arrive Tinténaic. Continue on D20 to Sens-de-Bretagne. Then take D794 to Vitré.
Arrive Vitré and go north on D179 to Fougères.
Arrive Fougères.

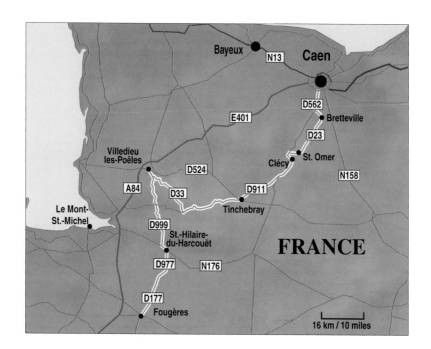

# Day 6  Fougères to Caen

Time to wrap this trip up with some nice twisties along river valleys and wooded hills. You can kick it in high gear today as there are few stops and just twisting asphalt to slow you down.

From Fougères take the D177 north which changes to D977. In St.-Hilaire-du-Harcouët turn left on N176 then right on D999. Continue on the D999 to Villedieu-les-Poêles. The D999 is a beautiful road heading north back into Normandy. When you arrive in Villedieu, you may want to stop and poke around. This town has been known for centuries as a guild town making all sorts of metal pans and lacework. The workers are called *sourdins* from the French word *sourd* meaning "deaf." The repeated hammering of pans made the locals deaf from the repetitive noise. It is now home to workshops with tradesmen marketing their wares. One other interesting note is that during WWII there was a lone German sniper who shot some U.S. soldiers entering the town. The sniper was killed, but the U.S. commander was so worried that he was about to order the town bombarded. The mayor convinced him otherwise by riding in an open jeep through Villedieu. Since no one shot, the U.S. commander obliged and this particular city was not damaged by WWII.

*Fertile farmlands spread over the rolling hills of northern France. Photo by John Ashley Hall.*

The next part of this journey takes you through what the locals call Suisse Normandie. A slight exaggeration since this area is no Switzerland, but nonetheless it does typify the type of road you will be on. Nice sweeping bends, hairpins, and twisties. The scenery as it sweeps by is second to none in this little enclave of Suisse Normandie. So head back on D999 from Villedieu then veer left on D33. Eventually, veer left again on D911 to Tinchebray and continue on to Clécy.

Clécy lies in the center of Suisse Normandie and is a beautiful little town overlooking the River Orne. This is a great place to stop for a break. After you rest up, continue north on D562 and turn right to St. Rèmy on D133. Just after St. Omer head north on D23 to Bretteville. At Bretteville veer left on D132, which turns into D562 to Caen. The roads in this area are remarkably smooth and twisty, and the scenery breathtaking. A perfect combination to end one of my favorite rides in France.

### Day 6 – Fougères to Caen  227 km/142 miles

Leave Fougères and take the D177 to Louvigné-du-Désert. Continue on D977 to St.-Hilaire-du-Harcouët. Turn left on D999 to Villedieu-les-Poêles.

Arrive Villedieu-les-Poêles, go back on D999 then veer off on D33. Continue on D911 heading east.

Follow D911 to D562 and on to Clécy.

Arrive Clécy. Continue north on D562, turn right on D133 to St. Rèmy/St. Omer.

After St. Omer turn left on D23 to Bretteville.

At Bretteville veer left on D132 then connect with D562 to Caen.

Arrive Caen.

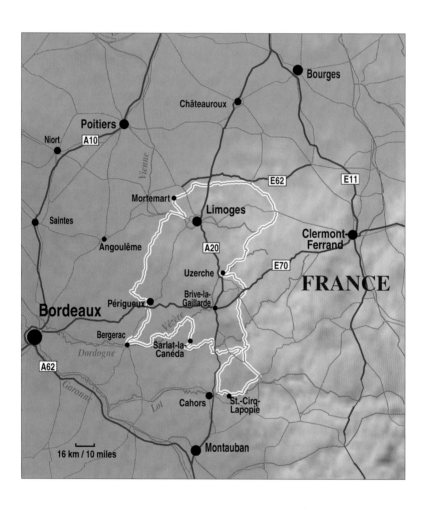

# The Medieval Walled Villages of Central France

**Distance:** *882 km/551 miles*
**Suggested Time Frame:** *5–7 Days*
**Highlights:** *Cro-Magnon caves, the Hundred Years' War, pilgrim trails, and medieval hilltop villages all come alive on this trip back in time through central France. Starting in Bergerac, the blacktop winds through the Dordogne, Lot, and Vézère River valleys to ancient towns and castles. Beautiful underground caves and caverns provide a glimpse of geological wonders under the earth's surface. Villages hang from limestone cliffs where once the French and English fought for close to a century. Sarlat-la-Canéda, Beynac-et-Cazenac, Castlenaud, Domme, and Rocamadour are all visited on this journey. The trip is completed by looping north to the low-lying Monédières Mountains and then over to the WWII memorial town of Oradour-sur-Glane. The beauty of France is all wrapped up in one great journey across the river valley of the Dordogne.*

An old arched stone bridge spans one of the many rivers in central France.
Photo by John Ashley Hall.

One of the reasons I enjoy Europe so much is the almost unlimited supply of history. And it's not just the last 200–300 years, but 700–1,000 years of history. For those of you who have read *Timeline* by Michael Crichton, this trip along the Dordogne River valley transplants you back several hundred years ago to villages and castles as portrayed in both the book and the movie. Medieval fortress towns line both sides of the river, as this was once the boundary between France and England. Beautifully restored townships perched on limestone cliffs overlook the perennially flowing Dordogne River to make this a filmmaker's paradise. Taking you even further back are caves discovered in 1940 once inhabited by the pre-historic Cro-Magnon man. And for those interested in more recent history, the town of Oradour-sur-Glane stands as an undisturbed memorial to its population totally massacred in June 1944 by the Nazis. Never rebuilt, burned out cars and bullet ridden buildings stand in stark contrast to green overhanging chestnut trees.

*Heading out for another day of exploring in central France. Photo by John Ashley Hall.*

*Buying fresh produce at the market is a whole lot cheaper than eating out every day. Photo by John Ashley Hall.*

This journey starts in Bergerac on small country roads hugging the Dordogne River to Sarlat, Beynac, Domme, and Rocamadour. The trip then jogs south to the Lot River and the hilltop town of St.-Cirq-Lapopie before heading north to the heart of France by Limoges, Uzerche, and Aubusson. Gently winding roads take you past small towns and eventually to the untouristy medieval village of Mortemart and the WWII memorial town of Oradour-sur-Glane. The countryside is lush, green, and at times contrasts sharply with the orange limestone cliffs. The total mileage is only 550 miles, but 5 to 7 days will seem inadequate by the end of your tour. Who knows, you may want to take a break from riding your bike and visit a few pre-historic cave dwellings or take a kayaking trip down the Dordogne River (highly recommended) . . . just keep an eye on where you're going because the scenery will only distract you.

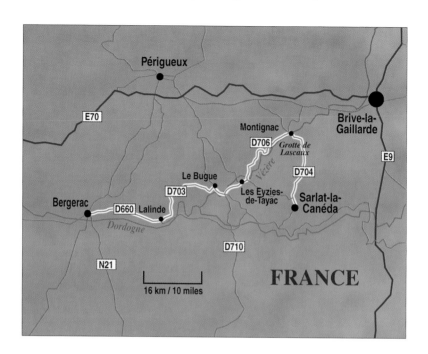

# Day 1   Bergerac to Sarlat-la-Canéda

Although it shares the same name, Bergerac is not the hometown of Cyrano de Bergerac. However, there is a statue in his honor just off the main square in the old town center. This small city lies on the banks of the Dordogne River and was destroyed during the Hundred Years' War back in the 1300s and 1400s. The *centre-ville* has been rebuilt and is filled with narrow lanes and quaint old buildings making it a pleasant area to sit at a cafe enjoying the gently flowing river and local citizenry. There is also a nice campground right on the river's edge and well within walking distance of town. It is called Camp Municipal la Pelouse, located on the south bank of the Dordogne right across from the town's central district.

From Bergerac take the D660 east toward Lalinde. At Lalinde, veer left on the D703 to Le Bugue. This is a great winding road and makes for a good time. So accelerate a tad and enjoy the asphalt before becoming immersed in France's medieval history. Turn left on D706 to Les Eyzies-de-Tayac. Right next to the Vézère River, this area requires a brief or . . . long visit depending on how many caves you want to see. The most famous one is Lascaux II located farther up on the D706 in Montignac. This Lascaux II is an exact replica of the famous Lascaux Cave some children discovered in

*The statue honoring Cyrano de Bergerac stands in the center of the town of Bergerac, even though the real Cyrano did not live in the town.*

1940 while rabbit hunting. The paintings sketched by early Cro-Magnon man are some of the world's best. Visitors are no longer allowed in the actual caves as human bacteria and humidity have already caused them to deteriorate.

After a visit to Lascaux II, turn right on D704 to Sarlat-la-Canéda. Sarlat is one of those towns where time has stood still. Except for the inescapable tourist, the whole town takes you back to times past. Old buildings, narrow lanes, and cobblestone roads give this town a unique charm. Look past the tourists and enjoy the wonder of this quaint village. Check out the *chambres d'hôte* listing at the tourist information or if you feel like camping again try the Camping les Perieres on D47 and only about ½ mile from town (you can easily walk to town). If possible try to be in town on market day—Wednesday or Saturday—it's a riot!

### Day 1 – Bergerac to Sarlat-la-Canéda  115 km/72 miles

Start in Bergerac. Take the D660 to Lalinde then the D703 to Le Bugue. Continue on D706 to Les Eyzies-de-Tayac.
Arrive Les Eyzies. Continue on D706 to Grotte de Lascaux.
Arrive Grotte de Lascaux. Turn right on D704 to Sarlat-la-Canéda.
Arrive Sarlat-la-Canéda.

# Day 2 Sarlat-la-Canéda to St.-Cirq-Lapopie

Today will be spent driving from town to town along the Dordogne River and then making a jog south to the Lot River and the old hilltop town of St.-Cirq-Lapopie. Start by heading south on D47 from Sarlat and then take the D57 and D703 to Beynac-et-Cazenac. Beynac is a classic medieval hilltop village. The castle on the hill housed the French while Castlenaud just across the river headquartered the English forces during the Hundred Years' War. Park down by the river, hike up the hill to Beynac, and then if you want to get some more exercise continue on across the river to Castlenaud. It's a very scenic hike as you gaze at the castle and the flowing river below.

From Beynac, continue on D703 to La Roque-Gageac, Domme, and Souillac. The ride is gorgeous with limestone cliffs and outcroppings framing these overhanging old French villages. La Roque is a frequent winner of the France's coveted "prettiest village award" and worth some photo stops. Domme is another classic town surrounded by 12th-century ramparts. It is set on a hilltop and offers great views in just about every direction. Right by the TI (main square) is an entrance to more underground caves used as a sanctuary during the various wars that ravaged this area. From Domme, continue on to Souillac and the tourist crowds should start to thin. Souillac is not on the main tourist agenda and makes a good spot to catch your

*The castle high on the cliff above the town of Beynac-et-Cazenac is a classic example of medieval architecture. Photo by Manfred Heyde.*

## Day 2 – Sarlat-la-Canéda to St.-Cirq-Lapopie   175 km/109 miles

Leave Sarlat going south on D47, D57, and D703 to Beynac-et-Cazenac.
Arrive Beynac. Continue south on D703 to La Roque-Gageac and onto Domme.
Arrive Domme. Take the D703 to Souillac.
Arrive Souillac. Go south on D820 then turn left on D673 to Rocamadour. Continue on D673 to Alvignac and Gouffre de Padirac. Take D60 to Gouffre de Padirac.
Arrive Gouffre de Padirac. Continue east on D673 then turn right on D807 to Labastide-Murat. Continue south on D32. Connect with D653 going south. Turn left on D662 to St.-Cirq-Lapopie.
Arrive St.-Cirq-Lapopie.

breath and grab some food before continuing on.

From Souillac, go south on D820 then left on D673 to Rocamadour. The road winds beneath this pilgrim town and ends up by several bus-filled parking lots. Although inundated with tourists, Rocamadour is not to be missed. Hanging precariously from steep cliffs, this town has been trampled by pilgrims from the Middle Ages to tourists in the 21st century. Once you see it, you will understand why!

Accelerate past the exhaust-fumed buses and continue on D673 and then take a spur road (if you are interested) to some more caves—the Gouffre de Padirac. This underground delight is one of France's most popular and takes you to lakes and rivers well below the earth's surface. Sometimes the lines are long getting in and as you can see this whole area is quite popular with Europeans, so you may want to plan to add an extra day if you really want to explore these towns and caves. You can stay near Rocamadour or just spend two nights in Sarlat. Throw in a kayaking trip down the Dordogne and you had better stay another day. *Chambres d'hôtes* and campgrounds abound in the area and are easily identified.

When you decide to continue, take the D673 east then turn right on

*Flowers add a dash of color to the old stone and mortar walls. Photo by John Ashley Hall.*

*St.-Cirq-Lapopie overlooks the Lot River from high on the south bank.*
*Photo by Draaen.*

D807 to Labastide-Murat. Go south on D32, continue south on D653, then left on D662 to St.-Cirq-Lapopie. These roads are great with just the right amount of twisties thrown in. St.-Cirq-Lapopie is an idyllic hilltop town perched on the south bank of the Lot River. It's a great place to spend the evening and unwind from another idyllic run through the French countryside. There is camping down by the river at Camping de la Plage. After a cool swim in the river, head up to town and have dinner overlooking one of France's most spectacular locations. Wander cobblestone lanes before heading back to camp for a well deserved night's rest. If you feel like splurging, stay in town at the Auberge du Sombral (remember, splurging to me is about 80 bucks for two!). Just call in advance as the entire town has only about 18 rooms—8 of which are at the Auberge.

# Day 3  St.-Cirq-Lapopie to Uzerche

Pulling yourself away from this hilltop town may be one of the more difficult chores on your trip through France, but today we start our journey into what I call the heart of France. Geographically located in the center of France, it is covered with rivers, lakes, mountains, and more charming (yet

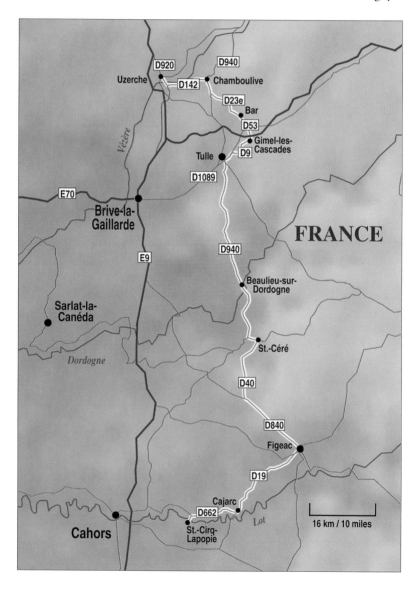

off the beaten track) towns. Begin by traveling on the tight turns of D662 to Cajarc then continue by turning left on D19 to Figeac.

Figeac is right on the River Céré and is another quaint, yet not so touristy town. The old center with timbered buildings and cafe awnings make it a mandatory stop. Visit the cathedral, sip a cool drink, and wander around a bit before heading on. From Figeac turn left on D840, then right on D40 and D940 to St.-Céré. Continue on D940 to Beaulieu-sur-Dordogne. Again, you are traveling through more beautiful scenery on gently sweeping country roads. Beaulieu is very picturesque and sits right on the river. The town is known for its Romanesque sculpture of Christ in front of the church.

Continue on D940 toward Tulle. At Tulle connect with the D1089 going northeast, and then take the D9 and D53e to Gimel-les-Cascades. The run to Gimel is a beautiful ride. Although only 2,000–3,000 feet in elevation, the countryside is mountainous and thickly forested. The winding road takes you past a magnificent waterfall and several lakes dot the landscape. Gimel is adorable and it may be very tempting to stay here. The waterfall, the Montane, is just outside of town. If you do want to stay, there is a hotel in the village or you can stay at a campsite by a small lake, the Etang de Ruffard, on the edge of town.

From Gimel take the D53 north to Bar, turn left (still the D53), then right on D23e. Connect with the D940, turn right and at Chamboulive take the D142 (left) toward Uzerche. Take the D920 to Uzerche. A typical French town, Uzerche is built slightly above the River Vézère. You should have more than enough time to wander its small lanes. Visit the TI just behind the main church. Find yourself a *chambres d'hôte* either in town or in the nearby vicinity, settle in, come back for dinner, and call it a day.

---

### Day 3 – St.-Cirq-Lapopie to Uzerche   181 km/113 miles

Leave St.-Cirq-Lapopie by continuing on D662 to Cajarc. Turn left on D19 to Figeac.

Arrive Figeac. At Figeac turn left on D840 then right on D40 and D940 to St.-Céré. Continue on D940 to Beaulieu and on toward Tulle.

At Tulle connect with the D1089 going northeast, then the D9 and D53e to Gimel-les-Cascades.

Arrive Gimel. Take D53 north to Bar. Continue left on D53 then right on D23e then right on D940. At Chamboulive take the D142 to Uzerche. Turn right on D920 to Uzerche.

Arrive Uzerche.

## Day 4   Uzerche to Mortemart

Today's ride starts with a nice run from Uzerche to Treignac. Take the D3 north and the road will gently curve through the Vézère River valley. Turn right to Peyrissac on D24 and the asphalt gains some curves, and then straightens out a tad as you approach the small town of Treignac. The Vézère River is no longer the calm, gentle river you remember seeing at Uzerche, but shows far more strength and speed. Treignac sits in the upper valley of the river and is home to world-class canoe and kayaking. This area is the gateway to the Monédières Mountains (more like glorified hills) and most of the homes are built from granite.

From Treignac take the D940 north, and then veer right on D69. The D69 will connect with the D992 to Felletin and the D982 to Aubusson. If you are interested in the European art of tapestry then definitely make a stop and drop by the museum. This area has been known for its tapestry weaving for centuries. The town itself is in a ravine next to the River Cruese.

Take the D942a north out of town until it connects with D942. Continue on D942 to Guéret. At Guéret head west on D914 and D4 to Le Grand-Bourg. The D4 turns into D711. Follow to Châteauponsac. Continue on D1 and at Rancor go southwest on D72, D83 and D5 to Mortemart. Take your time as you make this run. The roads wind gracefully across hills and farmlands.

*The rivers in central France wind through a scenic backdrop of hills, cliffs, and pastoral countryside. Photo by John Ashley Hall.*

Mortemart itself is a small village and off the main tourist track. It has a medieval market hall and is a very charming out of the way spot to recharge. There is a hotel in town (only 5 rooms). Keep a look out for *chambres d'hote* along the way. This is a perfect place to relax and sit at a small cafe at the end of the day.

### Day 4 – Uzerche to Mortemart   215 km/134 miles

Leave Uzerche by heading north on D3 then turn right on D24 through Peyrissac and Affieux to Treignac.

Arrive Treignac. Take the D940 north. Veer right on D69, which will connect with D992. Take D992 to Felletin and then follow D982 to Aubusson.

Arrive Aubusson. Take the D942a north out of town then connect with D942 to Guéret.

Arrive Guéret. Take the D914 and D4 west toward Le Grand-Bourg. The D4 turns into D711. Follow to Châteauponsac and continue on D1 toward Bellac. Before Bellac go south on D72, D83 and D5 to Mortemart.

Arrive Mortemart.

# Day 5  Mortemart to Bergerac

On June 10, 1944, a German SS Company entered the village of Oradour-sur-Glane and massacred the entire population. The men were machine-gunned down then burned in the local barn. The women and children were locked in the church and either burned or machine-gunned if they tried to escape. The town was never rebuilt and stands as a tribute to the horrors of war.

To get there, take the twisty route on the D204 south to Peyrelade and Cinturat. Turn left at the D9 intersection to Oradour. At Oradour visit the underground museum, walk the bombed-out streets, and remember what brutality lies in war. After visiting Oradour, go south on D3 then turn right

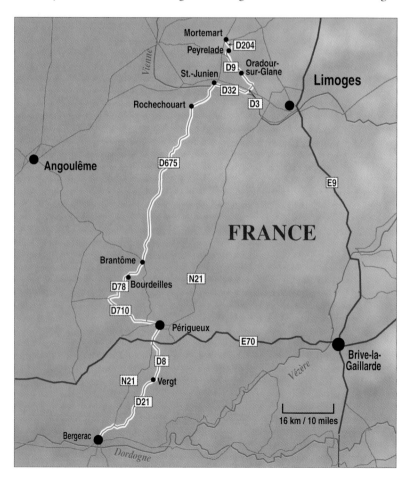

*Oradour-sur-Glane—a reminder of the horrors of war. Photo by TwoWings.*

(west) on D32 toward St.-Junien. Catch the D675 south to Rochechouart. Rochechouart is another small walled town deserving of a stop. The local chateau doubles as the actual town hall!

From Rochechouart continue south on D675 to Brantôme. At Brantôme connect with D78 through Bourdeilles then turn left on D710 to Périgueux. If you have time, visit the town center, otherwise take N21 south, and veer left on D8 just south of town. The road changes to D21 at Vergt and eventually takes you back to Bergerac. The ride from Rochechouart to Bergerac will be a smooth finish to, hopefully, a very worthwhile visit to the heart of France.

### Day 5 – Mortemart to Bergerac   197 km/123 miles

Leave Mortemart. Head south on D204 to Peyrelade and Cinturat. Connect with D9, turn left to Oradour-sur-Glane.

Arrive Oradour-sur-Glane. Go south on D3, turn right on D32, and follow to D675. Turn left on D675 and follow to Rochechouart.

Arrive Rochechouart. Continue south on D675 to Brantôme. At Brantôme connect with D78 through Bourdeilles and then turn left on D710 to Périgueux.

Arrive Périgueux. Take the N21 south then veer left on D8 and continue on D21 and back onto N21 to Bergerac.

Arrive Bergerac.

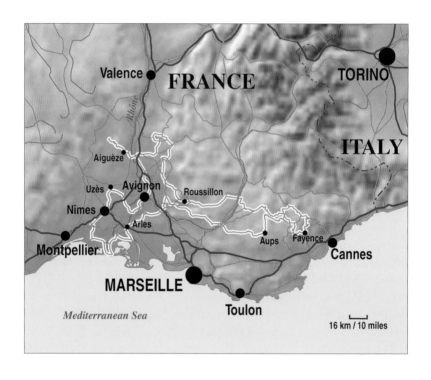

# A Week in Provence: Roman Ruins and Natural Wonders

**Distance:** *1075 km/671 miles*
**Suggested Time Frame:** *7–9 days*
**Highlights:** *This area in Provence, France, typifies the true meaning of Europe. Castles, walled cities, and a unique culture all mingle together to create one of the most rewarding rides on the continent. Small, narrow roads wind lazily beside Roman ruins, hilltop villages, and wide river gorges. The combination of history, culture, natural beauty, great cuisine, and smooth blacktop make this week in Provence a journey not to be forgotten.*

Ancient history and modern art merge in this small province of southern France. Once occupied in force by the Romans, this area has played host to popes, painters such as Van Gogh and Picasso, and most recently, the well-known author Peter Mayle. In his book *A Year in Provence,* Mayle restores an old home and provides an inside look into the unique culture, climate, and people of Provence. Not a bad read if you are interested in doing a little research before traveling on this loop.

Today the region is chuck full of ancient Roman ruins, old papal palaces, and gorgeous natural wonders. Our trip starts in Arles, heads down to the Camargue region along the Mediterranean coast, and then swings up to Pont du Gard, over to Avignon, former home of popes. From Avignon the road winds along the Ardeches Gorges then heads east to the small towns of Séguret, Sablet, and Gordes before heading to the Grand Canyon du Verdon and back to Arles through the Luberon hill country. About 670 miles in length, this trip will easily take 7 days and, who knows, you may do a "Peter Mayle" and find yourself a cottage for the whole summer!

# Day 1 Arles to Uzès

Get started in Arles. Find a nice *chambres d'hôte* and explore this old Roman city. Set next to the Rhône River, it was an important trading post during the Roman Era. Its winding streets hide medieval landmarks around each corner. The original Roman arena is still home to bullfights "à la Provence." If you have time, I would recommend you see one . . . no blood allowed!

From Arles take the D570 toward Stes.-Maries-de-la-Mer. Turn left on D36, right on D36b and D37, then left on C5 to Méjanes. Méjanes is a small village nestled next to the Vaccares Lagoon and is located in a very rustic, undeveloped area of France. Wildlife and fowl run free in this area providing the nature lover an opportunity to see a different side of France. Sort of like the old-west version of Europe. From here swing back up to D570 and on to Stes.-Maries-de-la-Mer, which lies in the heart of what is called the Camargue region of France. This is a protected wetland and home to

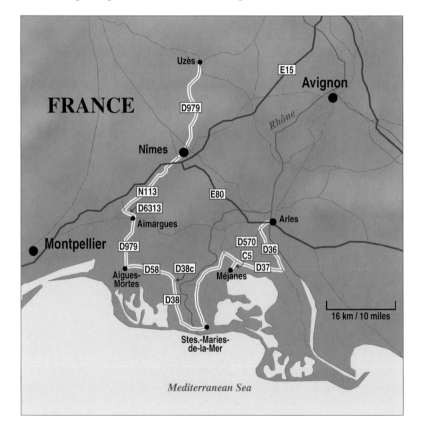

*The Camargue region in Provence is the marshy area near the mouth of the Rhône River. Wildfowl, horses, and cattle roam free in this protected area.*
*Photo by Rolf Süssbrich.*

### Day 1 – Arles to Uzès   173 km/108 miles

Start in Arles and take the D570 toward Stes.-Maries-de-la-Mer. Turn left on D36, right on D36b, and then right on D37. Catch the C5 to Méjanes.

Arrive Méjanes. Go back on D37, turn left on D570 to Stes.-Maries-de-la-Mer.

Arrive Stes.-Maries-de-la-Mer. Follow the signs to Aigues-Mortes on D38, D38c, and D58.

Arrive Aigues-Mortes. Follow signs to Nîmes on the D979, D6313 and N113. From Nîmes take the D979 to Uzès.

Arrive Uzès.

wild horses, flamingos, and other waterfowl. The *gardiens* (herdsmen) live in windowless stone homes with bull horns over the door to ward off evil spirits.

After a brief stop, follow the signs to D38, D38c, and D58 to Aigues-Mortes, an old fortress town built by Louis IX. For some great views of the Camargue, climb up the Tour de Constance and walk along the wall. The town is touristy but nice. Continue north and follow the signs to Nîmes on D979, D6313, and N113.

Nîmes is a larger city, but worth a brief stop if you want to see some more ruins. Just a tidbit of info, it was in this town that denim now used in jeans worldwide was originally manufactured.

From Nîmes follow the D979 to Uzès. The D979 is a gorgeous, winding ride through some gentle rolling hills and open, pristine countryside. Uzès is one of those off the beaten path fairy-tale-like medieval towns. Formerly a

*An expansive view of the salt marshes of the Camargue is visible from the ramparts of Aigues-Mortes, an important Mediterranean port in medieval times.*

The Tour Fenestrelle (Window Tower) is the only remaining part of the medieval structure of the Uzès catherdral. Photo by Marc Ryekaert.

vacation town for the wealthy textile owners from Nîmes, Uzès now has old towers, steeples, and spires lining the horizon. The chateau in town has been inhabited for more than a thousand years. This town makes for a delightful stopover. Wander the streets, do some window-shopping, and sip some regional wine. There are several accommodations in town, a decent hostel (Hostellerie Provençale) on Rue Grande Bourgade, and even a campsite off avenue Maxime-Pascal. And if you are there on Saturday, the colorful market is well worth your time.

# Day 2  Uzès to Avignon

From Uzès it is just a short jaunt to Pont du Gard east on D981. This aqueduct was built before Christ and was put together with no mortar, only finely cut stone. The best way to see it is on a canoe going underneath the huge structure. Very impressive. Very touristy. After cooling off under the aqueduct, continue on D986 south to Beaucaire and Tarascon. These two towns border either side of the Canal Rhône. Beaucaire is where "bloodless" bullfighting began. There is even a statue in town celebrating a bull (as opposed to a matador). Castles adorn either side of the river. In Tarascon, the cathedral is dedicated to St. Martha and is her supposed burial place (sister of the biblical Lazarus).

From Tarascon take the D970, then turn left on D35E to the abbey at St.-Michel-de-Frigolet. Continue on D35E to Barbentane then take the D35 and D570N to Avignon. If you have a moment stop at the abbey at St.-Michel-de-Frigolet. This religious convent was built in 1133 AD and is a mix of spires and basilicas. Inside there is a little cafe if you want a snack before heading on into Avignon.

Avignon is one of my favorite cities in France. Once the home of popes, the papal palace is well preserved and offers great views of the countryside and river valley. The square in front of the palace is often home to mimes

*The Palace of the Popes built in the 14th century dominates the view of the city and is one of several tourist attractions in Avignon. Photo by Mark Allred.*

and various street artists. I remember late one evening while sipping a warm drink in a nearby cafe, I heard a magnificent tenor singing opera in the deserted square. The sounds reverberated off the stone enclave like an acoustic laser show. It was one of those European moments I'll never forget and one of the reasons I keep going back.

Avignon is definitely worth a full afternoon and evening. There is a great campsite on an island in the river just outside of town. It's called Camping du Pont d'Avignon and is about a 20-minute walk to town (good exercise after riding your bike all day). It's right off the N580 as you cross over Ile de la Barthelasse.

### Day 2 – Uzès to Avignon   61 km/38 miles

From Uzès take the D981 to Pont du Gard.

Arrive Pont du Gard. Head toward Remoulins, then continue on D986 to Beaucaire and Tarascon.

Arrive Tarascon and continue on D970 to D35E and the abby at St.-Michel-de-Frigolet. Continue on D35E to Barbentane, then turn right on D35, then left on D570N to Avignon.

Arrive Avignon.

# Day 3  Avignon to Aiguèze

After a relaxing evening in Avignon, head out on the N7 north and then veer left on D17 to Châteauneuf-du-Pape. Yes, this is the home of that very famous (and very expensive) wine. Originally, the popes from Avignon were the primary customers of this exquisite wine. Now, thanks to wine critic Robert Parker, Jr., the wine is exquisitely priced. And please put the bottle in your saddlebag and enjoy it tonight, not while you're driving your bike.

From Châteauneuf-du-Pape follow the D68 straight to Orange. Once again you will encounter a magnificent Roman theater, which still seats 10,000 people. There is also a Roman arch in town celebrating the defeat of the Gauls by Julius Caeser. After a quick photo stop, go north on N7 then west on D944 to Pont-St.-Esprit. From here head north on N86 to St.-Just, then turn left on D290.

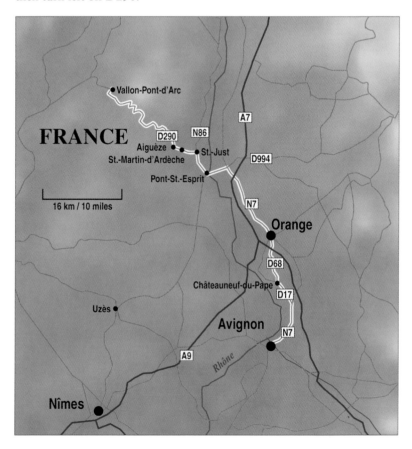

*Looking down at the "bridge to nowhere" in Avignon, France. The bridge was never rebuilt after being destroyed. Photo by Mark Allred.*

You're going to love D290! This blacktop winds crazily beside the Ardèche River and Gorge. It snakes past small villages and limestone caves, eventually climbing high above the river. Enjoy this run and zoom up the asphalt to Vallon-Pont-d'Arc, then turn around for another go of it, except this time stop at Aiguèze or St.-Martin-d'Ardèche for dinner and then spend the night here. I prefer Aiguèze, a small medieval village right at the entrance to the gorge. The old castle, cobbled streets, and towers make this an ideal layover. There is a nice camping spot not far from town called Les Ligades, about 100 meters from the river.

### Day 3 – Avignon to Aiguèze   141 km/88 miles

From Avignon take the N7 north then veer left on D17 to Châteauneuf-du-Pape. Continue on D68 north to Orange.

Arrive Orange. Continue on the N7 and then head west on D994 to Pont-St.-Esprit. At Pont-St.-Esprit go north on N86 to St.-Just. Turn left on D290 to St.-Martin-d'Ardèche and follow along gorge to Vallon-Pont-d'Arc.

Arrive Vallon-Pont-d'Arc. Turn around on D290 and go back to Aiguèze.

Arrive Aiguèze.

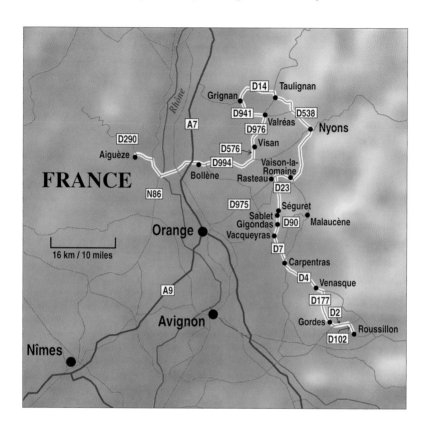

## Day 4  Aiguèze to Roussillon

Although you are only going about 120 miles today, there are numerous towns and villages along the way, and, hence, numerous potential stopovers. If you find one you like, by all means, stop, spend the night, and shorten the loop a tad to fit your timetable. This is what traveling is all about, finding what you like and making adjustments along the way.

After relaxing by the Ardèche River for a night, continue on D290, N86 and the D994 to Bollène. From Bollène, continue on D994, which becomes D94, then turn left on D576 to Visan. Visan is a small fortified village with the obligatory castle ruins and chapel. The road changes from D576 to D976 on its way north to Valréas. Valréas is a larger and, in my opinion, more charming version of Visan. There are two walls surrounding this town, an outer wall and an inner ring. There is a large church in the center, as well as a chateau. You may want to spend some time exploring the narrow, cobblestone streets. Don't get lost!

From Valréas, detour west on D941 to Grignan, then swing clockwise on D14 to Taulignan. Follow the winding D538 on to Nyons. All three towns have their own appeal. Grignan is perched just below a castle. Park in the lower area and walk up. Or if you are into olives, try Nyons and visit the Thursday morning market. From Nyons, continue south on D538 to Vaison-la-Romaine. Vaison makes a good base to do some exploring if you want to stay in this area. There are some good hotels in town and *chambres d'hôte* are bountiful. Otherwise continue west on D975 to Rasteau.

From here the real fun begins. Town after town, nestled on nice winding roads or perched on hilltops, are lined up like dominos just waiting to be visited, each one more picturesque than the last. Head south on D7 to Séguret, take D23 to Sablet, then D7 again to Gigondas, Vacqueyras, and Carpentras. End the day by weaving along D4 south, then right on D177 to Gordes and then take the D2 and D102 to Roussillon.

Roussillon is small, but charming and not as touristy or uppity as Gordes. It makes for a nice spot to overnight. Take a walk through the nearby Nature Park (I felt like I was at Bryce Canyon in Utah) and then sit at a cafe at the picture postcard square and unwind after your day of riding. The towns and names may all be blurred together, but oh, what a blur! A never-ending feast of history, culture, and charm. Blur away as far as I'm concerned!

## Day 4 – Aiguèze to Roussillon   184 km/115 miles

From Aiguèze head to Bollène on D290, N86, and D994. From Bollène take the D994 east, which turns into D94. Veer off on Route de Visan (D576) to Visan.

Arrive Visan. Head north on D976 to Valréas. At Valréas turn left on D941 to Grignan.

Arrive Grignan. Take the D14 to Taulignan then continue on D24 and the D538 to Nyons. At Nyons take the D938 and the D538 south to Vaison-la-Romaine just off the D975.

Arrive Vaison-la-Romaine. Continue west on D975 to Rasteau. Turn left (south) on D7 to Séguret. Continue on D23 to Sablet and then D7 again to Gigondas.

Arrive Gigondas. Continue on D7 south to Vacqueyras and Carpentras (there is a nice detour here to go up D90 to Malaucène).

Arrive Carpentras. Take the D4 to Venasque and then turn right on D177 to Gordes. Head east on D2 then right on D102 to Roussillon.

Arrive Roussillon.

# Day 5  Roussillon to Fayence

Leave Roussillon early and head on the D104, D4, and N100 to Apt. Since the town is known for its chocolates and candied fruits, stop and sample some treats. If you are there on Saturday, visit the crazy market in the town center (no motor vehicles allowed). From Apt continue on the N100 to Forcalquier. Take a hike up to the Citadel for a good view of the city and surrounding area. Narrow streets and squares adorn this gem of a town. Stay on the N100 then go south on D4 and connect with D15 and D6 to Riez. The road winds gently through lavender fields. This village was founded around the 1st century and surrounds a small hill. There is a park on the hilltop with commanding views. Some ancient Roman columns are nearby as well.

Continue on D952 to Moustiers-Ste.-Marie, a small village located at the entrance to the Verdon Canyon. The D952 is a great ride and runs by the canyon. If you are really into it, take a little detour on the D23 (Route des Crêtes) for a nice loop before continuing on D952 to Castellane. Castellane is at the opposite end of the canyon and is also touristy. There is an attractive town square lined with shops and cafes. Just remember as you explore this area that it is one of the most popular areas in Provence due to a host of outdoor activities available here.

From Castellane, take the N85 (Route Napoléon) to the D563 turnoff to Fayence. Another picturesque hilltop town, Fayence hosts several hotels as well as a TI, which can help you find a *chambre d'hôte*.

*The Verdon River has cut a gorge 25 km long through limestone creating a canyon up to 700 m deep, which attracts many hikers and rock climbers during the summer months. Photo by Dirk Beyer.*

## Day 5 – Roussillon to Fayence   210 km/131 miles

From Roussillon take the D104 to D4 and then head east on N100 to Apt. From Apt continue on N100 to Forcalquier.

Arrive Forcalquier and head east on N100, south on D4, then turn left on D15 and D6 to Riez. At Riez take the D952 to Moustiers-Ste.-Marie.

Arrive Moustiers-Ste.-Marie. Continue on D952 to Castellane. At Castellane veer right on N85 (Route Napoléon), then right on D563 to Fayence.

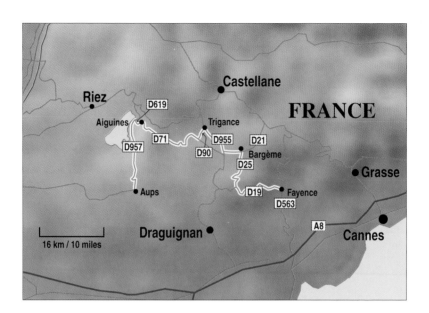

# Day 6  Fayence to Aups

Today is relatively short on distance and stops in just a few towns. Relax and enjoy the countryside. If you want to drive on, you can; otherwise get up late and stop early. From Fayence, head west on D19 and then north on D25. These are some neat little roads to get started with in the morning. When you get close to the D21, stay straight on D37 to Bargème, another medieval fortress village situated on top of a ridge. It's off the main road and somewhat isolated but the town offers up great views and is usually not too crowded. There is a charming little restaurant in town as well (I think the only one!).

From Bargème, head back on D37 to D21, turn right, and then connect with the D955 to Trigance. The hilltop castle in Trigance has views overlooking the Jabron Valley. A typical square lies right in the town center with all the amenities. The Bar Piccolo is another nice spot to grab a drink or something to eat while basking in a truly French-Provence setting.

Head south on D90 (another great little road), then left on D71 to Aiguines. This town is a bit larger and touristy, but definitely worth a brief stop and some exploring. The homes are old but not medieval and the town is a bit more colorful than the others. The local chateau, clock tower, and church give the town center a nice ambiance. Try the Rive Gauche if you still haven't eaten yet.

*Grabbing a quick bite to eat at the market is good—and cheap! Photo by John Ashley Hall.*

Continue on the D619 and D957 to Aups. Aups is not typically on the tourist circuit making it a nice break and a more traditional French agricultural community. The old town square and buildings with cafes and shopping are still there, except it is directed more toward the French citizenry, not the tourists. The hotels are reasonably priced and there are a couple of campsites just outside of town. Visit the TI for more information and directions.

## Day 6 – Fayence to Aups   117 km/73 miles

From Fayence head west on D19 then turn right on D25. Continue on D37 to Bargème. Head back on D37 to D21. Turn right and then follow D955 to Trigance.

Arrive Trigance. Head south on D90 then turn right on D71 to Aiguines. From Aiguines go south on D619 then connect with D957 to Aups. Arrive Aups.

# Day 7  Aups to Arles

Catch the D9 heading east from Aups, merge onto D30 then hang a left on D23, a right on D3 and D11 to the small town of Mirabeau. This is one of the longer runs without any stops . . . so enjoy it. The roads weave gently through the French farmland in fairly isolated countryside. Lift your visor and enjoy the sweet fragrance of lavender.

At Mirabeau, continue your ride on D973 west then right on D135 to La Tour-d'Aigues. Take D120 to La Motte-d'Aigues then the D27 and D56 to Lourmarin. At Lourmarin there is a chateau. Make this your first stop. The entire run from Aups to Lourmarin is about 70 miles and is an easy, pleasant morning ride. Maybe I just timed it right, but I found the traffic to be minimal and the countryside full of vineyards and olive groves.

From Lourmarin take the D943 north beside a sweet narrow river valley to Bonnieux. You had better stop here! After this morning's ride, walk up the 86 steps to the steepled chapel on top of the ridge and then rest under the century-old cedars. Walk or drive around town. Shops, cafes, and squares are built all along the way. This is one neat little town!

The D3 will take you to Ménerbes and Oppède, two more fortified villages. At Oppède, park just below the village then take another walk. You'll certainly get in your exercise today. From Oppède continue on D3, right on D2, then left on N100 to L'Isle-sur-la-Sorgue. This town is built around the Sorgue River and is worth a brief stop. The watermills, ponds, and canals give it a Venetian appearance. All they need are gondolas!

Continue south on D938 to Cavaillon, then veer west on D99 to St.-Rémy-de-Provence. Encircled by remnants of a 14th-century wall, this chic town encompasses itself in charm (and celebrities). Nostradamus was born

*The canals in Europe flow through the center of most towns making them a scenic place to stroll. Photo by Mark Allred.*

here, Van Gogh painted *Starry Night* here, Princess Diana once owned a place here, and I motorcycled here! From St.-Rémy, head east on D31 then turn left on D27 to Les Baux. If you want to brave the tourist crowds, be my guest and visit this tourist mecca—otherwise just breeze on by and enjoy this final run back to Arles. Hopefully, it's only been a week and you haven't missed your flight home!

### Day 7 – Aups to Arles   189 km/118 miles

From Aups take the D9 east and connect with D30. Follow D30 to D23. Turn left on D23 then right on D3 and D11 to Mirabeau.

Arrive Mirabeau. Take the D973 west then turn right on D135 to La Tour-d'Aigues. At the intersection take D120 to La Motte-d'Aigues. Continue on D27 and D56 to Lourmarin. Turn right on D943 to Bonnieux.

Arrive Bonnieux. Follow the D3 to Ménerbes and to Oppède. From Oppède continue on D3 and then turn right on D2. Turn left onto N100 to L'Isle-sur-la-Sorgue.

Arrive L'Isle-sur-la-Sorgue. Go south on D938 to Cavaillon. From Cavaillon take the D99 to St.-Rémy-de-Provence. From St.-Rémy go east on D31 then turn left on D27 to Les Baux. At Les Baux continue on D27 then D78 and D17 to D570n. Turn left on D570 to Arles.

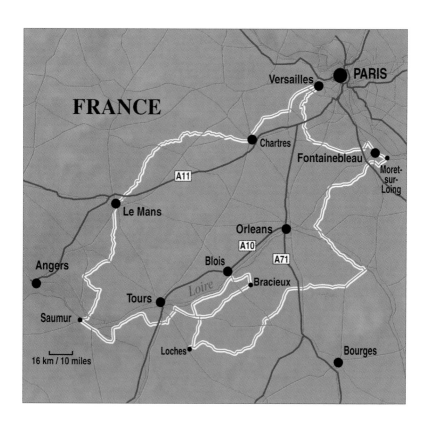

# Chateaux Country Along the Loire River

**Distance:** *1,000 km/625 miles*
**Time Frame:** *5–7 days*
**Highlights:** *This trip starts in Versailles, France's royal palace, wanders by Fontainebleau, Napoleon's residence, and then visits a myriad of chateaux in the heart of France. Interspersed are small medieval villages, vineyards, and an unusual detour into an area called Sologne, full of marshes, mists, and forests. After traveling this route you will better understand the meaning of excess and why the French royalty vacationed in the lush wonderland of the Loire Valley. At the tail end of this journey, you visit Le Mans and actually drive on the public portion of the circuit. Just be sure you don't get carried away on the Mulsanne straightaway!*

Originally a hunting lodge for the king of France, this royal residence mushroomed into a 400-room chateau, the largest in the Loire Valley. Photo by John Ashley Hall.

*Visitors admire the sumptuous elegance of the Hall of Mirrors at the Versailles Palace. Photo by Mark Allred.*

Have you ever wanted to stay on your own private island surrounded by the Loire River and have your own private view of a majestically illuminated chateau from your front window or maybe I should say . . . tent flap? Oh, and maybe I'm stretching it a little bit when I say "private," since you will be sharing the space and views with several fellow campers, but, hey, what do you expect for 8 bucks? Just point your camera up a little, avoid all those tent canopies and tell your friends this is where I stayed in Amboise or Saumur. I guarantee the picture will turn out great and your friends will be very impressed, especially after you tell them how much you paid to spend the night! Just remember, even though the Loire Valley exudes maddening excess and extravagance, you can still enjoy it on a relatively reasonable budget.

This tour takes you to some of the most remarkable royal homes ever built. Chateaux, castles, and vineyards line oak-canopied country roads as your motorcycle glides beside the Loire River and its tributaries. You can see why the French nobility chose this area to be their country getaway from Paris. The rivers, wooded lands, and vineyards are connected with small curving roads making this an ideal trip on a motorcycle. Total mileage is about 625 miles and takes 5 to 7 days. Start in Versailles, the home of Marie Antoinette, head down to Napoleon's former residence at Fontainebleau, then swing down to the Loire Valley abundantly endowed with chateaux, back through Le Mans for a visit to the motor-circuit, and end it with the grand cathedral in Chartres. Country roads meander through picture post-card scenery as you visit what was once France's showcase of conspicuous consumption.

*There are so many chateaux in the Loire valley that you lose count and can't remember their names. Photo by John Ashley Hall.*

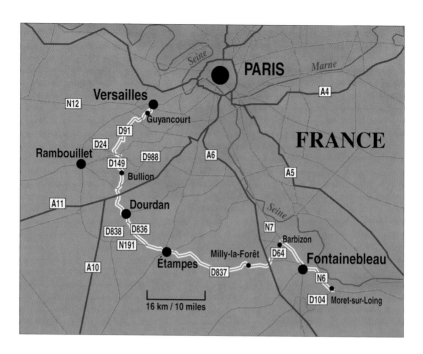

# Day 1  Versailles to Moret-Sur-Loing

Start this journey in Versailles, which is only about 10 miles from the center of Paris. The castle was the official residence of France's royalty from 1680 to 1790. Originally built as a hunting lodge, it eventually evolved into the grandest palace in Europe. Although a very popular tourist destination today, don't miss it and be sure to save some time to wander through the fairy-tale-like grounds surrounding the building.

From Versailles take the N12 out of town then turn left on D91 to Guyancourt. Continue past Guyancourt on the D91, turn left on D24 then after a couple of kilometers, turn right on D149 to Bullion. Connect with D988 to Dourdan. South of Dourdan at Les Granges-le-Roi veer left to Étampes. You will link up with N191 just west of Étampes. Drive though Étampes and then veer right on D837 to Milly-la-Forêt.

Milly-la-Forêt is the home of Christian Dior and has about 5,000 inhabitants. A quaint village nestled by a meandering stream, this is a perfect rest stop on your way to Fontainebleau. If you want to see more of this picturesque area, then continue on the D837 out of Milly-la-Forêt and then turn left on D64 to Barbizon. Nuzzled next to the Fontainebleau Forest, this village was the locale for many 19th-century artists who focused their painting

*The penultimate chateau is the one located in Versailles. This was the official residence of Marie Antoinette before she was beheaded. Photo by Mark Allred.*

style on landscape and nature. A small museum is located in town.

From Barbizon, head north out of town on the D64, and turn right on the N7. These roads weave a path through the forest of Fontainebleau. Thick and lush, there are several side roads if you want to do some exploring in this well-protected national woodland. Soon you will arrive in the actual town and will see the chateau at Fontainebleau. In my opinion, the grounds are as impressive as the castle itself. You may just want to wander beside the lakes and follow the footpaths through the gardens to stretch your legs. In

### Day 1 – Versailles to Moret-sur-Loing   136 km/85 miles

Start in Versailles. Go to the N12 then turn left on D91 south to Guyancourt. Continue to D24. Turn left on D24, then right on D149 to Bullion. Connect onto D988 to Dourdan.

After Dourdan veer left on D836 and then connect with N191 to Étampes. After Étampes take the D837 to Milly-la-Forêt.

Arrive Milly-la-Forêt. Continue on D837 then turn left on D64 to Barbizon.

Arrive Barbizon. Continue on D64 north to N7. Turn right to Fontainebleau.

Arrive Fontainebleau. Continue on N6 then turn left on D104 to Moret-Sur-Loing.

Arrive Moret-Sur-Loing.

some ways I prefer sitting on a bench looking from the outside in. Fontainebleau was chosen as the residence of Napoleon since Versailles was still considered too "Bourbon" to the French public.

After stretching your legs a bit, head east on the N6 from Fontainebleau and then turn left on D104 to Moret-Sur-Loing. Moret-Sur-Loing is another one of my favorite small medieval towns in France. Two fortified gates, stone walls and towers, a beautiful cathedral (consecrated by Thomas Beckett), and a typical town center with timbered buildings and shops give this town a surreal appearance. No wonder so many impressionistic artists came to this area for inspiration.

I would suggest spending the night around Moret-Sur-Loing. Two options are available. First off, visit the TI at the entrance of town in the Place de Samois and have them help you find a B&B. Or if you want to camp,

*Even the ceilings in the Versailes Palace are ornately decorated. Photo by Mark Allred.*

*The Fontainebleau Chateau has been the home of royalty since medieval times. It was restored to its current grandeur by Napolean Bonaparte who preferred Fontainebleau to Versailles. Photo by Carolus.*

there is a nice municipal campground about 6 to 7 miles northwest of town in Samoreau. The campground is called Camping Municipal La Grange aux Dimes. It borders the Seine River where you can watch an occasional barge pass by on its way to Paris. You will find it a very tranquil and scenic spot to catch up on some reading or play a few rounds of canasta before you crawl into your cozy sleeping bag.

# Day 2  Moret-Sur-Loing to Loches

Today will be spent on a pleasant drive through central France and the Sologne district. Rural landscape interspersed with two chateaux in Gien and Valençay provide great panoramas while you motorcycle along the smooth blacktop to the medieval town of Loches. Leave Moret-sur-Loing on the D104 to Villiers-sous-Grez then take the C9 and D16 to Larchant. At Larchant, turn left on D4 to Puiseaux. This road turns into D28. At Puiseaux follow the D26 to Pithiviers, home of France's almond cake. The roads flow over gently rolling hills and typical French countryside. The portions to Larchant and the run from Puiseaux to Pithiviers are especially scenic. Your speed will gradually accelerate as you approach Pithiviers.

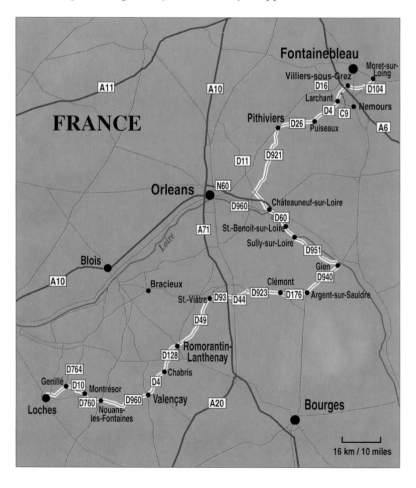

Try an almond cake in Pithiviers and then continue on the D921 south. This is another scenic stretch running through fields and agricultural lands. At the D11 intersection turn left. Cross the N60 and then in Châteauneuf-sur-Loire veer left on D960 then make a right on D60 to St.-Benoît-sur-Loire. After St. Benoît, continue on D60 then do a right on D948 and a quick left on D951 at Sully-sur-Loire. Continue on D951 to Gien. This run parallels the Loire River at some points and again provides some very scenic views.

Although bombed to a pulp during WWII, Gien has been restored to its former medieval status and is again a charming town along the Loire River. The town is known for its brick chateau and fine china and was the place where Joan of Arc met up with the king's army to help free France. Take a stop for a look from the bridge . . . other than the nuclear power plants spewing vapor . . . the views are excellent. Personally, I would take in the views of the Gien Chateau and pass on a tour.

From Gien, take D940 to Argent-sur-Sauldre. At Argent take the D176 toward Clémont. At the intersection, turn left on D79, then a quick right on D923. At the five-way junction, veer left on D44 and then connect with D93 to St.-Viâtre. You are now in the heart of the Sologne district. This is a rural area covered with agriculture, marshes, lakes, and forests. Almost eerie in its appearance, on a nice summer day, the scattered mist and occasional fog make this a truly unique driving experience for France.

### Day 2 – Moret-sur-Loing to Loches   256 km/160 miles

Leave Moret-Sur-Loing on the D104 to Villiers-sous-Grez. Take the C9 to D16 in Larchant. At Larchant turn left on D4 toward Puiseaux. D4 turns into D28. Follow to D26 and Pithiviers.

Arrive Pithiviers. Go south on D921 to the D11 intersection and turn left. In Châteauneuf-sur-Loire connect with D960, veer right on D60 toward St.-Benoît-sur-Loire. Turn right on D948 then left on D951 at Sully-sur-Loire. Continue on to Gien.

Arrive Gien. Leave on D940 to Argent-sur-Sauldre, then take the D176 toward Clémont. Turn left on D79 then right onto the D923.

Turn left on D44 and then connect on D93 to St.-Viâtre. At St.-Viâtre take the D49 south to Romorantin-Lanthenay.

Arrive Romorantin-Lanthenay and take the D128 then the D4 to Valençay.

Arrive Valençay. Take the D960 to Nouans-les-Fontaines. Continue on the D760 to Montrésor and then turn left on D11 and a quick right on D10 to D764. Turn left on D764 to Loches.

Arrive Loches

*Old stone arched bridges are common in the Loire River Valley.*
*Photo by John Ashley Hall.*

After St.-Viâtre, turn left on D49 to Romoratin-Lanthenay, the biggest town in the Sologne. Romoratin is a charming town and requires a short break to wander the town center and catch the views from the main street bridge. Great spot for a drink or an ice cream to cool you down. From here catch the D128 and D4 to Valençay.

In Valençay, we begin the journey into the vast chateaux estates populating the Loire Valley. The Valençay palace was built in the 16th century by the same architect who designed Fontainebleau. The castle was originally inhabited by French royalty. John Law, the famous Scotsman who introduced the system of credit, and then Talleyrand, Napoleon's foreign minister, also lived here. The grounds are spectacular, so stretch your legs and walk the estate. If you want, take a short tour of the interior. Personally, I prefer wandering the grounds, sitting on a bench, eating some dark European chocolate, and watching people go by . . . all with the magnificent chateau in the background.

Hopefully, you are not too tired to finish up the day with about another 30 miles to Loches. Take the D960 west from Valençay to Nouans-les-Fontaines where you connect with the D760. At Montrésor turn left on

D11 then a quick right on D10, which is a great little stretch of road that winds its way to the D764 at Genillé. At the intersection turn left to Loches.

Loches is that special kind of town that is just a tad off the beaten path and not nearly as touristy as some of the cities right in the Loire Valley. There is a castle overlooking the old town and two 15th-century gates with the remains of unbreached ramparts still standing as sentinels around the city. The Indre River, a tributary of the Loire, flows gently alongside this quaint village. I would suggest you drop by the TI at 7 Place de Wermels-kirchen and find yourself a cozy *chambres d'hôte* so you can enjoy a quiet evening and dinner in Loches.

*Pianos take on a new level in France. Photo by Laurie Taylor.*

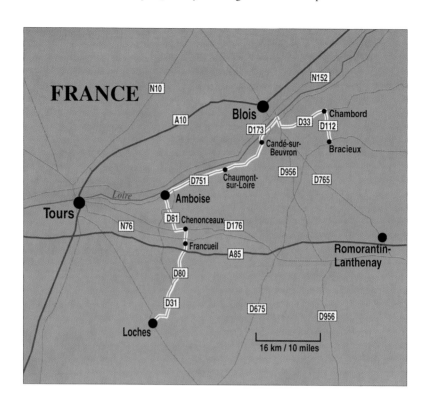

# Day 3  Loches to Bracieux

Two of France's most visited chateaux are located on today's ride—Chenonceau and Chambord. Three more are also along the way—Amboise, Chaumont, and Blois. So prepare yourself mentally since it is possible to over-do a good thing! The Chenonceau and Chambord chateaux are, in my opinion, worth going inside. Because today is loaded with chateau visits, I've shortened the ride to only about 60 miles using Chambord as the final stop. However, you need to choose where you want to stay. Quite honestly, staying in Loches for two nights is not a bad idea. Just do a loop back at the end of the day. Amboise has a great campground on a little island smack dab in the middle of the Loire River with great views of the chateau. Makes a very inexpensive evening with a beautiful castle in the background—especially at night. If you want to stay close to Chambord, I've also suggested a campground close to the chateau in Bracieux. So be a little flexible and adjust your schedule accordingly while being immersed in French chateaux!

*The chateau at Chenonceaux is built right out over the river. Photo by John Ashley Hall.*

Start by heading north out of Loches on D31. Veer right on the D80 to Francueil and Chenonceaux. Cross the Cher River and turn left on D176 (D40 on some maps). Follow the signs to the chateau. Chenonceau has truly one of the most magical settings of any of the French chateaux. The river flows gently below its arched foundation as the fairy-tale-like castle rises above the water. It seems like Sleeping Beauty should be making a

### Day 3 – Loches to Bracieux   100 km/62 miles

Leave Loches on D31 going north. Veer right on D80 to Francueil and Chenonceaux. Cross the river and turn left to Chenonceaux.

Arrive Chenonceaux. Leave on D176 then go north on D81 to D31. Turn left on D31 then right on D81 again to Amboise.

Arrive Amboise. Head out on D751 toward Chaumont-sur-Loire. At Candé-sur-Beuvron turn left on D173 along the Loire River. The road turns back into D751 as it enters Blois.

Arrive Bloise. Go south on D956. Veer left on D33 to Chambord. Turn right on D112 to Bracieux.

Arrive Bracieux.

*The Chambord Chateau has more than 300 fireplaces and was only occupied for about seven weeks. Talk about conspicuous consumption! Photo by John Ashley Hall.*

grand entrance any minute. Because the chateau is well visited, try to get there early to avoid the crowds and do visit the interior rooms. While parking my bike at the front entrance during my last visit, a couple came up and commented, "Now that's the way to see France." I couldn't have agreed more.

The next stop is Amboise. Turn left on D40 then right on D81. Continue to D31 and turn left, then right again on D81. Amboise is a touristy town set on both sides of the Loire River. The chateau rises grandly above the city and is its most prominent feature. The town itself is charming and pleasant to stroll around. You can park your bike by the river, wander through the castle, and then have lunch at one of the many restaurants downtown. Quaint eateries specializing in crepes adorn the streets. Another place well worth a visit is Clos-Lucé, the final home of Leonardo da Vinci. The creativity and foresight of this genius is noted in various drawings, inventions, and displays throughout the house. If you like this town check out the campground on the island, Camp Municipal de l'Ile d'Or, and spend the night.

From Amboise head east on D751 to Chaumont-sur-Loire. At Candé-sur-Beuvron turn left on D173 along the river and follow it to Blois. There are chateaux in both Chaumont and Blois. As I said before, you can over-do a good thing, but perhaps a drive-by look is worth it before you visit the mother of all chateaux in Chambord!

From Blois, go south on D956 then veer left on D33 to Chambord. Chambord is huge. The grounds are huge. And the crowds can be huge. Chambord is the most popular chateau in France and the immensity of this monstrosity will take your breath away. And just think, the guy who built it only spent 40 days here! Depending on what you want to see, you can definitely spend some time here. The grounds are fabulous and the interior rooms are probably worth a visit—there are more than 300 fireplaces. But you decide. Head back to Loches or Amboise if you want, or spend the night at Camping Municipal des Chateaux just beyond the southern wall of the park on D112 in the small village of Bracieux. It is a nice campground and seems a little less touristy than most others in the Loire Valley.

*The beautiful gardens surrounding the chateau at Chenonceaux are a pleasure to stroll through. Photo by John Ashley Hall.*

# Day 4  Bracieux to Saumur

Start the day by leaving Bracieux (after having a fresh croissant) on the D177 to Villesavin and D102 to Cheverny. Cheverny Chateau is still owned by the descendants of the original owners. They live on the 3rd floor but have opened up the lower levels and grounds to the public. Apparently, the French revolutionaries respected this family and let them be during the late 1700s. After a short stop, continue on the D52 to Fougères-sur-Bièvre, a small village with a very picturesque castle overlooking the village. Turn left on D764 toward Montrichard where you hook up with D176 to Chenonceaux. This is a great run from Bracieux as the roads wind gently by small villages, chateaux, and castle ruins.

Continue on D40 past Chenonceaux and connect with the D140. Just south of Montlouis-sur-Loire turn left on D85. Follow to the D17 and D121 to Villandry. The roads are sweet and the countryside is covered with vineyards. The Villandry chateau is worth a stop, not necessarily for the interior, but for the maze-like gardens surrounding the palace. They are very impressive and also provide some great views.

From Villandry turn left on D7 then right over the river to Langeais. The castle here appears more functional in its appearance with turrets and a drawbridge suggesting that more than just royal parties were held here. Head back over the river, turn right on D7 and follow to the D16 turnoff to Chinon. Chinon is a great little town adjacent to the Vienne River. Castle ruins lie atop a hill, so stretch your legs and hike up to the old fortification. There is a small pleasant garden and circle vision views awaiting you.

*The chateau and the town of Saumur are situated on the bank of the Loire River.*
*Photo by John Ashley Hall.*

From Chinon, cross the Vienne River on D749 then turn right on D751 to Saumur. The road turns into D947 before entering town. Saumur gracefully borders the Loire River, has its own chateau, and resonates an elegance of times past. The island in the Loire has both a hostel and campground. I prefer camping at Ile d'Offard. It's inexpensive and the view out your tent flap looks right over the city and the chateau. You can actually swim in the river here, so go for a refreshing dip, head to town for some delectable French cuisine, and then head back to your own personal view of Chateau Saumur. Not a bad day if I may say so myself!

## Day 4 – Bracieux to Saumur   189 km/118 miles

From Bracieux take the D77 to Villesavin. Veer left on D102 to Cheverny.

Arrive Cheverny. Take the D52 to Fougères-sur-Bièvre. Continue on D52 to D764. Turn left and follow to Montrichard. Turn right on D176 (also D40) past Chenonceaux and then connect with the D140.

Just south of Montlouis-sur-Loire turn left on D85. At the D17 intersection turn right. Follow the D17 to D121 and turn right to Villandry.

Arrive Villandry. Turn left on D7 then right on D57 to Langeais.

Arrive Langeais. Cross back over the river and turn right on D7. Follow to the D16 turnoff to Chinon.

Arrive Chinon. Cross over the Vienne River on D749 to St.-Lazare. Turn right on D751 and follow to Saumur (connects with the D947).

Arrive Saumur.

# Day 5  Saumur to Le Mans

From Saumur, head to Vernantes on D347, which turns into D767. Turn left at Vernantes on the D58 to Baugé. As you pass through the countryside take a close look at the church spires. You may see some that are twisted. Legend tells us that when two twin sisters married in this area on the same day, they swapped husbands for the ceremonial first kiss and the rooster at the top of the spire laughed so hard the spire twisted. I bet the sisters had a good laugh too!

Just before Baugé you will drive through the Forêt de Chandelais. Old oak and beech trees line the road as you approach town. Baugé itself has a 15th-century castle and convent where a supposed piece of the True Cross was brought to France by a Templar Knight.

From Baugé take the D817 then the D305 to Le Lude. Turn right on D306 to the village. Another beautiful chateau above the river is this area's claim to fame. Hopefully you haven't had a chateau overdose yet, and will at least take a quick look and a couple of pictures, before heading on to the Le Mans Circuit.

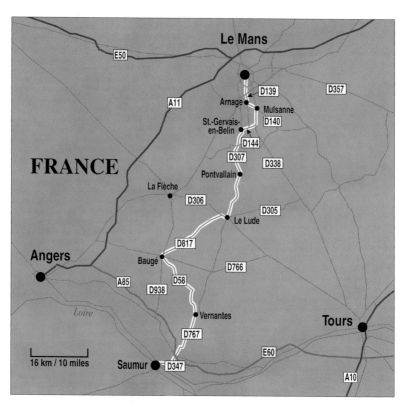

*Drive down a road in France and, voila, a cute little castle appears. I was half expecting to see Rapunzel's hair draped outside the wall. Photo by John Ashley Hall.*

Leaving town take the D307 north to Pontvallain. Continue to St.-Gervais-en-Belin and then turn right on D144, and continue to the D338. Turn left on D338 and at Mulsanne turn left on D140 toward Arnage. At the roundabout, turn right on D139 to the Le Mans Racing Circuit Grandstands. If you haven't noticed already, you have been driving on the actual world-renowned raceway used for the 24-hour race held in June each year. If you're lucky, you can watch test runs, which are open to the public from the grandstands. Enjoy!

Although I try to avoid the larger cities, Le Mans is one place you should visit. Take the D139, struggle through the outer perimeter congestion, and go to the center of town. The old town is charming and is like an old medieval city encircled by a modern metropolis. The old cobblestone streets, wood timbered buildings, and classic cathedral are in stark contrast to what you just drove through. Several Hollywood movies have been filmed in old town Le Mans.

Remember as you approach Le Mans to keep a look out for *chambres d'hôte* and try your luck at getting your own room. You should be an expert by now. One other piece of advice, unless you want to see the races—don't come here in June or around race time—it's a madhouse!

### Day 5 – Saumur to Le Mans   115 km/72 miles

From Saumur take the D347, which turns into D767, to Vernantes. Turn left on D58 to Baugé.

Arrive Baugé. Take the D817, which turns into the D305, to Le Lude. Turn right on D306 to Le Lude.

Arrive Le Lude. Take the D307 north to Pontvallain  Continue on D307 to St.-Gervais-en-Belin. Turn right on D144 then left on D338. At Mulsanne turn left on D140 toward Arnage. Just before Arnage, turn right on D139 to the Le Mans Racing Circuit Grandstands.

Arrive Grandstands. Continue on D139 to Le Mans.

Arrive Le Mans.

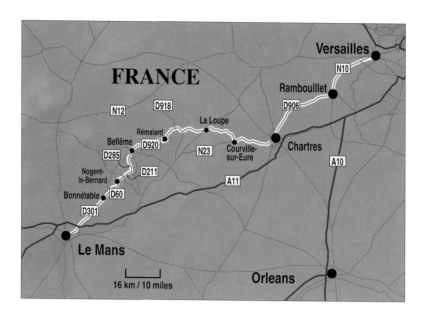

# Day 6   Le Mans to Versailles

This last day will be spent traveling through countryside blanketed with farmlands, forests, and some great weaving blacktop. The roads north of Le Mans wind gracefully back to Versailles through Chartres, home of a huge cathedral, and Rambouillet, the summer retreat of France's presidents.

Leave Le Mans on D301 heading northeast off the ring road. Then veer right on D60 and take the D211 and D285 to Bellême. Continue on D920 and finally N23 to Chartres. After getting into the rhythm of these roads you may not want to stop, but Chartres is home to what Rodin called "the Acropolis of France," or Chartres Cathedral. Truly spectacular with more than 2,000 figurines and one-of-a-kind stained glass windows, you had better stop and see it. The town itself is pleasant and dates back to Roman times. Visit the cathedral, then grab some baguette, salami, and brie, and have a picnic just behind the church. Maybe you'll even have time for a nap.

From Chartres, take the D906 to Rambouillet for one last look at . . . yes . . . one final chateau. The Chateau Rambouillet was originally a fortified manor built in the 1300s, but is now the summer retreat for French dignitaries. The grounds and surrounding forest are just as you would expect for a presidential retreat. Continue on N10 back to Versailles to complete your loop, and you have now seen more chateaux than you ever thought existed and survived! Congratulations, *mon ami!*

The tall spires of the Chartres Cathedral are visible from miles away as you approach the city. Photo by John Ashley Hall.

## Day 6 – Le Mans to Versailles   205 km/128 miles

From Le Mans take the D301 northeast off the ring road. Veer right on D60 toward Nogent-le-Bernard and then take D211 and then D285 to Bellême.

At Bellême take the D920 to Rémalard. Continue past Rémalard on D920 then turn right on D918. Changes back to D920 toward La Loupe. Stay on D920 to Courville-sur-Eure.  At Courville-sur-Eure take the N23 to Chartres.

Arrive Chartres. Take the D906 going northeast to Rambouillet. At Rambouillet take the N10 to Versailles.

Arrive Versailles.

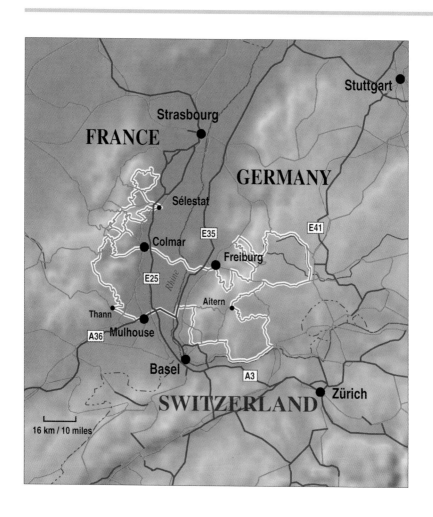

# Villages of the Mountainous Alsace-Lorraine and Germany's Black Forest

**Distance:** *755 km/472 miles*
**Suggested Time Frame:** *4–5 days*
**Highlights:** *Travel through the French Alsace-Lorraine with its numerous vineyards, castle ruins, and colorful villages, then connect with the mountainous Route des Crêtes on your way to the Schwarzwald, the world renowned German Black Forest. Then loop around the Schwarzwald and visit several traditional German towns and hot springs. In my opinion there is nothing better than hitting an alluring spa after an intoxicating drive on some smooth black asphalt.*

This journey through the Vosges Mountains and the Black Forest starts and ends in Colmar, one of the best small cities in all of Europe and one of my favorites. Nestled in the French Alsace-Lorraine, this traditional European enclave was not bombed during WWII and is home to twisty cobblestone lanes and colorful tiled roofs. Built on the confluence of two rivers, Colmar is a classic European city where canals, arched bridges, town squares, and markets all coalesce into a perfect blend of history and culture.

You will be visiting two countries on this trip, France and Germany. Begin in the French Alsatian countryside and wander through numerous vineyards and small towns before tackling the Vosges Mountains on the Route des Crêtes. Built during WWI as a supply route to protect the French from a German attack, the Route des Crêtes is now a breathtaking run across an alpine mountain ridge. This journey then crosses into the German Black Forest for some great runs through this legendary area of southwest Germany before looping back to Freiburg and Colmar. Save some room in your saddlebag, you may want to buy an original German cuckoo clock in Triberg!

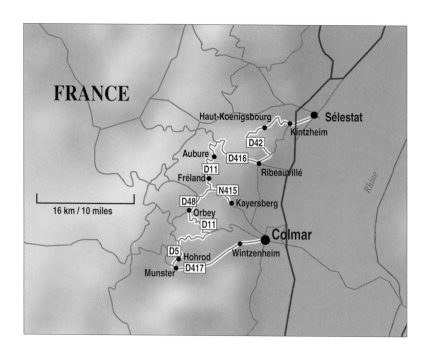

# Day 1 Colmar to Sélestat

Colmar is one of those charming cities you could easily fall in love with and spend your whole summer based here while exploring the surrounding countryside. Purposely not bombed during WWII, this city of 70,000 twists and turns on pedestrian-friendly lanes lined with half-timbered, red-tiled houses. The town center, though thoroughly touristy is not to be missed. Colmar is Europe at its best and provides you with an ambiance you will not soon forget.

I usually stay at the campsite about 2 kilometers outside of town—just the right distance for an invigorating walk in the morning. There is a huge grocery store just down the street providing fresh croissants and cheese. The tent area is right next to the Ill River with trees providing good cover. It's called Camping Intercommunal de l'Ill and is located on the N415 on the east side of town.

After a brief stint in Colmar, head west on D417 to Wintzenheim. Continue on to Munster, home of the renowned Alsatian cheese. You will be traveling through a narrow valley bordered by the burgeoning Vosges Mountains just ahead. Just past town turn right on D5 toward Hohrod, Orbey, and Kayersberg. Follow D5 north then veer left on D11 and D48

*The tables are set for dinner in Colmar, France. Photo by Mark Allred.*

north to Orbey. At Orbey continue north on D48 then turn right on N415 to Kayersberg. The scenery is green and the road winding. You will probably see two mountains in the not too distant horizon—Le Petit Balloon and Le Hohneck, both around four- to five-thousand feet high. These are the

### Day 1 – Colmar to Sélestat   74km/46 miles

Start in Colmar. Head west on D417 to Wintzenheim. Continue on to Munster then turn right on D5 to Hohrod. Veer northwest on D11 then D48 to Orbey. Continue on D48 north to N415. Turn right to Kayersberg.

Arrive Kayersberg. Head back on N415 (west) to D11 to Fréland and Aubure. After Aubure connect with D416 and turn right. After Ribeauvillé turn left on D42 to Haut-Koenigsbourg at Orschwiller.

Arrive Orschwiller. Continue on D42 to Kintzheim and onto Sélestat. Arrive Sélestat.

highest mountains in this mini-alpine region and make for some great motorcycle roads.

Kayersberg is a small medieval town and the former home of Albert Schweitzer, the famous doctor and humanitarian. It's a pleasant spot to take a break with its castle ruins, fortified bridge, and church. If you have time, drop by the Albert Schweitzer museum.

From Kayersberg, head back on N415 going west and then turn right on D11 toward Fréland. Continue on to Aubure then turn right on D416. The road wiggles through the Alsatian countryside. Vineyards abound in the area. If you are a connoisseur of wines, drive leisurely and take a few samples. Just be sure you put them in your saddlebag to try after you have settled in and found your accommodations for the night. Ribeauvillé is also a very pleasant town along this route and is not as touristy as other villages in this same area. If you feel like stretching your legs, hike up to the castle overlooking the town.

*Kayersberg in the Alsace-Lorraine looks like a town from a Hans Christian Andersen fairy tale. Photo by Mark Allred.*

*The canals of Colmar add to the serene ambiance of this delightful city.*
*Photo by Toby Ballentine.*

After Ribeauvillé, turn left on D42 to Orschwiller and the Castle Haut-Koenigsbourg. The castle is worth a visit. It is located high on a hill and offers great views of the surrounding plains. Originally built around 1150 AD, it was reconstructed in 1899 by German Emperor Wilhelm II. The D42 continues east to Orschwiller, Kintzheim, and eventually Sélestat.

Sélestat is slightly more cosmopolitan than other small cities in the Alsace, but it has a very charming medieval town center. Old churches, colorful roof tiles, and a 15th-century library adorn this town. Keep your eyes peeled for some *chambres d'hôte* (you are an expert by now) or visit the TI on Boulevard du General Leclerc. There is also a campsite, Les Cigognes, south of the town center behind the ramparts.

# Day 2   Sélestat to Thann

From Sélestat take the D424 toward Villé. At the D203 intersection, turn right and continue on the D253 to Andlau. This small village is typical of the many Alsatian communities you will encounter on the trip. Half-timbered homes, an old Benedictine abbey and church, all dominated by castle ruins above the town.

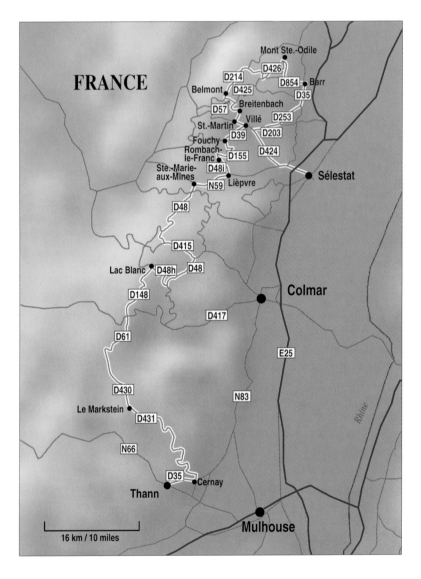

FRANCE

Mont Ste.-Odile
D426
D214
Belmont   D425        D854   Barr
D57                     D35
Breitenbach
D253
Villé
St.-Martin        D203
D39
Fouchy
Rombach-       D155   D424
le-Franc
Ste.-Marie-   D48i              Sélestat
aux-Mines     N59   Lièpvre

D48

D415

Lac Blanc   D48h   D48

D148

D417                 Colmar

D61

E25

D430

Le Markstein              N83
D431

N66

D35
D35   Cernay
Thann

Mulhouse

Rhine

16 km / 10 miles

*The Lièpvrette River cuts through the Vosges Mountains from Ste.-Marie-aux-Mines to Sélestat, France. Photo by Christian Amet.*

Continue just a short distance on D35 to Barr. More cobblestone streets and windows decked with colorful flowers await you. Wander around a bit, then head west on D854, D426, and D426a to Mont Ste.-Odile. This short sprint up the mountain will get your juices flowing (as long as it is not

### Day 2 – Sélestat to Thann   202 km/126 miles

Leave Sélestat on the D424 to Villé. Just before town turn right on D203. Continue on D253 and D35 to Barr. Turn left on D854 and then take D426 and D426a to Mont Ste.-Odile.

Arrive Mont Ste.-Odile. Head back on D426 west and connect with D214. Turn left (south) and after Belmont turn left on D57 to Breitenbach. Road turns into D425. At St.-Martin turn left on D424 (east) to Villé. Turn right on D39 to Fouchy. Just after Fouchy turn left on D155 to Lièpvre At Rombach-le-Franc the road turns into D48i. At Lièpvre turn right on N59 to Ste.-Marie-aux-Mines.

Arrive Ste.-Marie-aux-Mines. Take the D48 south to N415. Turn left on N415 and then right on D48.  Head west on D48h to Lac Blanc and then take the D148 south. The D148 turns into D61, D430, and D431 on its way to Cernay. Arrive Cernay. Turn right on D35 to Thann. Arrive Thann.

*The cobblestone streets in the small villages in Alsace-Lorraine are very enjoyable to explore on an evening stroll. Photo by Mark Allred.*

too busy). This mountaintop retreat of cloisters, chapels, courtyards, and terraced viewpoints offers a quiet repose and tranquil setting. Take a few minutes and enjoy the serene environment and wonderful views. This is a pilgrimage center and oftentimes is busy, but the setting more than offsets any traffic you may encounter.

Head back on D426 and get ready for some more great riding. The road down the hill and onto Cernay twists and turns like a snake's back. The scenery is some of the best you will find in Europe as you ride between valleys and mountain crests. After a short distance on D426, connect with D214 and head south. Soon after Belmont, turn left on D57 to Breitenbach. The road turns into D425. At St.-Martin turn left on D424 to Villé.

Villé lies in a small valley and has architecture going back to the 12th century. Continue south on D39 to Fouchy. Just after Fouchy turn left on D155 to Lièpvre. At Rombach-le-Franc the road turns into D48i. This is a great little run. At Lièpvre turn right on N59 to Ste.-Marie-aux-Mines.

Ste.-Marie-aux-Mines is famous for silver mining and weaving. Most of the ore has been mined, but you can take a tour of the old mineshaft. It's a cute little town and if you decide to take the tour, you may want to spend the night.

From Ste.-Marie-aux-Mines, continue south on D48 to N415. Turn left on N415 and then right back on D48. Just after Orbey, veer right on D48h to Lac Blanc and then take D148 south. This is the official Route des Crêtes, originally built during WWI as a defensive supply route against a German attack. It's a beautiful road and rides the collar of the Vosges Mountains. You will pass various mountain peaks as you drive along this twisting ridgeline. It is over 80 kilometers long and is often closed in the winter months. The road turns into D61, D430, and D431 on its way to Cernay.

At Cernay turn right on D35 to Thann. Thann is a small city (pop. 8,000) that borders the River Thur. During WWI, this town was won back by the French at great cost in 1914 and is now a quaint town known as the south end of the "Wine Route." Old timbered homes, wall remnants, and towers make this a pleasant overnight stay before continuing on to Germany's Black Forest. There is a TI in town where you can ask for accommodations or just keep an eye out for *chambres d'hôte.*

*What's not to love about breakfast in France? Photo by Marl Allred.*

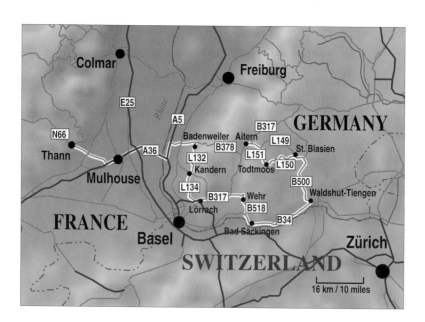

# Day 3   Thann to Aitern

Today's journey takes you to Mulhouse and the fabled Black Forest, or Schwarzwald, located in southwest Germany. To get the day started, head east on N66 from Thann to Mulhouse. Though Mulhouse is primarily an industrial city, it does host a couple of museums worth seeing. One of the best automobile museums I've ever seen is the Musée National de l'Automobile. It is located here and if you are interested in classic European cars you had better plan a visit. Bugattis, Rolls-Royces, Maseratis, Alpha-Romeos, Gordinis etc., make this a must-see for any car enthusiast. Train enthusiasts can also make a stop at the Cite du Train where a century of French locomotives are on display.

Continue from Mulhouse on the A36 into Germany. Turn left on A5 toward Freiburg, but before reaching the city take the B378 to Badenweiler. Badenweiler is one of several bath complexes located in the Black Forest. It is geared primarily to the tourist and offers all sorts amenities. As you continue your drive through the Schwarzwald, you will see many towns that are picture postcard perfect. It may take a little self-discipline to keep your hand on the throttle, so stop wherever you like. Many tourists spend their entire

*Market day in the town square of Mulhouse, France, is a day for shopping and chatting with friends. Photo by Mark Allred.*

## Day 3 – Thann to Aitern   200 km/125 miles

Leave Thann on the N66 and follow signs to Mulhouse.

Arrive Mulhouse. Take the A36 into Germany, and then turn left on A5 toward Freiburg. Before Freiberg take the B378 to Badenweiler.

Arrive Badenweiler. Head south on the L132 to Kandern.

Arrive Kandern. Continue on L134 then follow L141 to Lörrach.

Arrive Lörrach. Take the B317 east and then the B518 to Wehr.

Arrive Wehr. Continue on B518 then left on B34 to Bad Säckingen.

Arrive Bad Säckingen. Continue on B34 to Waldshut-Tiengen.

Arrive Waldshut-Tiengen. Take the B500 north to St. Blasien.

Arrive St. Blasien. Take the L150 to Todtmoos. From Todtmoos take the L151 north and the L149 and B317 to Aitern.

Arrive Aitern.

vacation here, traveling between baths, taking hikes, and visiting historical sites. So be flexible and if you find a nice *gasthaus* use it as a base and do some exploring on your own. You won't regret it!

After Badenweiler, head south on L132. The road sweeps gently across the western edge of the forest and onto Kandern. This town is typical of what you will find here—ruined fortresses and baroque palaces. Continue on L134 then turn left on L141 to Lörrach. Visit the Castle Rotteln about 2.5 miles north of town. Destroyed in the 17th century it is one of the largest fortresses in southwest Germany. Take the B317 east and then the B518 to Wehr. Wehr also has some old fortresses nearby, Werach and Barenfels. There are great views to be seen from the Fortress Werach.

Continue on B518 then turn left on B34 to Bad Säckingen. This town lies right on the border of Germany and Switzerland. A wooden pedestrian bridge crosses the Rhine at this point linking the two countries. Continue on B34 to Waldshut-Tiengen. This town boasts some great 16th- and 17th-century architecture and may require a bit longer stop. If you like it here, spend the night and take the Rheinfalle excursion to where the Rhine River

*On those sunny summer days, the lush green countryside is unforgettable.*
*Photo by Mark Allred.*

*As you travel through the Black Forest you will see many of these beautifully frescoed storefronts. Photo by Mark Allred.*

actually begins. A huge waterfall roars thunderously where the Rhine starts its journey north across Germany.

From Waldshut-Tiengen, go north on B500 to St. Blaisen where you will find an old Benedictine abbey built in the 1700s. At St. Blaisen connect with L150 to Todtmoos and then L151 and B317 to Aitern.

Aitern is a hillside village a bit off the tourist track and makes a nice place to spend the night. Splurge and stay at one of the rustic guest houses. Flowers will grace your balcony and cows will wander aimlessly through meadows. Visit a local *gasthaus* for dinner, then crawl in your feather tick and enjoy the fresh, clean air of the Schwarzwald.

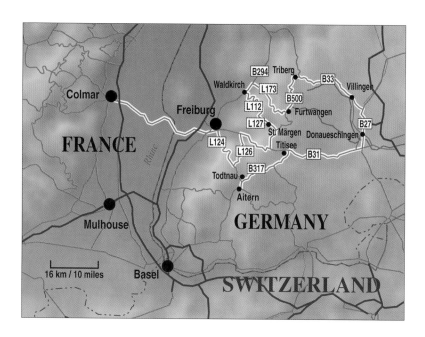

# Day 4   Aitern to Colmar

Leave Aitern on the B317 going north to Todtnau. Surrounded by mountains and a beautiful waterfall, the setting of this town is idyllic. One of the nearby mountains, the Hasenton, has a summer chair lift to catch a view from the top. From Todtnau continue on the B317 to Titisee. Titisee is the tourist capital of the Black Forest. The lake, mountains, and various recreational activities make this a base for many tourists.

From Titisee, take the B31 east to Donaueshingen and then start circling back by taking the B27/33 to Villingen and Triberg. These towns were either vacation resorts for past royalty or old fortress towns now catering to tourists. If you want to take a short hike, walk to the waterfall from Triberg. The water cascades down more than 500 feet.

Take the B500 from Triberg to Furtwangen. Both towns are known for their cuckoo clocks and Furtwangen even has a museum dedicated to more than 100 timepieces.

The next part of this trip takes you on some great asphalt through several more typical Schwarzwald villages. I will leave the sightseeing to you. If you see a particular town that suits your fancy, by all means stop and take a gander. Usually, I just stay on my bike and do some "seatseeing" and enjoy the run to Freiburg. But the choice is yours.

*Walking down the cobbled lanes of Colmar looking for a restaurant makes for a great evening activity! Photo by Mark Allred.*

## Day 4 – Aitern to Colmar   280 km/175 miles

Leave on B317 to Todtnau.

Arrive Todtnau. Take the B317 northeast to Titisee.

Arrive Titisee. Take the B31 east to Donaueschingen.

Arrive Donaueschingen. Take the B27/33 to Villingen.

Arrive Villingen. Take the B33 west to Triberg.

Arrive Triberg. Take the B500 south to Furtwangen.

Arrive Furtwangen. Take the B500 west then go right on L173. Turn left on B294 to Waldkirch.

Arrive Waldkirch. Take the B294 through town and at the L112 turn left (south). Connect with L127 and continue on to St. Märgen.

Arrive St. Märgen. Continue on to B500 and go south. Turn right on B31 toward Freiburg.  Turn left on L126 then right on L124 to Freiburg.

Arrive Freiburg. Continue on B31 west to Colmar and into France.

Arrive Colmar.

*Interested in a cuckoo clock? The Black Forest is known for them. You'll want to ship it home, though . . . not a good idea to put it in your saddlebag. Photo by Toby Ballentine.*

Just outside Furtwangen off of the B500 go right on L173 and wind your way up to Waldkirch. From Waldkirch take the B294 and at the L112 turn left and head down the L127 to St. Märgen. This is a great little loop that only gets better. Continue south on B500 then turn right on B31 then left on L126. Make a final right on L124 to Freiburg. You will love this run and if the roads aren't too busy you will have a peg-scratching good time!

If you have time, Freiburg is certainly a good stop. It is an old university town that was totally destroyed during WWII, but has been rebuilt showcasing its old glory. The city is also very pedestrian friendly with many

*Not only are the roads great but the bratwurst and sauerkraut along the way is delicious, too. Photo by Ron Ayres.*

streets closed to traffic. Small *bachle* (tiny streams) flow down many of the streets.

From Freiburg finish up your trip by taking the B31 back into France and home again to Colmar.

# Germany

Motorcycling in Germany is definitely *wunderbar* (wonderful!). Driving is very similar to the States. Signage is frequent and understandable and, for the most part, the drivers are courteous. In addition the roads are well maintained and often use a rubberized asphalt creating an almost vibration-free ride on a bike. Just remember to keep right when traveling on the autobahn. Before you know it, you'll see blinking headlights in your rear view mirror and if you don't move back to the right lane quickly, the other vehicle will be kissing your rear tire! For the most part, the journeys in this section use the secondary or "B" roads, but the temptation to drive on the speed-limitless autobahn will be too great to resist—just be careful!

Campgrounds are plentiful in Germany. They are very clean and often have separate showers and provide washers and dryers. Stores and small outdoor restaurants are often located on the premises as well. The Germans are natural outdoorsmen and, as a result, there are many hiking trails and nature reserves next to the campgrounds, which make for some great morning walks. Don't forget your lederhosen!

Shopping can be a pain sometimes, since stores are frequently closed in the afternoons. Little quick marts at gas stations are becoming more and more commonplace, so if you get in a bind, pull in for some gas and check out the chocolate section. They not only have dozens of candy bars but bread with chocolate filling . . . like my mom always said . . . gotta have a sandwich for lunch! This is my type of country!

Germany is a great place to start your European odyssey on a motorcycle since bikes are easily rented in the gateway cities of Frankfurt and Munich. Plus these two cities are right in the heart of some of the best motorcycle regions in all of Europe. The Mosel/Rhine River Valleys are near Frankfurt and the Alps are just south of Munich. The best time of year to come is from May through September. And since there are no toll roads here, traveling is a breeze (and free). Happy *fahrvergnügen* and *auf wiedersehen!*

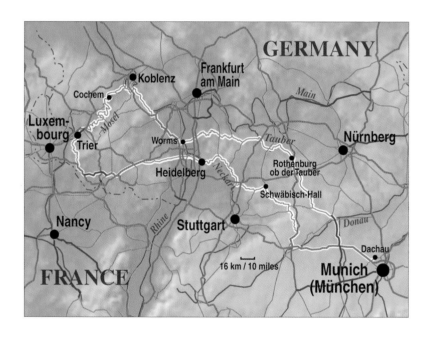

# Germany's River Valleys and Castles Galore

**Distance:** *1225 km/766 miles*
**Suggested Timeframe:** *7–9 days*
**Highlights:** *If you want to see castles then this is your tour. The river valleys of the Mosel, Rhine, and Neckar have more castles than you can count. Throw in one of the best-preserved medieval walled cities in all of Europe—Rothenburg ob der Tauber—and you have the recipe for one great trip. The roads hug the rivers, weaving through some of the most beautiful countryside in Germany. If you are interested, a side trip to Dachau, the infamous WWII concentration camp is also included.*

*The towns along the Mosel River exude a unique charm not seen elsewhere in Europe. The combination of vineyards, mountains, old towns, and a flowing river make it a perfect run on a motorcycle. Photo by Toby Ballentine.*

Narrow cobbled lanes lined by timbered homes are commonplace in the Mosel River Valley. Just the right fit for a motorcyclist. Photo by Rachelle Ballentine.

When I was a teenager, my parents took our family to Cochem on the Mosel River. We camped right on the river and our tent looked up at the castle built high on a hill overlooking the village. It wasn't so busy back then, but even at that age I grew to appreciate the joys of travel and the German culture. My parents then drove us to Rothenburg ob der Tauber and we took the Romantische Strasse to Dachau, just north of Munich. As we walked around the infamous concentration camp, my dad, a veteran of WWII and part of occupational forces in Germany, told me that due to the lack of un-bombed structures, the Army had used the SS officers quarters at Dachau to train personnel coming over from the States. Being an officer, my dad had been one of the instructors. He then shared his experiences and the hardships in Germany at that time. This made quite an impression on a teenage boy who at the time was only thinking about motorcycles and the opposite sex.

This journey will make you glad you are not only thinking about motorcycles, but actually riding one. And hopefully the opposite sex (your better half) will also be along for the ride. You'll be visiting four river valleys, the Mosel, Rhine, Saar, and Neckar. The black asphalt winds beside riverbanks covered with castles and traditional German towns. Many castles were built by robber barons extracting tariffs from the frequent barge traffic plying the rivers. I also take you on a detour to Dachau, the infamous WWII concentration camp. I would advise you to take the time to see this memorial to the millions of Jews and POWs killed during WWII. From Dachau, you head back up the Romantische Strasse to Dinkelsbühl and Rothenburg, two beautifully intact medieval fortress towns. The journey then follows the Tauber River to the old city of Worms, back up the Rhine and over to Cochem on the Mosel River.

*We are on our way to the old castle town of Heidelberg located next to the Neckar River. As you can see the roads in Germany are well marked. Photo by John Ashley Hall.*

# Day 1 Cochem to Trier

The trip begins and ends in the lovely village of Cochem on the Mosel River. This town has all the amenities of a typical German village—a hilltop castle, timbered buildings, cobblestone lanes, and from what I understand, some of the best wine in Germany. Set on the riverbanks between the Eiffel and Hansbruck mountains, this is a great spot to get acclimated to the German culture. A neat little municipal campground, Campingplatz am Freizeitzentrum is within walking distance of town and is a convenient place to stay while in Cochem. And, geez, what a view!

From Cochem, head toward the Luxembourg border on B49 and B53. The road winds along the banks of the river making this a perfect run on a motorcycle. The hills rising from the river floor are covered with vineyards. As you proceed on to Trier, you will drive through the towns of Beilstein, Zell, Traben-Trarbach, and Bernkastel. If you can, take a few moments and explore these small towns. All of them are worth a stop (that's why you're

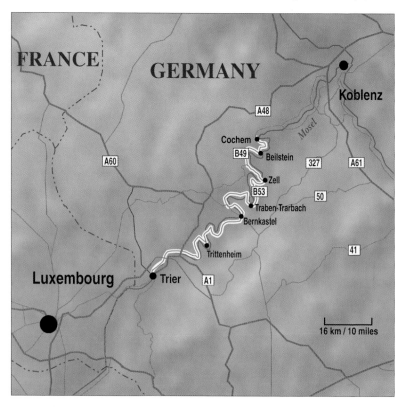

*The Town of Cochem on the Mosel River is one of my favorite places in all of Germany. Photo by Toby Ballentine.*

only traveling 70 miles today).

Beilstein has only 180 official inhabitants and is a little less visited than the other towns along the Mosel. Find a parking spot next to the river, walk to the market square and if you want a great view of the valley then climb up to the castle. The towns of Zell and Traben-Trarbach are also worth a visit. Take your time and mosey through each of these small villages. They are small and can be easily seen along the way. Ever wonder where Snow White lived? It must have been around this area!

### Day 1 – Cochem to Trier   112 km/70 miles

Start in Cochem, take the B49 then B53 along the Mosel River to Beilstein, Zell, Traben-Trarbach, Bernkastel, and Trier.
Arrive Trier.

Bernkastel is probably the most picturesque of the bunch. A multitude of timbered structures, a parish church, and *rathaus* (town hall) surround the town square. A fountain set in its center adds even more charm. Grab an ice cream and sit beside the gushing water as you watch scads of tourists go by.

The final stop for today is the ancient city of Trier. It will probably be later in the afternoon by the time you arrive, so set up camp at Campingplatz Trier-City which is on the B53 just outside of town. It's about a 15-minute walk to town from the campsite. Get situated then put your walking shoes on and take a stroll along the river to Trier.

Trier is Germany's oldest city and was the Roman Empire's capital of its Western Region. There is still one city gate left standing, the Porta Nigra.

*Stop for a drink and some apple strudel in one of the quaint towns along the Mosel River. Photo by Cherise Ballentine.*

*Looking down on Cochem from the bridge over the Mosel River. Photo by Toby Ballentine*

But the real fun is the lively and bustling square in the center of town. Vendors, mimes, flower stalls, cafes, tourists, and townspeople all converge, making this town square an absolute delight. So stretch you legs, walk into town, find yourself a nice cafe, and sit outside eating dinner while you enjoy the sights and sounds of Trier!

# Day 2  Trier to Heidelberg

Today you will be covering a bit more distance than yesterday. There are several towns along the way, but I would recommend you just stop at Saarburg and then cruise over to Heidelberg. Spend most of the late afternoon and evening exploring this ancient (and unbombed) city nestled on the banks of the Neckar River.

Start by heading south from Trier on B51. You will soon arrive in the quaint town of Saarburg bordered on both sides by the Saar River. Water flows freely through the village in the form of small canals and waterfalls. Visit the town center, have brunch at one of the many cafes, and then take a stroll up to the castle. As most of the castles in this area are built above the towns, you will be rewarded with some stunning views of the Saar River Valley.

Don't get too carried away in Saarburg because you need to save some time for Heidelberg. From Saarburg catch the B51 toward Merzig, and then connect with A8 and then A6 to Kaiserslautern. From Kaiserslautern take the B37 to Heidelberg. The A8 and A6 are autobahns. I figure when in Germany you need to fully experience all aspects of the German culture, so pull on that throttle a tad as you merge onto the fast lane! Just remember to keep right except when passing or you will have a very irate driver blinking his

*The center of a typical German town often includes a church surrounded by a town square and marketplace. Photo by John Ashley Hall.*

lights two inches behind you!

When you arrive in Heidelberg, head toward the Campingplatz an der Friedensbrücke in the town of Neckargumünd about 8 clicks east of Heidelberg at the intersection of B45 and B37. The campground is right on the Neckar River and is very peaceful. Otherwise keep an eye out for a *zimmer frei*. In my opinion, the hotels are too expensive in Heidelberg . . . too many tourists, but still a nice place to visit.

Heidelberg was not destroyed during WWII and is now a university/tourist town. The Karl-Theodor Bridge spans the Neckar River and connects the city. A castle clings to a hill overlooking the valley. Cobblestone streets wind up and down, past shops and cafes. So go for a walk. Drop by Perkeo's restaurant and grab a bite. Apparently, back in the good old days, Perkeo was the court jester and keeper of the king's wine cellar and helped himself to more than his fair share. Story goes that he died when he drank a glass of water! Go figure.

### Day 2 – Trier to Heidelberg   242 km/151 miles

From Trier head south on B51 to Saarburg.

Arrive Saarburg and continue on B51 to Merzig. At Merzig connect with the A8 and then the A6 to Kaiserslautern.

Arrive Kaiserslautern. Take the B37 to Heidelberg.

Arrive Heidelberg.

# Day 3   Heidelberg to Schwäbisch-Hall

The Burgenstrasse, or Castle Road, is a tourist route through Europe's castle country from Mannheim to Prague. The portion you will be following on this journey is along the Neckar River and is one of the most rewarding on the entire circuit. Back in the good old days (Middle Ages), the waterways of Europe connected cities and hamlets and were used as the main thoroughfares, not the roads. That's why so many castles are built along the rivers and canals. The Rhine, Danube, and even Mosel are well known and well traveled. The Neckar is not as well known and a bit less traveled. The towns along the way may still be busy, but not like Cochem or Heidelberg. Regardless, today's trip is only 69 miles, allowing some time to stop and explore.

Start by taking the B37 out of Heidelberg and then proceed on the Burgenstrasse (Castle Road). This road winds back and forth next to the river, making it perfect for a motorcycle. Meander beside the Neckar and a castle here or there will pop up on a hilltop providing some of the best scenery you will see in Europe. Continue driving on B37 through Eberbach and on down to Neckarzimmern. Stop here, stretch your legs, and visit the Burg Hornberg Castle. Climb up some of the castle towers for a great vantage point. The next town Gundelsheim also boasts a castle, the 16th-century Schloss Horneck.

*This photo was taken while driving beside the Neckar River. Deciding when to stop can be a very difficult decision . . . so keep your camera ready. Photo by John Ashley Hall.*

One town that I particularly like on this route is Bad Wimpfen. Although no castle overlooks the river, the town is an old walled city with its own medieval tower. It has very typical German architecture and for whatever reason is off the main tourist track. The locals have hidden this little gem all to themselves!

As you continue, B37 turns into B27 and eventually arrives in Heilbronn. My brother was stationed just outside of town during his stay in Germany during the Vietnam War (father like son). From Heilbronn take the B39 and B14 to Schwäbisch-Hall. Schwäbisch-Hall is another off-the-beaten-track German town. Its buildings are characteristically built in the German/Swiss style and blend in beautifully with the setting. Charming covered wooden bridges cross the River Koch to pedestrian-friendly island parks. I'd recommend taking a break from camping and find yourself a nice room in the local *gasthaus* or a nearby *zimmer frei*.

## Day 3 – Heidelberg to Schwäbisch-Hall   110 km/69 miles
From Heidelberg continue on B37 to Eberbach and then connect with B27 to Heilbronn.
Arrive Heilbronn. Take B39 and B14 to Schwäbisch-Hall.
Arrive Schwäbisch-Hall.

# Day 4  Schwäbish-Hall to Dachau

For those of you interested in seeing one of the most infamous Nazi concentration camps in Europe, I would recommend this approximately 150-mile detour to Dachau located just north of Munich. This side trip fits nicely into this loop, since you can take the Romantic Road back from Dachau to Dinkelsbul and Rothenburg ob der Tauber on Day 5.

From Schwäbish-Hall follow B19 to Gaildorf and Aalen, and then continue on B29 then B19 south again. B19 takes you through Heidenheim then connects with the autobahn (A7) heading south. Eventually connect with A8 in the direction of Augsburg/Munchen. Take the B471 to Dachau (east of the A8).

Today, Dachau is a sterile and cleaned up version of the Nazi war machine. This was the first of several concentration camps built throughout Europe during WWII. All sorts of "undesirables" were imprisoned here. Jews, Jehovah's Witnesses, homosexuals, gypsies, and Christian clergy opposed to the war were used as forced labor to manufacture armaments and other war goods. Tens of thousands were massacred. Personally, I would suggest you make this detour and see this horrific site, especially in this day

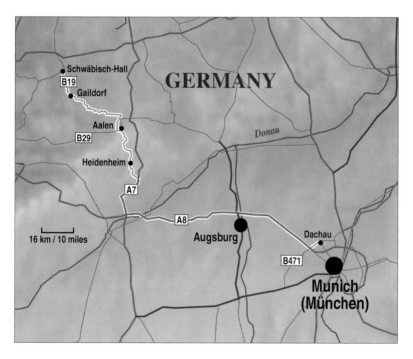

*This sign at Dachau translates to WORK MAKES YOU FREE. It really meant "Free to be Slaughtered by the Nazis." Photo by John Ashley Hall.*

and age when political pundits deny these events even happened. Seeing is definitely believing.

Dachau is only about 20 kilometers northwest of the large Bavarian city of Munich. A myriad of *zimmer freis, pensiones, gasthauses,* and campgrounds are located in this area. If you want to stay close by go to Campingplatz Nord-West between Dachau and Munich just off the B304. If you have time and want to add another day to the trip then visit Munich, home of the BMW Motorworks and the original Oktoberfest!

## Day 4 – Schwäbisch-Hall to Dachau   232 km/145 miles
From Schwäbisch-Hall follow B19 to Gaildorf and Aalen.
Continue on B29 then back onto B19 to the A7 south.
Go direction Augsburg/München on A8.
Turn left on B471 to Dachau.
Arrive Dachau.

# Day 5  Dachau to Rothenburg

Originally, the Romantische Strasse, connected the Rhine with the major Roman trade route over the Alps to Italy. Today, it is one of the most scenic (and most visited) signpost routes in Germany. The trip back north to Cochem from Dachau follows a portion of this road to Dinkelsbühl and Rothenburg ob der Tauber.

From Dachau head back to the A8 on B471. On the A8 go toward Stuttgart, and then take the B2 to Donauwörth and the B25 to Dinkelsbühl. The road will wander through some of the most fertile farmland in Germany. As this is a popular route, buses loaded with tourists may slow you down a bit, but, oh well, you're going slowly anyway while you enjoy the scenery. Brown ROMANTISCHE STRASSE signs mark the road, making it hard to get lost.

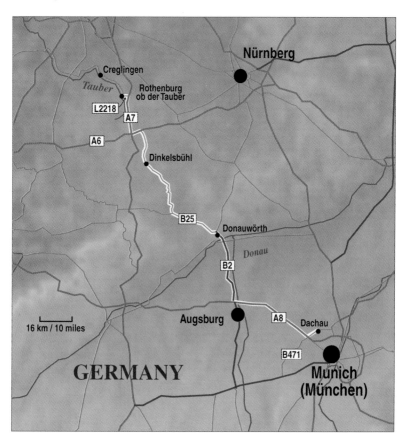

*Welcome to Rothenburg! One of the best preserved medieval walled cities in Germany. Photo by Bradley Clark.*

There are various sites along the way, but the most rewarding are Dinkelsbühl and Rothenburg. Dinkelsbühl is a typical German medieval town with towers, gates, and walls. Definitely worth a stop to have lunch and wander around a bit before heading to the granddaddy of all medieval fortress town—Rothenburg ob der Tauber.

## Day 5 – Dachau to Rothenburg   195 km/122 miles

From Dachau take B471 back to A8 and head toward Stuttgart. Take B2 to Donauwörth then go straight on B25 to Dinkelsbühl.
Arrive Dinkelsbühl. Continue north on B25. Turn left on A6 then right on A7 to Rothenburg ob der Tauber. Turn left on L2218.
Arrive Rothenburg ob der Tauber.

Continue on B25 out of Dinkelsbühl. Turn left on A6, then connect with A7 north. Rothenburg is easily accessible right off the A7. Usually, when I go I try to arrive late afternoon, head over to the very pleasant Campingplatz Tauberromantik and set up camp. The campground is well kept and only about one or two kilometers from town (northwest of Rothenburg on the way to Creglingen). By the time you set up camp and start to wander up to Rothenburg it is early evening and most of the tourists

*The Romantic Road is one of the most famous in Europe. Originally a medieval trade route, it runs through the heart of southern Germany. Though it can be busy during the peak summer months it is not to be missed. Photo by Toby Ballentine.*

*The narrow cobblestone streets in Rothenburg were built long before the modern automobile was invented. Photo by Bradley Clark.*

are on their way out. The bulk of the visitors only come for the day before heading south to Munich or north and west to Heidelberg and the Rhine River. The town will still be busy, but nothing like midday.

Undoubtedly, Rothenburg caters to the tourist industry, but there is nothing to compare to this gem of a town. The originality of the architecture, buildings, and walls puts this town in a class all by itself. Many people just spend a couple of hours wandering the cobblestone streets; I would recommend a couple of days. There is much to explore and, more likely than not, some sort of festival will be going on that you shouldn't miss! This is one town where you will definitely want to play tourist. It's that much fun!

## Day 6  Rothenburg to Worms

After getting enough of Rothenburg (hard to do), follow the L2268 and L2251 along the Tauber River to Creglingen. The roads on today's journey twist and turn along the Tauber and Main Rivers through some of the most beautiful countryside in Germany. This trip will reconfirm your faith in why we ride motorcycles. The asphalt is pristine and the small towns less visited than the more popular Rhine and Mosel river valleys.

Creglingen was originally founded by the Celts more than 2,000 years ago. It is a small village, but the architecture captures the essence of this very German region. Drive slowly through town, stop if you like, or just continue on to Bad Mergentheim. There is a great little square in this town for a stop and to relax. Formerly tied to the Teutonic Order, Bad Mergentheim is home to a medieval castle and some well-known mineral-rich hot springs.

From Bad Mergentheim, continue on B290 to Tauberbischofsheim. Set in the Tauber valley beside its namesake river this is another town well worth a brief stop. In particular, you may want to visit the Chapel of St. Wolfgang and read the legend about Johann Klinger and a stone he found in his field. (Visit the chapel yourself and get the rest of the story.)

From Tauberbishofsheim, take the B27 to Walldürn, then cruise on the B47 to Amorbach and Michelstadt. Walldürn has an impressive basilica and Amorbach's church is built around a gorgeous baroque organ. Each of these

*Castles beckon you around each bend. This one rises above the valley with both foreboding and grandeur. Photo by John Ashley Hall.*

towns evokes all that is typical of old Germany, but Michelstadt is one of the most charming. It is a small town, only a few city blocks in size, but very well preserved. The half-timbered houses, city wall, and fountain-filled town square tempt you to stay a bit longer. So . . . time to make a choice. You can continue on the B47 to Worms, known for its history surrounding Martin Luther, or just stay put and enjoy the small town ambiance of Michelstadt. Either way, you can't lose. Your choice!

## Day 6 – Rothenburg to Worms   189 km/118 miles

Leave Rothenburg ob der Tauber on L2268 and L2251 along the Tauber River to Creglingen and on to Bad Mergentheim.

Arrive Bad Mergentheim and continue on B290 to Tauberbischofsheim.

Arrive Tauberbischofsheim and then take B27 to Walldürn. Continue on B47 to Michelstadt and Worms.

# Day 7  Worms to Cochem

From Worms take the A61 and then connect with B9 to Bingen. Bingen dates back to the Roman times. As you drive up the Rhine, you will see a funky looking structure called the Mouse Tower. Apparently, the evil king from this area was devoured by mice in the infamous tower. Yuk!

Continue on to Bacharach and then take a break. This is another pleasant medieval town now surviving off tourists. The shops, church, towers, and walls make this an enjoyable layover for lunch or a pastry. Visit the town square and then climb the tower up on the hill for some great views.

The next stop, St. Goar, has one of the biggest castles in Germany—The Rheinfels Castle. The only problem is it's in ruins, but pretty good ruins! If you want to tour a castle and get a good idea how they operated, survived, and defended themselves then take a tour of the Rheinfels Castle. It's got all the amenities from gardens to dungeons.

From St. Goar continue on B9 to Boppard, and then head west on L209 then right on B327. At L207 turn left, then left again on B416. This should

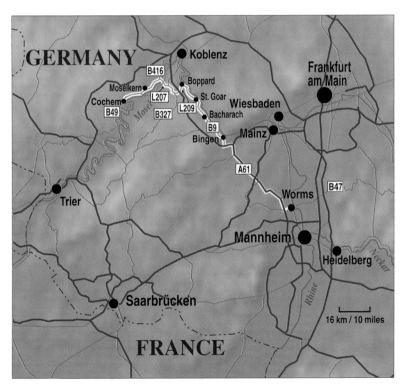

*Burg Eltz is just off the main road in the Mosel River Valley. Rather than drive to the parking lot by the castle, park your bike at the trailhead and take the two- to three-mile hike to the entrance. Photo by Toby Ballentine.*

get you back to the Mosel River and the town of Moselkern. Not far outside of town is another castle worth a serious look—Burg Eltz.

The castle is just off the river and looks like the castle you've always imagined. Set next to a stream that feeds into the Mosel, a dark forest and an occasional mist provide a very realistic backdrop. Still owned and inhabited by the original family, Burg Eltz is worth a visit and even a tour if you still have time. Otherwise, just sit out front, enjoy the view and take a few pictures.

Burg Eltz is located just a few kilometers outside Cochem where this whole journey began—a perfect way to end your loop through the river valleys of Germany.

### Day 7 – Worms to Cochem    146 km/91 miles

From Worms take the A61 toward Koblenz, and then take B9 to St. Goar/Rhein.

Arrive Bacharach. Continue on B9 to St. Goar and Boppard.

Arrive Boppard. From Boppard go east on L209 and then right on B327.
    At L207 turn left then left again on B416 to Moselkern and Burg Eltz.

Arrive Burg Eltz and follow road to Cochem.

# The Famous Alpine Road and Sound of Music Tour

**Distance:** *1145 km/715 miles*
**Suggested Time Frame:** *8–9 days*
**Highlights:** *The famous Alpenstrasse takes you through Southern Bavaria and Mad King Ludwig's castles. Small towns with fresco-adorned chalets sit beside azure lakes and snowcapped mountains. The roads are narrow but well-maintained and well-marked, making this an easy route to follow and enjoy. The ride back through the Austrian Tyrol is a bit less touristy, but just as magnificent.*

*The Castle Hohenschwangau was the childhood home of King Ludwig and is located just across from the Neuschwanstein Castle. Photo by Mark Allred.*

The small towns of Bavaria and the Austrian Tyrol are incomparable. There is a uniqueness and charm that can only be found in this part of the world. Several years ago while traveling through this area, our family stopped in a town called Zell am Zee and didn't leave for two weeks. At the time, I didn't realize this was the final stop for Stephen Ambrose's Band of Brothers during their trek across war-ravaged Europe. What a great place to recover from the horrors of the war!

This ride combines the snow-capped Alps with Cinderella-like castles and black asphalt that gyrates like a dancer's hips making this one of the most popular journeys in all of Europe. It starts in Lindau on the Bodensee (Lake Constance), follows the Alpenstrasse through southern Germany and then loops back across the Tyrolean Alps. Towns with names like Füssen, Berchtesgaden, Garmisch, Salzburg, Hallstatt, Kitzubühel become alpine paradises that pull you in and won't let you go. Hope you brought your cell phone to call home and extend you vacation another few weeks!

*This type of frescoed storefront in Oberammergau, Germany, can be seen throughout Bavaria and Tyrol. Photo by Mark Allred.*

*Walt Disney copied his Snow White castle after Neuschwanstein Castle in Füssen, Germany. Do you see the similiarity? The castle had been a childhood dream of King Ludwig, who tragically died before the castle was even finished. Photo by Mark Allred.*

Most of the days cover relatively short distances. There are too many towns and street-side cafes begging you to stop. If you want to speed the trip up, be my guest, combine the days and do this trip in four days. Personally, I prefer two weeks. Castles, old salt mines, misty gorges, and alpine lakes all wrapped together with just the right amount of history and good food provide all the necessary ingredients for a full-fledged vacation retreat. Many Europeans spend their entire four-week vacation hiking, exploring, and traveling through this area.

# Day 1  Lindau to Füssen

Start in Lindau, one of the loveliest resorts in Germany. Situated on a small island accessible by a narrow causeway, Lindau is immaculately dressed. A beautiful promenade overlooking the Bodensee and the Swiss Alps make this an idyllic location to get started. From Lindau, take the B12 and the B18 northeast to Wangen im Allgäu.

Wangen im Allgäu lies on the Argen River and has been around since the 800s AD. The Ravensburg Gate is the prime landmark in town. Narrow streets and motif-adorned homes make this a great first stop. Continue west on B12 to Isny im Allgäu then take the B309 and B310 on to Füssen. I would suggest setting up camp before seeing Füssen and the surrounding area. I usually camp in Schwangau at Camping Brunnen am Forggensee. This is a very nice five-star camping resort right on the lake with views of the water and the Neuschwanstein Castle. If possible, spend two nights here. Visiting the castles, the town of Füssen, and then hiking up to Mary's Bridge and around the Alpsee make for a full day. Use Rick Steve's book as a guide.

*This is another picture of Neuschwanstein Castle taken while hiking up to the entrance. No matter how you look at it, this castle is a beauty.*
*Photo by Toby Ballentine.*

### Day 1 – Lindau to Füssen   107 km/67 miles

Start in Lindau. Take the B12 and then the B18 to Wangen im Allgäu.

Arrive Wangen im Allgäu. Take the B32 south, then head west on B12 to Isny im Allgäu.

Arrive Isny im Allgäu. Continue on B12 and then the B309 and B310 to Füssen.

Arrive Füssen.

## Day 2  Füssen to Garmisch-Partenkirchen

Once again, another short day of driving, but still filled with great rides, scenery, and traditional Bavarian villages. Today you will be visiting a small chapel with an eye-poppin' interior, another one of Mad King Ludwig's castles and then end the day at Garmisch-Partenkirchen, home of the 1936 Winter Olympics. Start by going north on B17 toward Steingaden, then turn right on St2059 and St2559 to Wieskirche (the church in Wies). Follow the signs—you won't miss it. Wieskirche has a non-descript exterior, but don't be fooled, the interior will knock your socks off. The parking lot is usually full of tourist buses and cars, but this is why we drive motorcycles—you can find a parking spot just about anywhere.

The pilgrims started coming to this remote church in the mid-1700s when, miraculously, tears were seen on a wooden carving of Christ. Due to the thousands of visitors since that event, this church and shrine were built to house the carving. The interior is one huge painting. Don't miss this!

From Wieskirche, head back to St2059 then turn right and right again on B23 to Oberammergau, the home of the famous once-in-a-decade Passion Play. Oberammergau escaped the devastation of the Bubonic Plague in 1634 and in commemoration re-enacts Christ's life once every 10 years. Continue on B23 south then turn left on St2060 to Linderhof. At Linderhof is another castle built by King Ludwig. He also built a grotto on the grounds where special invited guests could come and listen to a

*The interior of this small church in Wies is unbelievable. Glad we stopped! Photo by Toby Ballentine.*

Wagnerian opera.

When you've had enough, turn around and connect again with B23 and head on to Garmisch. The town is nestled right below the Zugspitze, Germany's highest mountain. There is a convenient campsite about two miles west of town on B23 and close to the ski lifts. Set up camp and then wander a bit through town and take the lift up the Zugspitze. I could tell you about an experience my brother and I had skiing the Zugspitze as teenagers, but I'll save that for the next edition (plus my brother might have my head if I shared it). It's about a one-and-a-half-hour trip one way, so be sure you have enough time.

### Day 2 – Füssen to Garmisch-Partenkirchen   85 km/53 miles

Leave Füssen on B17 north toward Steingaden. From Steingaden turn right on St2059 and St2559 to Wieskirche.

Arrive Wieskirche. Turn around and at St2059 turn right and then at B23 turn right to Oberammergau.

Arrive Oberammergau. Continue on B23 south. Turn left on St2060 to Linderhof.

Arrive Linderhof. Turn around and then follow B23 to Garmisch-Partenkirchen.

Arrive Garmisch-Partenkirchen.

## Day 3  Garmisch-Partenkirchen to Tegernsee

The roads for the next couple of days hug the Bavarian Alps and wind through some of the most picturesque countryside in the world. The Alpenstrasse rings true to its name! From Garmisch take the B2 east, and then turn left on B11 to Wallgau. Wallgau sits in the Isar Valley surrounded by mountains. I would suggest a brief detour north to the Walchensee. This lake has a deep blue azure color and is ringed by summits and conifers. This is also the lake where King Ludwig drowned. Take a few pictures, then head back to Wallgau and follow the Alpenstrasse from Wallgau to Vorderriß. The road follows the Isar River and eventually links into the B307. Follow the signs toward the Tegernsee. The B307 follows the east shore of the lake through Rottach-Egern and Tegernsee to Gmund, while the B318 branches left to Bad Wiessee and continues up the west shore of the lake.

These properties along the Tegernsee are some of the most expensive in Germany. Wooded shores, hiking trails, boating, and skiing make this both a summer and winter haven. So, find yourself a *gasthaus* or camping spot of your liking then go for a carriage ride in Bad Wiessee, wander the upscale neighborhoods of Rottach-Egern, or just grab your crumpled up

*Linderhof is the only one of the "fantasy" castles King Ludwig built that he inhabited before his untimely death. Don't miss visiting the grotto built exclusively for personal performances by the composer Wagner. Photo by Mark Allred.*

paperback book and enjoy a good read as you sit on a bench beside the Tegernsee.

### Day 3 – Garmisch-Partenkirchen to Tegernsee   80 km/50 miles

From Garmisch take the B2 east, and then turn left on B11. Just after Wallgau turn right to Vorderriß (Alpenstrasse) and then connect with B307. Connect with B13 and then B307 again. Eventually head north on B318 to Bad Wiessee.

Arrive Bad Wiessee. Head back on B318 and follow the road around the lake to Rottach-Egern and Tegernsee.

Arrive Tegernsee/Gmund.

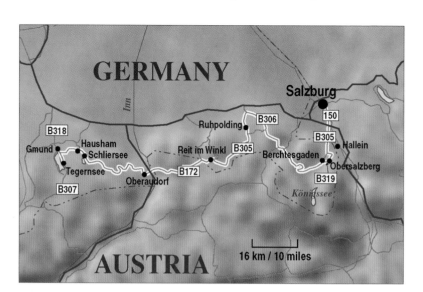

# Day 4  Tegernsee to Salzburg

Just north of the small town of Tegernsee and south of Gmund, head east on the Alpenstrasse to Hausham, then go south on B307 to Schliersee. The lake and town are, once again, picture postcard perfect. If you're off to an early start, stop at a pastry shop for some strudel and hot chocolate. The road winds through some sharp hairpins then meanders to Oberaudorf and Reit im Winkl on the B172. Reit im Winkl is a popular resort with its primary industry being tourism. This typical alpine village is active in both summer and winter. Take a hike up the Grünbühel for views of the Kaiser Mountains. From Reit im Winkl continue on the Alpenstrasssse B305 to Ruhpolding, home of the St. Georg Parish Church. Take a look, then continue south on B305 to Berchtesgaden.

There is much to see and do around Berchtesgaden. It was once a popular resort for the Nazi elite and the home of Hitler's Eagle's Nest. If you want to see the sights in this part of Bavaria, then find a camping spot or *gasthaus* and spend the night. You could easily spend a day visiting the Salzbergwerk (salt mines), Kehlsteinhaus (Eagle's Nest), and the Königssee. The Königssee is a gorgeous lake with no road around it. A monastery resides on the opposite end of the lake and is only accessible by boat.

The trip on to Salzburg is on B319 via the small town of Obersalzberg. This is a well-known road in Germany and is often used as a motorcircuit, so don't be surprised if you get caught behind some vintage automobiles!

*Hohensalzburg Castle, built in the 11th century, lies watch over the city of Salzburg.
Photo by Toby Ballentine.*

After swinging around the U-shaped B319, reconnect with B305 and head north to Salzburg. Just west of the 150 and south of the autobahn is a nice campground called the Panorama Camping Stadtblick. It's about 4 km outside of town and built on a terraced slope. Find a grassy spot, set up camp, and more likely than not, you'll end up with views of Hohensalzburg Castle.

One day in Salzburg is the minimum. After a visit to the castle, Mirabell Palace, wandering downtown, and taking a *Sound of Music* Tour, your day will be shot. Also, one of my favorite salt mine tours is the Dürrnberg Salt Mines in Hallein, about 8 miles south of town.

---

### Day 4 – Tegernsee to Salzburg   181 km/113 miles

Just north of Tegernsee and south of Gmund head east on the Alpenstrasse to Hausham. At Hausham go south on B307 to Schliersee.

Arrive Schliersee. Continue on B307 and connect with B172 in Oberaudorf and on to Reit im Winkl.

Arrive Reit im Winkl and take the B305 and B306 to Ruhpolding and on to Berchtesgaden.

Arrive Berchtesgaden. Take the B319 toward Obersalzberg then go north on B305, which becomes 160 then 150 as you enter Salzburg.

Arrive Salzburg.

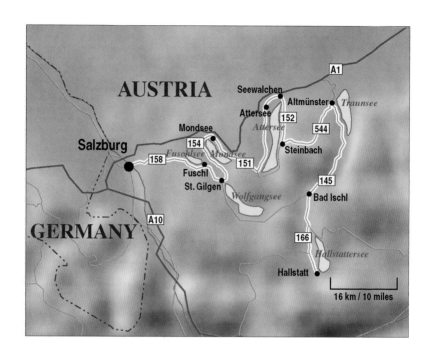

# Day 5  Salzburg to Hallstatt

From Day 5 to Day 8, this journey wanders blissfully through the Salzkammergut and the Austrian Tyrol. Known for its unparalleled beauty, this region of small towns, lakes, and ski resorts offers you some of the best motorcycling the world has to offer. When you open up your visor, smell the fresh alpine-scented air, and gaze on the color-filled scenery—you'll think you've been transplanted to a painted canvas. The landscape may seem surreal and you may have to pinch yourself to be sure it is not a dream.

From Salzburg take road 158 to Fuschl overlooking the Fuschlsee, then head north on road 154 to Mondsee. The road hugs the lake then wraps around the top back down to where you can connect with 151 north again to Attersee. Just follow the road to Seewalchen, then swing south on 152 to Steinbach. At Steinbach connect with 544 to Altmünster, then go south along the lake on road 145 to Bad Ischl. Continue south, bear right on 166 and follow the road to the Hallstattersee and the picturesque village of Hallstatt.

Each of these towns is idyllically set beside a deep azure alpine lake with mountains soaring in the background. Old churches, monasteries, and lakeside cafes invite you to stop each step of the way. The small town of Hallstatt is the epitome of Tyrolean beauty and has been named a UNESCO World Heritage

*The epitomy of the quintessential alpine village, Hallstatt, is a World Heritage Site that clings tenaciously between a rugged mountain and an azure lake. You may have to pinch yourself to make sure this isn't a dream! Photo by Laurie Taylor.*

Site. There is a campsite called the Campingplatz Klausner-Holl just south of town. After setting up camp, drop by the local supermarket, buy some dark rye bread, salami, and Swiss cheese, and then head to the park just alongside the lake. If you have a good book, bring it along for company, then have dinner, entertainment (your book), and the best view in Europe for less money than taking the family to McDonald's.

### Day 5 – Salzburg to Hallstatt   184 km/115 miles

From Salzburg take road 158 to Fuschl.
Arrive Fuschl. Take road 154 north to Mondsee.
Arrive Mondsee. Take road 151 to Attersee.
Arrive Attersee. Take road 151 then 152 south to Steinbach. Connect with road 544 to Altmünster then follow 145 beside the Traunsee to Bad Ischl. Continue south, bear right onto 166, and follow the road alongside the lake to Hallstatt.
Arrive Hallstatt.

## Day 6   Hallstatt to Kitzbühel

After a relaxing day in Hallstatt, go north back to road 166 and then turn left. Continue south to A10, take the A10 south a short distance, then get off at B163 to St. Johann im Pongau. This is a well-known ski area in Austria, but also home to the Dekanatskirche St. Johannes, a remarkable neo-gothic cathedral. Another nice detour, just south of town, is a well-known gorge and waterfalls, the Liechtensteinklamm.

From St. Johann go north on road 311. Take 159 to Bischofshofen, then west on B164 to Saalfelden am Steinernen Meer. Connect with road 311 to Lofer. At Lofer take B178 to Erpfendorf and St. Johann in Tirol. At St. Johann continue south on road 161 to Kitzbühel. This is the heart of Austrian ski country. Bischofshofen is known for its ski jumping, while St. Johann and Kitzbühel are famous world wide for their downhill skiing. Geranium-filled windowsills and fresco-adorned houses line the asphalt as you drive through this alpine dreamscape.

Kitzbühel was originally a midpoint on the Bavaria-to-Italy trade route. The nearby salt mines contributed to its value as well. Nowadays, Kitzbühel

*I could drive through the lake district of Austria (Salzkammergut) all summer long! Photo by Mark Allred.*

is a chic ski resort that caters to an upscale clientele. But don't worry, there are several campsites around town that are quite affordable for the traveling motorcyclist on a tight budget.

### Day 6 – Hallstatt to Kitzbühel   182 km/114 miles

From Hallstatt go back to the road 166 intersection and turn left (west). Follow 166 all the way to A10 (south). Hop on A10 for a short ride, then get off at road B163 (west) to St. Johann im Pongau.

Arrive St. Johann im Pongau. Go north on 311, then take 159 to Bischofshofen. At Bischofshofen go west on B164 to Saalfelden am Steinernen Meer. Connect with 311 to Lofer.

Arrive Lofer. Take the B178 to Erpfendorf and St. Johann in Tyrol. Then connect with 161 to Kitzbühel.

Arrive Kitzbühel.

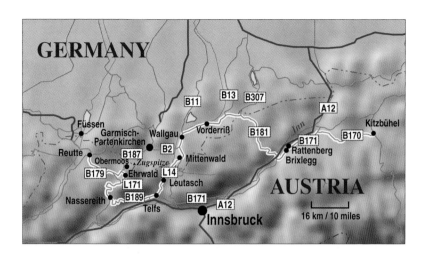

## Day 7   Kitzbühel to Reutte

Get up late and head west from Kitzbühel on B170, then turn left on road 171 to Rattenberg and Brixlegg. Rattenberg is a small, well-preserved medieval town. Park your bike just outside of town and then walk in to the pedestrian-friendly town center. Stroll around a bit and visit the burgher's house and baroque-style church. Hop back on your bike and then meander on through Brixlegg. As you cruise along the blacktop, you'll see several castles on either side of the road. Stop if you like, otherwise just drive slowly and enjoy the scenery.

After Brixlegg, take the B181 back into Germany and connect with the Alpenstrasse again. Head west through Vorderriß and Wallgau. At Wallgau turn left on B2 and go south to Mittenwald, another charmer of a town. As you take L14 from Mittenwald to Leutasch, the asphalt re-enters the Leutasch area of Austria. This high plateau is relatively wide open with several small hamlets along the way. Mountains line the perimeter, cows graze in the highlands, and hikers regularly visit the many trails in this area.

From Leutasch take the L35 to Telfs. The road will weave gently across the open fields and then veer in a southwesterly direction through the small hamlets of Telfs, Barwies, and Nassereith. At Telfs follow the B171 then connect with B189 to Nassereith. Continue north on B179. Eventually you will pass a lake, then cross over a small pass, the Fernpass, to Ehrwald. You are now on the south side of the Zugspitze (Garmisch is on the other side). If you didn't make it up the mountain on Day 2, take the speedy cable car from the village of Obermoos. It only takes about 8 minutes to get to the top!

*Nothing like coming home to the local gasthaus and a warm plate of weinershnitzel after a long day of riding. Photo by Mark Allred.*

From Ehrwald take the L171 then the B179 to Reutte. Reutte is a more relaxed Tyrolean town and caters mostly to local tourists. It's also very close to Füssen if you missed seeing King Ludwig's Neuschwanstein Castle. There is a nice campground, Camping Reutte, less than a mile outside of town.

### Day 7 – Kitzbühel to Reutte   234 km/146 miles

From Kitzbühel head west on B170 then veer left on 171 to Rattenberg and Brixlegg. Take B181 toward Germany and connect with B13 and B307 to Wallgau (via Vorderriß).

Arrive Wallgau. Take B2 to Mittenwald.

Arrive Mittenwald.

From Mittenwald take the L14 back into Austria to Leutasch.

Arrive Leutasch. Take the L35 to Telfs then the B171 thru town to B189. Follow B189 and connect with B179 at Nassereith to Ehrwald and then on to Reutte.

Arrive Reutte.

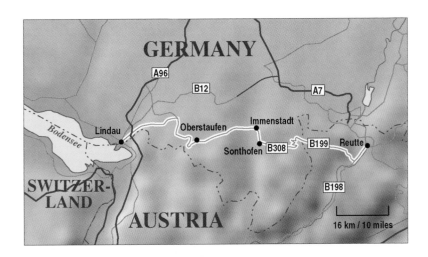

# Day 8  Reutte to Lindau

From Reutte, Austria, take the B198 then the B199 back to Germany. Reconnect with the Deutsche Alpenstrasse (B308) to Sonthofen. The B308 winds back to Lindau through the towns of Immenstadt and Oberstaufen. If you want to stop at just one town, stop at Immenstadt. Built next to another typical alpine lake, the town has a neat baroque parish church and

*The snowcapped Alps serve as a backdrop to the green valleys that lie around each corner in Bavaria. Photo by Bradley Clark.*

*The Tower Mangenturn guards the Lindau Harbor on Lake Constance. Built on an island,*
*Lindau is nestled right on the borders of Germany, Austria, and Switzerland.*
*Photo by Mark Allred.*

townhall. There are also some 17th-century castle ruins just outside of town
(just what you want to see . . . another castle!).

You'll have more than enough time to drive back to Lindau to enjoy your
evening there. This is your last night, so splurge and stay in town and then
dine at one of the cafes along the promenade. Enjoy your meal as a gentle
breeze blows off the lake and read another chapter of this book as you plan
your next motorcycle adventure across Western Europe.

## Day 8 – Reutte to Lindau   93 km/58 miles

From Reutte take the B198 to the B199 into Germany. Then take B308
to Sonthofen.

Arrive Sonthofen. Follow the B308 to Immenstadt, Oberstaufen and
Lindau.

Arrive Lindau.

# Austria and Switzerland

You're going to love these two small countries. Austria and Switzerland are situated in some of the most picturesque countryside in the world. Pictures don't ever do this area justice! And to make it even better, the roads in both countries are fabulous—a perfect combination for a motorcyclist. The blacktop is usually well maintained and marked, making your ride through the Austrian and Swiss Alps a dream come true. The only hitch is that driving on the expressways is almost unavoidable. So just remember when you cross the border, you need to purchase a sticker (vignette) that allows driving on these roads. Instead of collecting tolls, Austria and Switzerland charge road fees via the vignette. I wouldn't chance not buying one—the fine is substantial and then you have to buy a sticker anyway. Vignettes can be purchased at the border, post offices, and gas stations.

Camping is excellent in these countries. The facilities are almost always spotless and well-kept. Since camping is so popular here, the sites are often in very picturesque surroundings. When the weather cooperates, I have often slept outside my tent with views of waterfalls cascading down towering cliffs. Not bad for $10 to $15 per night!

The cost of living is a bit higher here, especially in Switzerland. Camping and shopping at the local grocery stores really does make a difference! No way could I afford staying in hotels or eating out. Austria uses the euro and Switzerland has its own currency, the almighty Swiss franc! The exchange rate is even worse than the euro (as I said, camp and shop and you'll be fine). I would recommend flying into Munich, Germany, or Zürich/Bern, Switzerland. Actually, even Milan, Italy, will work. All are close to this area and offer affordable motorcycle rentals. One final note—be prepared for inclement weather—afternoon thundershowers are quite common.

# Heaven on Earth: Into the Heart of Switzerland

**Distance:** *806 km/504 miles*
**Suggested Time Frame:** *5–6 days*
**Highlights:** *The Swiss have created a culture engineered to taking care of its favorite visitor—the tourist. The cog railroads, funiculars, massive tunnels, and roads combine to make Switzerland accessible to all. But not without a price—Switzerland is a bit more expensive than her neighbors. That's why camping is so ideal here—great locations at a great price. This trek will take you across various regions starting in the conservative eastern area of Appenzell all the way to the old French canton near Aigle and Gruyeres. And no matter which direction you steer, there is no such thing as a bad road!*

You may not like to hear this, but Switzerland is not just about roads. The Swiss have created an enclave where time in some respects has stood still. I presume a traveler from 100 years ago would easily recognize many of the sights on this trip and probably not even get lost! Though a bit more expensive than its neighbors, Switzerland has been a sanctuary for hundreds of years—and its culture still shows it. It's a trip back in time.

This route takes you deep into the country and bypasses the major tourist destinations of St. Moritz and Zermatt. Rather it takes you to a few of the less visited regions—Appenzell, Chur, Aigle, Thun, and Brienz to name a few. But remember, regardless of where this journey takes you, the roads will not disappoint. This is a country where getting lost is not a mistake, but a blessing. So use this chapter as an outline, then turn off your GPS, get lost and see if you can find a boring road . . . I don't believe there is such a thing in Switzerland!

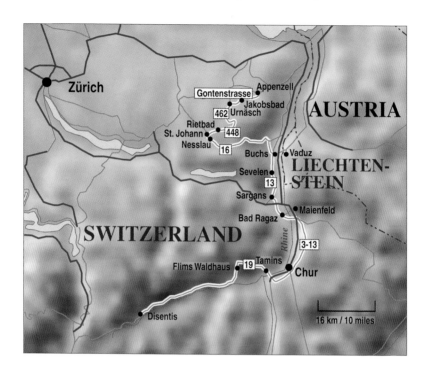

# Day 1   Appenzell to Disentis

We will start in the very traditional region of Switzerland—Appenzell. For many years this area has been (and still is) a very conservative bastion of the Swiss. From politics to culture to costume-clad townsfolk, this region is covered with bell-swinging cows and a somewhat peculiar smelling cheese.

    The town of Appenzell itself is pedestrian friendly and caters primarily to the tourist trade. What is most appealing, however, is the countryside. This area is stereotypical Switzerland and draws hikers and vacationers from all over the world. There is a campground just above town that provides splendid views of the surrounding area—I'd recommend you stay there. Follow road 448 outside of town then take the Enggenhuttenstrasse south to the campground.

    It may be hard to pull yourself away from this picturesque haven, but far more awaits as you motorcycle deeper into Switzerland. From Appenzell, head west on the Gontenstrasse to Urnäsch. On the way you will drive through the small town of Jakobsbad. There is a summer bobsled ride there that will remind you of Disneyland's Matterhorn. Just be sure to remember which handle is the brake! Continue on through the small, but pleasant

*Looking down from Wengen across the valley to the Jungfrau makes you believe you have found Heaven on earth. Photo by Toby Ballentine.*

village of Urnäsch and then veer south on road 462. Turn right on 448 and follow it as it swings west through Rietbad and St. Johann.

At St. Johann turn left on road 16 to Buchs and then south on Road 13 to Sevelen, Sargans, and Bad Ragaz. The area around Bad Ragaz is often referred to as "Heidiland" due to the children's classic, *Heidi,* being set here.

### Day 1 - Appenzell to Disentis   173 km/108 mile

Start in Appenzell and take the Gontenstrasse to Urnäsch.

Arrive Urnäsch. Veer south on road 462 and then right on road 448 to Rietbad and Nesslau. Then take road 16 to Buchs.

Arrive Buchs. Continue south on road 13 to Sevelen. At Sargans connect with the 3-13 to Bad Ragaz and Chur.

Arrive Chur. Take road 13 west to Tamins and then connect with road 19 to Flims Waldhaus and on to Disentis.

Arrive Disentis.

The town of Maienfeld is just east of Bad Ragaz. If you are a big Heidi-groupie then spend some time visiting the area. In my opinion, it's a bit overdone.

From Bad Ragaz, continue on 3-13 south to Chur. Nestled beside the Brambrüesch Mountain, Chur is one of the oldest towns in Switzerland. The gothic town center and 800-year-old cathedral are worth visiting. If

*The first tunnel in Switzerland was built in the early 1700s over the Gotthard Pass and the Swiss haven't stopped since. Even the shorter ones are fun on a bike. Photo by Ron Ayres.*

*This is a typical road in the Swiss Alps. And they seem to go on forever.*
*Photo by Ron Ayres.*

you want a drink, try the outlandish Giger Bar—named after H.R. Giger, the creator of *Alien.*

Continue on road 13 and then merge onto 19 at Tamins. You are about to embark on one of the most memorable motorcycle rides in all of Europe. The mountains, valleys, glaciers, and hairpin passes all converge to make this a one-of-a-kind motorcycling delight. From Tamins follow 19 to Flims-Waldhaus and then eventually to Disentis.

Disentis/Sedrun is where the mighty Rhine River begins its descent into Germany and on to the North Sea. The area is pristine and makes a superb overnighter before heading over some truly Swiss-like passes on Day 2. There are a host of hotels, *zimmer freis,* and campgrounds to select and you can't go wrong! Just bundle up in your sleeping bag, as it does get a little chilly at night.

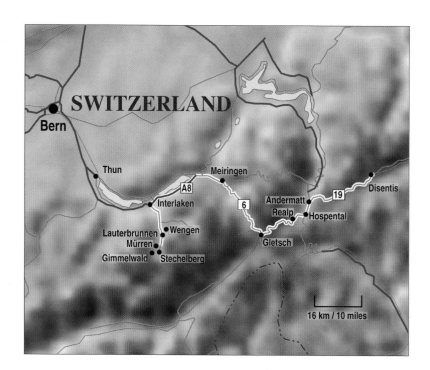

## Day 2   Disentis to Lauterbrunnen

Prepare yourself for a day of unforgettable motorcycling with three unbelievable mountain passes and ending with camping overnight beneath the mammoth Jungfrau in Lauterbrunnen. Start by continuing on road 19 over the Oberalppass. The asphalt tops out at about 6,500 feet then winds down to the small town of Andermatt—home to the hard core skier. Continue along 19 to Hospental and its namesake castle, then on through the Ursenen Valley to Realp. The road then works its magic up and over the Furkapass. This pass has been in a couple of James Bond movies and starts by climbing up the Fuchsegg (nine sharp bends) and then slides down to the village of Gletsch. There is a lot of twisting on this road, both of your bike and your neck—the views of Switzerland are at their best. Glaciers, lakes, valleys, and mountain peaks fill the horizon. This is one pass that will be forever embedded in your memory.

At Gletsch, turn right on road 6 over another pass, the Grimselpass, and continue to Meiringen. If you are a Sherlock Holmes fan, this is a mandatory stop. Meiringen is home to the Reichenbach Falls and is the presumed spot where Holmes met his unfortunate demise. Even if you are not a

*Be alert driving over the passes in the Swiss and Italian Alps. Snow and ice are still a hazard in the summertime. Often snow is still being plowed and is several feet deep beside the road. But as you can see, the dangers are well worth it! Photo by Ron Ayres.*

Sherlock fan, the waterfalls are worth seeing.

Continue on A8 and you will eventually end up in Interlaken, a nice, but tourist infested town. I prefer to stay south of town in the valley right beneath the Jungfrau and Eiger mountains. This whole area is geared to the summer/winter visitor. The Swiss engineers have built funiculars, cog trains, and cable cars to take you to mountain retreats and backcountry

### Day 2 - Disentis to Lauterbrunnen   142 km/89 miles

From Disentis continue on road 19 to Andermatt, Realp and Gletsch. At
    Gletsch turn right on road 6 to Meiringen then left on A8 to Interlaken.
Arrive Interlaken. From Interlaken head south to Wengen/
    Lauterbrunnen/Jungfrau.
Arrive Lauterbrunnen.

Yikes! That's my daughter up there! Sure hope that paraglider knows what he is doing. All my kids took turns gliding down from Wengen past the Staubach Falls in Lauterbrunnen. Photo by Toby Ballentine.

alpine villages. Several of the towns in this area are not even accessible by motorized vehicle. There is a nice campground in Lauterbrunnen that is right next to a local waterfall. This is usually where I stay.

If you have time spend two nights here and experience the Alps at their best. Take the cog train up the Jungfrau or the cable car to the Schilthorn and eat at the Piz Gloria restaurant or just wander around this hiker's paradise. One word of caution—neither of these popular trips up the Jungfrau or Schilthorn are cheap! You can easily spend $100 to $200 per person (including your meal). So if you are on a tight budget, do what I do and drive your bike up to Stechelberg just up the road from Lauterbrunnen, take the

*Ever heard of having the road all to yourself? Well, don't count on it, but when you do there is no place better than in the Alps. Photo by Ron Ayres.*

cable car to Gimmelwald (great little rustic town) and Mürren, then catch the funicular up the Allmendhubel and hike back down to Gimmelwald. The scenery is almost as spectacular. There is a restaurant on top of Allmendhubel, if you want to eat there, or while hiking down to Gimmelwald, stop at one of the alpine huts along the way offering drinks and food. Couldn't ask for a better setting and it's about one-fifth the cost of going up the Jungfrau!

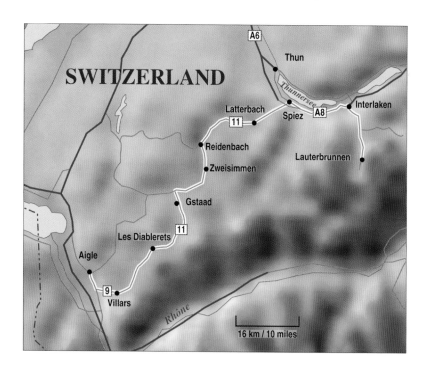

# Day 3 Lauterbrunnen to Aigle

After a couple of relaxing days in Lauterbrunnen, load up your bike and head back to Interlaken. Turn left on A8 and drive to Spiez. You will be driving along the Thunnersee, one of the most beautiful lakes in Switzerland. Spiez is located by a small bay and as you approach the town on the Seestrasse an elegant castle rises above the town. Stop by the castle and adjacent church, grab a pastry, and enjoy the views across the water. There are usually a number of small sailboats and yachts plying the horizon.

From Spiez take road 11 west toward Gstaad. This is a pleasant run through several small villages and valleys. The road will veer south to Reidenbach. The next village you approach is Zweisimmen. It lies in a wide valley and is the gateway to the Gstaad-Saanenland region. If you have time, there is a beautiful lake, the Seebergsee, not too far away that is worth a visit.

From Zweisimmen follow the signs to Gstaad. Gstaad is another chic stomping ground for the rich and famous and I'm not sure why. The town is rather small and has no more charm than any other town in the area. Stop if you like, otherwise drive on by the pricey boutiques and continue south through Les Diablerets. You're going to love this part of the road as it winds

*By offering a snack, the author found a friend near Wengen, Switzerland. Yes, I still have all my fingers! Photo by Cherise Ballentine.*

gracefully to the small resort town of Villars. Follow the signs to Aigle on Route de Villars and road 9.

Aigle lies on the edge of the Vaudois Alps in the Rhône Valley. The town seems more French than Swiss. You can easily see the influence from its larger western neighbor in both architecture and ambiance. Once closely associated with the French, it was integrated into the Swiss cantons around 1476. The town is mostly known for two things—the chateau-like castle with its steep spires and, from what I understand, some of the best wines in the region. So find yourself a place to stay (you should be an expert by now), take a tour of the castle and then find a comfortable cafe to dine. Enjoy another relaxing evening in another charmer of a town (far better than Gstaad, if I may say so myself).

### Day 3 - Lauterbrunnen to Aigle    136 km/85 miles

From Lauterbrunnen head back to Interlaken. Turn left on A8 to Spiez.

Arrive Spiez. From Spiez take road 11 to Latterbach and on to Reidenbach. Follow road 11 to Gstaad.

Arrive Gstaad. Continue south to Villars. From Villars take road 9, the Route de Villars, on to Aigle.

Arrive Aigle.

# Day 4  Aigle to Thun

Today the trip loops to Gruyères and then circles back to Spiez and Thun. It's another beautiful run, especially from Gruyères to Reidenbach. Start by taking road 11 north from Aigle toward Les Mosses and Château-d'Oex. This is a small road that winds neatly up the valley. As you approach Château-d'Oex veer left and follow the sign to Gruyères on road 190.

Gruyères is situated in the foothills of Mount Moleson and is a very popular tourist destination. The town's castle is well preserved and definitely worth a visit. You will need to park your bike just below the hillside as no motorized vehicles are allowed in town. Walk down the main street and you will eventually end up at the castle. As you walk along, try some of their very famous gruyère cheese.

From Gruyères, continue on to Epagny then don't miss the turnoff (on the right) to Broc and Charmey. This is road 189 and is another off-the-beaten-path beauty that follows the Jogne River. Toward the end there are some great twisties that lead back to Reidenbach over the Jaun Pass. Try some more cheese in the charming village of Charmey (I bet I know how it

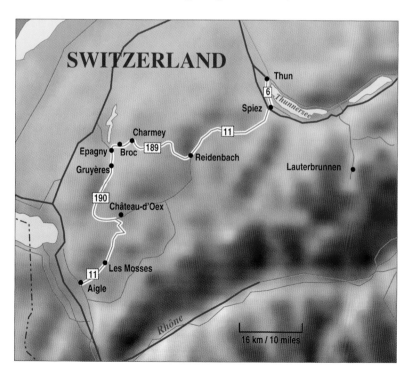

*Lake Thun is one of the largest lakes in Switzerland and surrounded by the Bernese Alps, it is very picturesque. Photo by John Ashley Hall.*

got its name) just after Broc.

Once over the pass, head back to Spiez on road 11, then follow road 6 along the Thunnersee to Thun. The lake is gorgeous with mountains framing the backdrop. Thun is one of my favorite spots in Switzerland. Though not quite as touristy as some other Swiss cities, Thun has all the elements of a small Swiss city—a castle, lake, mountains, and a nice park to enjoy all of the above. So settle in, buy some fresh bread, local cheese, some slices of meat and a little fruit, head over to the park, and enjoy a mini-feast of both food and scenery.

### Day 4 - Aigle to Thun   142 km/89 miles

From Aigle take road 11 to Les Mosses and then veer left on road 190 to Gruyères.

Arrive Gruyères. Continue on to Epagny, then take road 189 to Broc, Charmey, and Reidenbach. At Reidenbach take road 11 back to Spiez. From Spiez continue to Thun.

Arrive Thun.

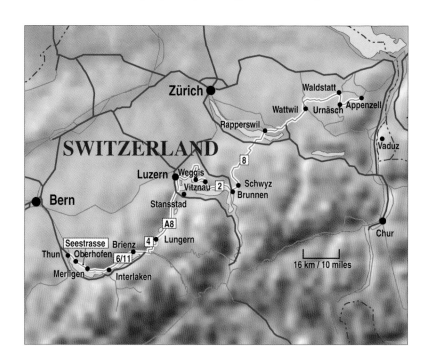

## Day 5    Thun to Appenzell

Although it doesn't seem very far, 133 miles is a long distance to cover due to the several tempting stops along the way. Not only will it be hard to pull yourself away, but Luzern, in particular, may require you to extend this one dayer into an overnighter. From Thun follow the Seestrasse along the north side of the lake. This is without a doubt one of the most heavenly rides you will ever encounter. The views of azure lake with the Jungfrau and Eiger mountains in the background are breathtaking. Follow the road through the quaint villages of Oberhofen and Merligen. Continue along the shoreline to Brienz located at the northeast end of the Brienzersee.

Brienz has been around for a thousand years and hasn't changed much over the last 200 to 300. Still charming, still quaint, and yes, still touristy . . . but that's because it's been that way for a long, long time. There's a nice old hotel right on the lake if you want to splurge and really play tourist. Otherwise, continue on road 6/11 and the road 4 over the Brünigpass and on to the lovely little town of Lungern with its own picture perfect lake. The road connects with A8 and eventually connects with Luzern (this route is called the Golden Pass Route).

*The covered bridge across the River Reuss in Luzern, Switzerland, connects the two parts of the city. Photo by Mark Allred.*

Luzern, is . . . well, Luzern. Split in half by the River Reuss, Luzern is connected by its landmark covered wooden bridge making this town very pedestrian friendly. Medieval squares, outdoor frescos, and cafes are all wrapped into one heck of a nice Luzern bouquet. Spend the night if you want to, and then take a walk around town. In the evening stroll down the lakefront just as the lights begin to dance on the lake's surface. It's a sight not soon to be forgotten.

### Day 5 - Thun to Appenzell   212 km/133 miles

From Thun follow the Seestrasse on the north side of the lake through Oberhofen to Merligen.

Arrive Merligen. Continue on the Seestrasse to Unterseen and then on to Brienz.

Arrive Brienz. Follow road 6/11and 4, then take A8 to Luzern.

Arrive Luzern. Follow road 2 around the lake to Weggis and Vitznau and on to Brunnen.

Arrive Brunnen. Take road 2/8 to Schwyz.

Arrive Schwyz. Continue on road 8 to Einsieden and on to Rapperswil.

Arrive Rapperswil. Continue on road 8 to Wattwil and then on to Waldstatt. At Waldstatt turn off to Urnäsch and back to Appenzell.

Arrive Appenzell.

One other side trip from Luzerne that I have done more recently is a visit to Fortress Fürigen. This is not your typical medieval castle or ruins, but rather a 20th-century military complex built to protect the Swiss from modern day military invasions. Built in 1941, this complex has been kept secret until the early 1990s when the Cold War era and the threat from the Soviet Union finally came to an end. It houses one of Switzerland's several fortress cities utilized in an elaborate network to keep potential invaders at bay. For many years, the Swiss, determined to maintain their neutrality through strength, organized a system of forts to protect its citizens, and make it extremely costly for outsiders to invade this little mountain country. This particular fortress has just recently become declassified and is now open to visits (count on the Swiss to turn this into a tourist stop). If you are into military history, this is well worth a visit. It is located by the small town of Stansstad not far from Luzern.

*Switzerland to the motorcyclist is smooth asphalt twisting through rolling green pastures tucked among rocky snow-covered peaks. Photo by Cherise Ballentine.*

*This typical Swiss town has a future motorcyclist racing down the main street. Photo by John Ashley Hall.*

Continue from Luzern on road 2 along the north side of the lake. You will pass through the towns of Weggis, Vitznau, and Brunnen. Veer right on road 2/8 to Schwyz and then road 8 to Rapperswil. Eventually road 8 ends up in Wattwil and Waldstatt where you turn right to Urnäsch and back to Appenzell. All of these towns are typical Swiss villages and worth a stop if you have time. If you don't, just keep on driving, lift your visor up, and enjoy the sights, smells, and feel of your final ride through the heart of Switzerland.

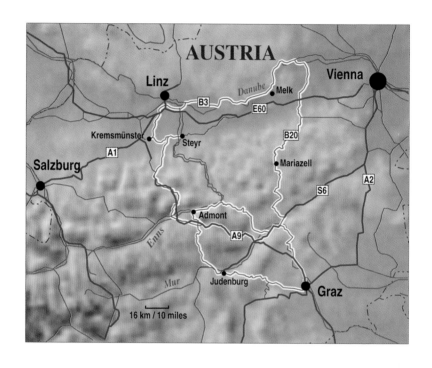

# The Blue Danube and Alps of Central Austria

**Distance:** *859 km/537 miles*
**Suggested Time Frame:** *4–5 days*
**Highlights:** *Follow the world-renowned blue Danube through some of Europe's most beautiful countryside in the Wachau Valley, then head south into the heart of Austria. Old towns surrounded by the Austrian Alps make this a scenic and cultural adventure into the center of this small county. Visit a WWII Nazi death camp in Mauthausen, and then veer south to Graz, a UNESCO World Heritage Site, before heading back to Melk on one of the best motorcycle roads I've ever been on. As an extra bonus, drop by Mount Erzberg, home of the Erzberg Enduro Rodeo and the world championship King of the Mountain motocross course.*

Maybe you've waltzed to Johann Strauss's *Blue Danube*, but have you

*The Austrian landscape will enchant you. Photo by Dave Rogers.*

done the Blue Danube twisties on a motorcycle? Well, get your dancing boots on because this ride carries you beside the world famous Danube River as it flows eastward across Austria and ultimately into the Black Sea. The section of the river that this journey takes you on is known for its remarkable beauty and, bless my soul, the Austrians were kind enough to build a sweet little piece of asphalt right beside it. The asphalt hugs the Danube River and takes you across some of the most magnificent countryside in all of Europe. Similar to the river valleys of Germany, charming towns and castles line this corridor, teasing you to stop at each bend. Ultimately, you head south into an older and less visited part of Austria. Graz, Admont, Eizenerz and Mariazell are but a few of the typical Austrian towns you will visit on this sojourn through the central Alps of this small, yet culture-rich little country.

This trip starts and ends in Melk. Begin in the beautifully situated Melk

*Anyone feel like a hike through the Alps? Here are the perfect traditional outfits. You'll look just like the Family Von Trapp! Photo by Laurie Taylor.*

*The roads in the Austrian Alps run through quaint villages tucked up against the steep slopes. Photo by Laurie Taylor.*

Campsite on an island in the Danube looking up to the world famous abbey. Once again, just a tent flap away lies one of the most beautiful views in all of Europe—all for a measly $10 per night. Continuing west down the Danube, you pass numerous vineyards nestled next to charming old villages and castles, such as the one where Franz Ferdinand lived and is buried (the Archduke killed in Sarajevo triggering WWI). At the furthest western point of this journey, the blue Danube suddenly turns red as you arrive at Mauthausen, a notorious WWII Nazi death camp. From here, head south into the little visited Styrian Alps of central Austria all the way down to Graz, a UNESCO World Heritage Site, and then head north to Mount Erzberg, home of the Erzberg Motorcycle Rodeo located in its very own 2,000-year-old iron ore quarry. Each year, the town of Eisenerz hosts a very serious motorcycle enduro race to determine the king of some very vertical-looking mountains. After taking a tour of the quarry, swing back up to Melk through Mariazell on one of the most twist-worthy roads in all of Europe. By the end of this trip, you will have spent a very pleasant four to five days journeying across some of Austria's most picturesque and less crowded tourist destinations and, who knows, you may want to dust off those old enduro boots when you get home!

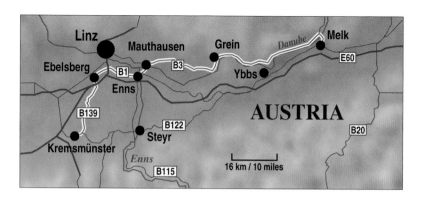

# Day 1  Melk to Kremsmünster

Start and end this Austrian tour in the small town of Melk. Melk lies on the south side of the Danube and is best known for the Stift Melk, or world-renowned Benedictine abbey. Originally built around 1100 AD, the abbey was beautifully restored in the early 1700s. It overlooks the Danube from a bluff offering great views of the valley.

I would recommend staying in either a local *zimmer frei* or at the very pleasant campsite located on an island in the Danube just down from the abbey. There is a restaurant that offers good fare and views of the monastery. It's located just off B1 across the bridge at the foot of the abbey. While in Melk enjoy the town square and local baroque architecture. Take a walk to Schloss Schallaburg (castle) or follow the Leopold Bock-Weg to a beautifully restored 16th-century palace and, of course, don't forget to visit the abbey. This is a charming town where you can relax and really feel the culture of old Austria.

From Melk, you will be following the Danube for about 60 miles. The B3 hugs the shoreline making this one of the most beautiful rides in Europe. The scenery melds with small villages, castles, and roadside cafes creating another quintessential motorcycle ride. Just beware of bicyclists—this is a popular bike route—so be alert!

If you feel like stopping along the way, several towns worthy of a visit are Ybbs, Grein, and Mauthausen. This area is called the Wachau region, known for its beauty and history. As a matter of fact, if you are interested in WWI, Archduke Franz Ferdinand, whose murder in Sarajevo triggered the onslaught of WWI, is buried at his castle, Artstetten, located on the way to Ybbs. There is a very well done exhibit at the castle discussing the events leading up to the war and the eventual decline of the Hapsburg monarchy.

*Flowing rivers and lush green countryside make for a winning combination in central Austria. Photo by Toby Ballentine*

Continue on B3 and then plan to make a stop at Mauthausen. Mauthausen was another one of Nazi Germany's infamous death camps. The camp is open to the public and offers an inside look into the grotesque treatment of both Jews and political undesirables. Though smaller than some of the other camps, this was labeled a category three, or *rückkehr unerwünscht* (return not desired), death camp. Most of the prisoners were brutally treated and worked to death in the local rock quarry.

From Mauthausen cross the Danube to Enns. Originally settled in the 2nd century AD, Enns is full of history boasting old buildings, basilicas, and a castle. Enjoy a short visit, and then continue on B1 toward Linz. At Ebelsberg head south on B319 to Kremsmünster. This is a lovely old medieval town with its own Benedictine Abbey and a nice place to spend the night. There are numerous *zimmer freis* nearby making finding a bed and breakfast a breeze. So, build up a little courage, go knock on a door, say *"Guten tag"* and go for it. A smile and a billfold is often all it takes to get a nice clean room and a warm feathertik blanket!

### Day 1 – Melk to Kremsmünster   146 km/91 miles

Start in Melk on the Danube then follow B3 along the river through Ybbs and then on to Mauthausen.

Arrive Mauthausen. Cross the Danube to Enns.

Arrive Enns. Go back to B1 and head west toward Linz. At Ebelsberg go south on B139 and L562 to Kremsmünster.

Arrive Kremsmünster.

# Day 2  Kremsmünster to Judenburg

From Kremsmünster, follow the B122 east out of town then take the L561 to Bad Hall. Like all Germanic towns starting with "Bad," this small village is known for the healing powers of a hot brine spring mixed with iodine and bromine. So if you are having some heart problems, please, be my guest and try the miraculous healing powers of this hot stinky water! If your heart is feeling fine, continue on B122 to Steyr.

Steyr hosts the main manufacturing plant for most of the BMW engines built in Europe, but still preserves the charm of a typical medieval city. The

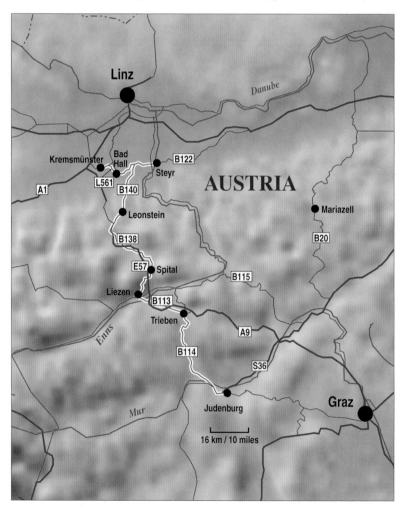

*This is a traditional home in the Tyrolean Alps of Austria. The workmanship is exquisite. Photo by Laurie Taylor.*

### Day 2 – Kremsmünster to Judenburg   206 km/129 miles

From Kremsmünster follow the B122 east out of town then turn right on L561 to Bad Hall.

Arrive Bad Hall. Continue on B122 to Steyr.

Arrive Steyr. Go back on B122 then turn left (south) on B140. Connect with B138 and head south to Liezen.

Arrive Liezen. Connect with B113 east to Trieben.

Arrive Trieben. Go south on B114 to Judenburg.

Arrive Judenburg.

*Even though it can get cold when the clouds descend, the small alpine villages never fail to be a treat to the eyes. Photo by Ron Ayres.*

downtown's square is surrounded by colorful facades and narrow lanes overlooked by the Castle Lamberg. It is a great place to grab a drink before continuing on to Judenburg. From Steyr, head back on B122 (west) then veer south on B140. You will pass through the small towns of Untergrünburg and Leonstein before connecting with B138. Go south toward Liezen. The B138 through Spital, Liezen, and then farther on to Judenburg is a delight to ride. The Styria Alps exude a remote, yet refined beauty when contrasted with the more rugged Swiss Alps. The route was originally blazed by the Celts and later by the crusaders on their way to the Holy Land. Sure am glad I'm doing it on a motorcycle!

After Spital, the asphalt winds over the Pyhrn Pass and on to Liezen. At Liezen head east on B113 to Trieben and then south on B114 to Judenburg. Once again you won't be disappointed—these are some great motorcycle roads! Just north of Judenburg is the small village of Aoden Tauern. Legend has it this is where snowboarding got started. Roughly 2,000 years ago, the Romans attempted sliding down the mountains on their shields . . . and it's all downhill from there!

The scenery here is spectacular as you twist and turn within the corridor between the Tauern Mountains. Eventually, you end up in the small town of Judenburg. This town was founded in the 11th century and prospered under the influence of Jewish merchants. Set in the Settler Alps, Judenburg makes a nice waypoint and is loaded with *zimmer freis*. Make yourself at home and plan to spend the evening here.

*Time to take a break at one of the many "refreshment cottages" you will find while traveling across the Alps. Photo by Ron Ayres.*

# Day 3 Judenburg to Admont

Today is the start of a double loop through three different mountain ranges of central Austria—the Stub Alpen, Eisenerzer Alpen, and the Seckauer Tauern—three gorgeous areas in and through the heart of old Austria. Start your morning cruising down the B77 from Judenburg to Köflach. This is a great stretch of road, which winds majestically through the Stub Alps and then down to the small town of Köflach. Just north of town is the village of Piber—the current home of the famous Lipizzaner stallions used in the Viennese Spanish Riding School.

At Köflach continue on B70 to Graz. Graz is a fairly large city (population more than 250,000), but I would recommend a stopover in the downtown district—a designated UNESCO World Heritage Site. When my parents lived and worked in Klagenfurt, I would often visit this part of Austria and really grew to appreciate Graz. My mom would often take us here and give us the cultural tour of this stately city. The town center blends renaissance, Balkan, and Germanic architecture into its own unique flavor.

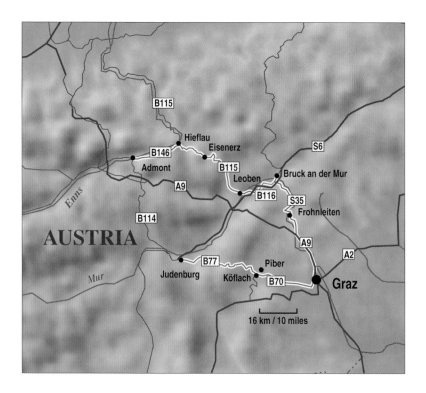

*The Schloßberg (castle mountain) is a hill in the middle of the city of Graz with a castle on top. In addition to these stairs, there is an elevator and a funicular railway to take you up. Photo by Jean François Riemer.*

It's a great place to walk around and if you like the taste of it, spend the night, visit the armory museum (one of the largest in the world), and then hike up to the remains of the Castle Schloßberg for some expansive vistas.

### Day 3 – Judenburg to Admont   200 km/125 miles

From Judenburg follow the B77 to Köflach and then the B70 to Graz.
Arrive Graz. Follow the A9 and S35 north to Frohnleiten and on to Bruck an der Mur.
Arrive Bruck an der Mur. Go west on B116 to Leoben.
Arrive Leoben. Take the B115 to Eisenerz.
Arrive Eisenerz. Continue on B115 and B146 to Admont.
Arrive Admont.

The icon for the city of Graz is the clock tower on the top of the Graz Schloßberg. The surrounding gardens are part of the public park at the top of the mountain. Photo by Diliff.

After a brief respite in Graz, catch the A9 and then the S35 north to Frohnleiten and Bruck an der Mur. Frohnleiten sits right on a bend of the river. It was destroyed by Napoleon in the early 1800s and is now a resort town. Continue on to Bruck an der Mur and then head west on B116 to Leoben. The loop swings back to the northwest on B115 to Eisenerz— home of the Erzberg Rodeo. For all you enduro riders, this is a must-see. The local iron ore quarry is used as a massive enduro and mountain climb-ing course. This area has been mined for close to two thousand years and now draws some of the world's best enduro riders as they attempt to scale vertical-looking quarry walls. Each year the fastest rider gets crowned "King of the Mountain" and becomes a local celebrity. The quarry is open to the public and tours are available. If you have the time it is quite interesting and worth a visit.

The town of Eisenerz lies in a beautiful valley next to the quarry between the Eisenerzen Alps. If you decide to skip the quarry, slowly meander through town and grab a drink before heading on. The next stretch of road between Eisenerz and Admont is to die for. It cuts a ribbonesque route through the mountains and, especially from Hieflau on, the B146 hangs above the Enns River making this a delight to ride. The road eventually opens up to the Enns Valley and the small town of Admont.

Admont makes a perfect layover. Set in a serene valley, this little town has all the appropriate amenities—a cute town square, church, abbey, and you're not going to believe this, but one heck of a library! Situated in the abbey, this library has just recently been restored and it will knock your socks off. Baroque paintings on the wall, beautiful marble floors, statues, and some pretty old books from what I understand. Almost made me want to become a full-time librarian. The only problem is they won't let you check any of the books out. Anyway, take a look. It's the best-looking library I've ever seen.

*This is a typical campground in Germany and Austria. The sites are clean and well kept and views are definitely worth the $10 price! Photo by Toby Ballentine.*

# Day 4   Admont to Mariazell

From Admont take the L713 south to Trieben. This road is a sweet little two-laner that cuts right through the mountains. From Trieben go east on the E57/A9 and then take the S6 back to Leoben and Bruck an der Mur. If you missed either of these towns heading to Admont, you've got a second chance to drop by on this return trip. Once enclosed by medieval walls, Leoben has a well-preserved old town and some of the finest gothic-style buildings in all of Austria, several built by wealthy iron merchants. In Bruck there is one merchant's home still standing called the Kornmesserhaus, built in a very elegant gothic style and considered one of the best in this area.

From Bruck, go north on B116 and B20 to Kapfenberg. The next part of this trip is a motorcyclist's dream. Starting in Kapfenberg and ending in St. Pölten, the black asphalt winds and gyrates through the low-lying Alps of

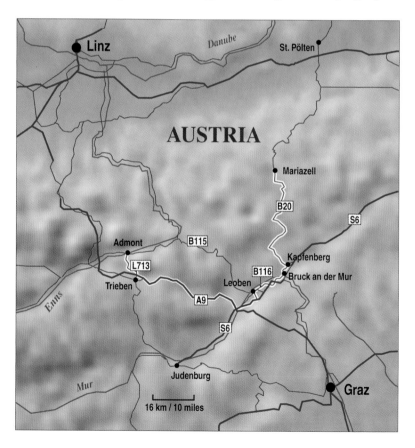

*The Kornmesserhaus in Bruck an der Mur was designed in the Venetian style and built in the 15th century by Pankraz Kornmess. Photo by Marion Schneider and Christoph Aistleitner.*

central Austria. The smooth curves turn into tight twisties after Mariazell making this back end ride to Melk a real kick. If you feel the zone, then just continue on to St. Pölten and finish up the ride to Melk. Otherwise take the more leisurely option and spend the night in Mariazell as a halfway point.

Mariazell is a famous pilgrimage destination, just as Lourdes is in France. The sanctuary of Maria Geburt, a very well known 12th-century statue of the Madonna, is located here. The town itself is a typical Austrian village with all the amenities. *Zimmer freis* and a local campsite are nearby making it easy to find a spot to spend the night.

### Day 4 – Admont to Mariazell   158 km/99 miles

From Admont take the L713 to Trieben.
From Trieben turn left (east) on the E57/A9 and the S6 to Leoben. Continue on B116/S6 back to Bruck an der Mur.
At Bruck an der Mur go north on B116 and B20 to Kapfenberg.
Arrive Kapfenberg. Continue on B20 to Mariazell.
Arrive Mariazell.

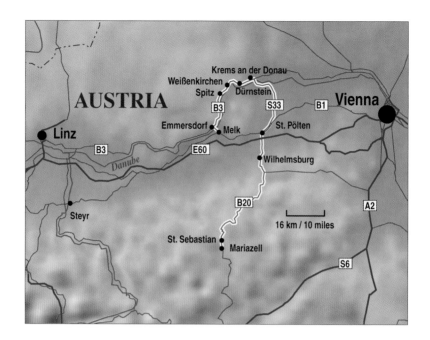

# Day 5  Mariazell to Melk

Today, I saved the best for last. The road north of Mariazell to St. Pölten twists and turns to your heart's delight. And not only that, but north of St. Pölten is the town of Krems which marks the eastern entrance into the Wachau Valley. This area is world renowned not only for its wine, but its unsurpassed beauty. I believe the entire region is a designated UNESCO World Heritage Site. This is also a very popular bicycle route, so be courteous to your fellow two-wheelers.

From Mariazell, continue north on B20. One of the first towns you enter is St. Sebastian. This is a cute little town that is right next to the Erlaufsee Lake. The lake is crystal clear and surrounded by beaches and lawns. There are some nice walking trails if you feel like some early morning exercise. After St. Sebastian, the road quickly turns into some luscious hairpins on its way to St. Pölten. This is a wonderful motorcycle road and requires your full attention. About ten clicks south of St. Pölten is the town of Wilhelmsburg, another quaint village. St. Pölten is just up the road and is the capital city of the area. Baroque facades are mixed with modern government buildings creating an interesting contrast between the old and the new.

*The mustard grown in the Danube river valley near Krems is famous for its mild sweet flavor. Kremser Mustard is produced by Mautner Markhof, a company founded in 1690. Photo by John Ashley Hall.*

After St. Pölten catch the S33 to Krems an der Donau. Krems is the eastern gateway to the Wachau/Danube region. The town is more than 1,000 years old and on a nice day is an irresistible teaser that beckons you to settle in and stay awhile. The problem is as you continue on B3 toward Melk, smaller versions of Krems entreat you the same way . . . all inviting you to stay. Dürnstein, Weissenkirchen, Spitz, and Emmersdorf are all old beauties ideally situated along the Danube. So mosey on down, take your pick, and bask in this quaint string of old towns while motorcycling along the banks of Johann Strauss's *Blue Danube*.

## Day 5 – Mariazell to Melk   149 km/93 miles

From Mariazell take the B20 north to St. Pölten.
Arrive St. Pölten. Follow the S33 north to Krems an der Donau.
Arrive Krems. Take the B3 back to Melk.
Arrive Melk.

# Italy

When renting a motorcycle in Italy, I would fly in to Milan, which is located in the northern part of Italy and is right in the heart of some great riding country. Access to the Lake District, Alps, coastal cities, and Tuscany is very convenient. If you are planning to visit Marches and Umbria then Rome makes a good alternative. I know Italy has a reputation for crazy drivers, but they are really quite good (surprised?). In all my years of driving there, I rarely saw an accident. Plus, Italy must have more scooters than all of Europe combined! You will see them everywhere. This is good for two-wheelers like us because it makes the Italians a bit more aware and mindful of motorcyclists. Nonetheless, drive carefully in Italy. The secondary roads I take you on are decent but often not of the same caliber as those in other European countries. Be prepared for a bump or two and keep a lookout for loose gravel. Unless noted otherwise, the typical speed limits are 30 mph around town and 55–60 mph on the major thoroughfares (not the toll roads).

Camping is great in Italy. Once again there are literally thousands of campgrounds available from the northern Alps to the boot of Sicily. In northern Italy the facilities are clean and well kept, but the farther south you go the more unpredictable the quality. Most campsites have a market and small dining area as well. Otherwise drop by the local market for some fresh bread and local cuisine.

Due to its more southerly latitude the riding season is much longer in Italy than the rest of Europe. Motorcycling as late as the first part of November and as early as March is usually quite tolerable . . . and often quite nice. Actually, late fall and early spring are often the best times to motorcycle in Tuscany and Umbria. Just remember, Italy may require a bit more driving patience than up north, so slow it down a notch or two. What's the hurry? *Arrivederci!*

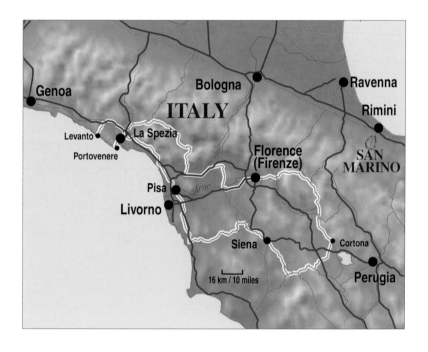

# Hill Towns of Tuscany: Birthplace of the Italian Renaissance

**Distance:** *838 km/524 miles*
**Time Frame:** *6–7 days*
**Highlights:** *Start in the beautiful city of Siena, then swing across vineyards and rolling fields as you visit the hill towns of Tuscany. Montepulciano, Cortona, Arezzo, Lucca, San Gimignano rise like pantheons as you cruise beside vineyards and rolling hills. Spend a day in Florence, and then journey up to the remote villages of Cinque Terre along the Ligurian coast before heading back through Pisa to Siena.*

*Rolling hills and vineyards dot the Tuscan countryside. Old buildings add even more charm to this rural setting. Photo by Laurie Taylor.*

*We are heading to Riomaggiore, the southernmost town of the Cinque Terre. The five villages of the Cinque Terre are all connected by a walking trail along the Ligurian coast. Photo by Laurie Taylor.*

Remember the Andrea Bocelli PBS Special that came out a few years ago? He is a famous Italian tenor who sings in an amphitheater overlooking the rolling hills of his native Tuscany. The singing, setting, and photography are spectacular. Well, just imagine driving through this scenery on a motorcycle enjoying the smells and sights of this extraordinary region . . . and go ahead sing your heart out because no one can hear you anyway! All that is best about Europe is heaped into a very delectable riding treat in this culture-filled journey. Road after road leads you to small quaint villages hanging tenaciously from limestone cliffs. Being able to drive your own bike right up to the ancient walls and enter the city on two wheels is a dream come true! Just stop singing once you park the bike.

    This journey starts in the smaller version of Florence, the city of Siena. Siena is not as crowded yet exudes an aura similar to its bigger sister. Stroll

*It's time to stop for some lunch and the motorcycles are as colorful as the flowers!*
*Photo by Ron Ayres.*

the main square and sip an afternoon drink while you watch the tourists
and locals go by. From here you will explore the heart of Tuscany as you
wander small two-laners and visit Cortona, Arezzo, Lucca, Florence, and
the list goes on. One of the best parts of this trip (and one of my favorite areas of Europe) is driving north to Levanto and visiting the Cinque Terre—
five villages perched on the windswept Ligurian coast. Park your bike in
Levanto, then take the boat and the walking trail to these charming villages
nestled by the ocean. After pulling yourself away from Cinque Terre, head
down to the Leaning Tower of Pisa before circling back to Siena.

# Day 1 **Siena to Cortona**

Start in Siena. For the past 400 years the town's population has not changed—it is still around 60,000. Once a rival with Florence (population 500,000), Siena is the sleepy little backwater to its more formidable neighbor. The Black Death put an end to any hope of Siena establishing itself as a major power when one third of its population died during the plague. Now it's a thriving old tourist center with all the amenities.

Although well-visited, Siena is not to be missed. The center, or *campos,* is automobile-free and a haven for the strolling pedestrian. Visit the cathedrals, towers, and museums at a leisurely pace. Sit at a cafe along the red brick square enjoying the twilight hours and locals wandering about. But most important, don't miss the ancient alleyways off the main square and the several smaller cathedrals. The art and atmosphere of this city transport you to another time and place—inhale the scents and bask in one of the cradles of the Italian Renaissance.

I usually stay at Siena Colleverde Camping located on the northeast side of town. It's a little difficult to find but well-signed. The tent sites are great and offer up wonderful views of the city—especially at night. I would recommend leaving your bikes at the campsite and either taking the bus or walking the 1.6 miles into town.

*The "Duomo di Siena" (Cathedral of Siena) towers above the surrounding tiled roofs. The cathedral was originally built in the 13th century with later additions by Michelangelo and Bernini. Photo by Patsy Scott.*

From Siena follow the SR2 south toward Montalcino. On the way, if you feel like a small detour, go right on SS451 to the Abbey of Monte Oliveto Maggiore. This is a small cloister still inhabited by monks that typifies a traditional Tuscan monastery. The setting in the rolling hills, the artwork, and tranquility combine to convert even the most ardent non-believers. Other than the celibacy part, even I may have signed up! Veer slightly off the main road and follow the signs to Montalcino. This town is a small hilltop village

### Day 1 – Siena to Cortona   115 km/72 miles

Starting in Siena go south on SR2 then veer off on road to Montalcino. Arrive Montalcino. Take road back to SR2 and then continue on SS146 to Pienza and Montepulciano.

Arrive Montepulciano. Take the SP17 and SP32 to Cortona.

Arrive Cortona.

surrounded by medieval walls and is known primarily for its wine. The cobble streets climb up to the main plaza and Romanesque church. Park your bike in the visitor parking just outside the main entrance then take a stroll into town—the walk will do ya good!

From Montalcino take the road back to SR2 then continue on SS146 to Pienza and Montepulciano. The road twists slowly through green Tuscan hills as town after town unveils itself around each corner. The town of Pienza was the birthplace of Pope Pius II and, as a result, in the 15th century the town was remodeled in his honor. The town square's piazza is a bit more elegant than others and the architecture more eye-catching than many other neighboring towns. Continue on to Montepulciano. This small village is centered around two streets and is another gem of a Tuscan hill town. Wander around a bit and at the very least climb the clock tower for some magnificent views.

*Here is an interesting storefront in Siena. We are not sure what to think about the boar's head on the left. Photo by Patsy Scott.*

*Hill town after hill town adorn the Tuscan landscape. Photo by Mark Allred.*

Turn left on SP17, which changes number as it crosses the A1 Autostrata to SP10, then SP32 as it approaches Cortona. This stretch of road wanders aimlessly through truly traditional Tuscan countryside. Rolling hills, small villages, the smell of freshly baked bread . . . you'll want to pull up your visor and smell the ambiance as it rushes across your face. Eventually, the road ends up in the well-known Tuscan town of Cortona. Cortona is best known nowadays as the classic hill town made famous in the book and movie *Under the Tuscan Sun.* The town is a bit more well-worn than its neighbors, but exudes its own unique personality. You get the sense that this is the real Mc-Coy and not some artificial tourist town. The sights to see here are just as enchanting; when the sun sets, the surrounding fertile hills glow like translucent chardonnay. I can see why Frances Mayes decided to settle in a villa here!

Another benefit of Cortona is the charming San Marco Youth Hostel that is located right in town. It's an old convent that has been restored and converted into a very pleasant and inexpensive hostel. For the whopping amount of $20 per night you can stay right in town (includes breakfast, too). Since you may be arriving later, the hostel's location will allow you more time to stroll the back streets of the classy little town. Bring a copy of Frances Mayes book. Who knows who you may run into!

# Day 2/3  Cortona to Florence (Firenze)

Today the road continues to wind through the majestic hill country of Tuscany. There are several stops along the way, the primary one being Florence at the end of today's drive. Florence is a larger city, but deserves at least 1–2 days, so plan accordingly. Start the journey by taking the SR 71 north to Arezzo. This town is about 20 miles away—an easy morning ride! Plan to stop for some breakfast pastries and enjoy the birthplace of Petrarch. The heart of this medieval town is centered on the Piazza Grande. Castle-like mansions surround the square. Romanesque churches abound with their requisite supply of sculptures and frescos. The Church of San Francesco houses one of the most famous frescos—the *Legend of the Cross*. So play tourist for a bit then hop back on your bike and continue north on the

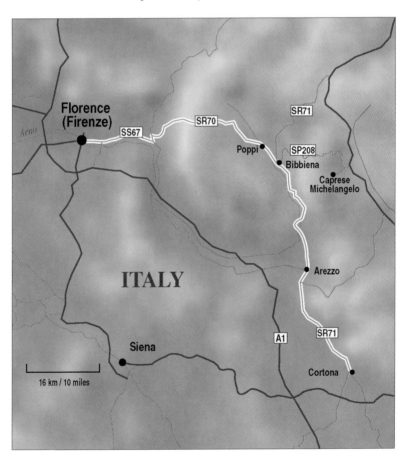

*During an afternoon walk through a typical Italian city, I will oftentimes just grab*
*some provolone, prosciutto, and fresh rustic bread, and sit on a neighborhood bench*
*for dinner. Photo by Toby Ballentine.*

### Day 2/3 – Cortona to Florence (Firenze)   125 km/78 miles

From Cortona go north on SR71 to Arezzo.
Arrive Arrezo. Continue on SR71 to Bibbiena. At Bibbiena continue on
SR70 to Poppi.
Arrive Poppi. Take SR70 to SS67 to Florence.
Arrive Florence.

*The buildings of the Florence cathedral in the historical center of Florence are part of a UNESCO World Heritage Site. The exterior facade is made of small pieces of different colored marble. Photo by Brian Jenkins.*

SR71 to Bibbiena. The landscape becomes more wooded as you approach this town. It's worth a stop, so grab a drink, then if you feel up to it make a quick detour to Caprese Michelangelo, the birthplace of that great artist. Although not officially on my designated route map, Caprese Michelangelo is about 22 miles from Bibbiena on SP208.

Continue on SR70 to Poppi. Due to its prominence on a hill overlooking the surrounding plains, Poppi is visible from miles away. This town is another typical Tuscan village with old homes and churches. The rest of the drive follows SR70 and SS67 to Florence. As you approach the city follow the signs to Piazzale Michelangelo then to Camping Michelangelo. It's conveniently located only a couple of clicks from Ponte Vecchio and has some great tent sites in an olive grove overlooking the old section of Florence. Once again—low cost with a five-star view—what a deal!

Although Florence is a larger city compared to most in my book, it is not to be missed. I know, I know . . . it's busy, hot sometimes, and touristy, but the historical and cultural sites are definitely worth the hassle. To make your stay a little easier, don't fight the traffic in town, but leave your bike at the campsite and put on your walking shoes. The Ponte Vecchio Bridge is close by and from there you can get to the Accademi where Michelangelo's *David* is located, visit the *duomo* (Santa Maria del Fiori Cathedral) with its huge nave, and the Uffizi Gallery. Be sure to climb the dome for some great views and then wrap up the day with a stroll down pedestrian friendly Viadi Calzaiuoli.

*Not only is the food great, but the menus are not too bad looking either! Even if you don't speak Italian, you will still recognize most of the items. If not, be adventurous, point at something and take a chance! Photo by Toby Ballentine.*

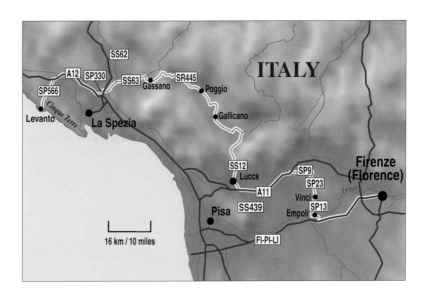

# Day 4/5 Florence to Levanto

Time to give your legs a rest after walking them off in Florence, so hop back on your bike and take the FI-PI-LI to Empoli. Empoli has been in existence since Roman times and is still an agricultural center. From Empoli continue north on SP11 and S13 to Vinci. This town is, yes, you got it, the birthplace of Leonardo da Vinci. Visit his original home and the local museum, then continue north on SP23 and SP9 to A11. This run between Empoli, Vinci, and the freeway is an absolute delight. It gyrates back and forth through some of the most beautiful scenery in all of Tuscany. As the road and bike find their rhythm, you are drawn further and further into the ambiance and past of Italy.

Continue west on A11 and then follow the turnoffs to Lucca, one of the best-kept secrets in Italy. Not overly visited, Lucca is one of the better-preserved medieval towns in Tuscany. The city is still surrounded by fortress walls and ancient ramparts. If you really want some exercise, walk atop the wall around the entire city. Along the way, visit the churches and medieval homes. Of particular note is the Torre Guingi—a 130-foot tower with an oak tree growing from its roof.

After Lucca, head out on the SS12 north and SR445 toward the small towns of Gallicano, Poggio, and Gassano. The road weaves through the Parco Alpi Apuane, a natural reserve noted for its sharply clustered mountains near the western seaboard of Italy. It makes for a great ride as you twist

*Be careful when you drive on the roads along the coast. Not only will the views distract you, but the Italians are notorious for passing anywhere —even around blind corners. Photo by Ron Ayres.*

### Day 4/5 – Florence to Levanto   280 km/175 miles

From Florence take the FI-PI-LI to Empoli.

Arrive Empoli. Go north on SP11 and SP13 to Vinci.

Arrive Vinci. Continue north on SP23 and SP9. Go west on A11 then take SS439 to Lucca.

Arrive Lucca. Take the SS12 north then the SR445 swinging in a north-westerly direction through Gallicano, Poggio, and Gassano. Connect with SS63 going west. Follow SS63, SS62 and SP70 and SP330 toward La Spezia. Veer north on A12 then take SP566 to Levanto.

Arrive Levanto.

and turn on your way towards the coastal area of La Spezia and the Cinque Terre. Eventually link up with the SS63 going west then follow the LL63, 62 and SP70 and SP330 toward La Spezia. Just before town veer right on A12 then head west on SP566 to Levanto.

Levanto is a small town located just north of an area called Cinque Terre. This is one of the most unique areas in all of Italy and is well worth a two-night visit. Five small towns cling tenaciously to the coastal highlands fostering a surreal setting that can only be appreciated if actually visited. The villages are accessible by boat, train, or trail. Being somewhat of a hiker, I prefer walking from town to town. Start this adventure by driving to Levanto just north of the Cinque Terre. There are several campsites here, but the one I stay at most frequently is the Camping Acqua Dolce. Olive trees and terraces provide an inviting backdrop to this campground. It can be busy during the summer months, but the staff can usually find room for a motorcyclist and his tent. After setting up the tent I usually enjoy the evening in Levanto, then the next day catch the boat to Monterosso. From Monterosso, I spend a day hiking to the various other villages before

*Not a bad day for a motorcycle ride along the Italian coast. Photo by Ron Ayres.*

*Colorful umbrellas crowd the beach near Cinque Terre, Italy. Photo by Mark Allred.*

heading back to Levanto. Be careful though, this area can become very seductive. There must be something in the air, because you'll have a hard time leaving.

# Day 6 Levanto to Pisa

Time to finish up this trip and began the trek back to Siena through the world famous city of Pisa. So pack up your hiking shoes and put on your motorcycle boots! Head back the same way you came on the SP566 and A12 to La Spezia. Feel free to drop by this old harbor town. It is larger and a bit more industrial than most but still has a unique appeal. One site in particular worth seeing is the St. George Castle built on a rise overlooking the old town. Another tidbit of information about La Spezia is that it served as the departure point for thousands of Jews to Israel just after WWII. The famed boat *Exodus* was part of that fleet. At one point La Spezia was actually called Door to Zion.

Continue south on the very scenic SP530 to Portovenere. The road hugs the rugged coastline ultimately arriving in this very lovely Ligurian town. There is a small church and a ruined castle along its windswept shoreline.

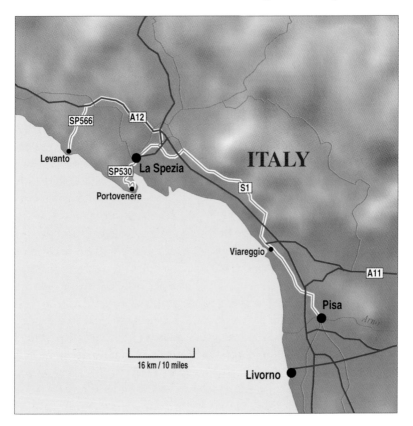

*It definely looks like it is leaning to me. Better not park your bike too close!*
*Photo by Bradley Clark.*

Once the site of a Roman temple dedicated to Venus, it is now a sleepy village typical of the Ligurian coast. From here head back on SP530 then connect with the S1 to Pisa. You will follow this road along the Riviera della Versilia. There are numerous opportunities to stop and one of the most typical is Viareggio. Known for its famous papier-mache floats and carnival, Viareggio is a typical resort town with about six miles of sandy beaches. An

---

### Day 6 – Levanto to Pisa   158 km/99 miles

From Levanto head back to A12 on SP566 then go back to La Spezia.
From La Spezia go south on SP530 to Portovenere.
Arrive Portovere. Turn around and follow the S1 to Pisa.
Arrive Pisa.

old fortress still protects the harbor.

From Viareggio, continue on the S1 all the way to Pisa. Although known for its very famous leaning tower, Pisa is loaded with historic churches and palaces. Once a rival to other city-states, Pisa's prominence peaked early in the 13th century. After the Pisoran navy was defeated around AD 1290, the city never recovered. It is now known for its Piazza dei Miracoli (Field of Miracles), where the *duomo* (cathedral) with its leaning bell tower, the *baptistry*, and the Camposanto (Holy Field) cemetery are located. By the way, the leaning tower is a little straighter now (by about a half a foot), thanks to about 10 years of work, 30 million dollars, and various novel fix-it schemes.

There is a very nice campground just one km from the tower. It's called the Pisa Campground (duh!) and is just off the S1 as you approach town from the north. I would encourage you to go there first, set up camp on the grassy knoll, and then walk to town. Do not try to fight the traffic and drive

*The outside of the 12th-century church and baptistery in Pisa are quite impressive, but just wait until you go inside, the grandeur and immensity will astound you!*
*Photo by Bradley Clark.*

*From the top of the Cathedral, you can see the city of Pisa spread out below you, basking in the warm Italian sunshine. Photo by Bradley Clark.*

into town. The walk is only about 10–15 minutes. If you're lucky you may even have a view of the leaning tower from the campsite—a million-dollar view for the price of a few bucks! Bet you're glad you bought this book!

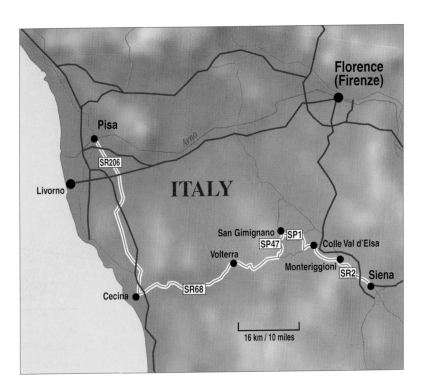

# Day 7  Pisa to Siena

Today is the last leg of your journey and only covers around 100 miles. There are two or three cities along the way that I would encourage you to stop at and enjoy, so plan accordingly in order to not arrive too late at Siena. Start by leaving Pisa and heading south on SR206 to Cecina. Head east from here on SR68 to Volterra. This road is a sweet two-laner that eventually winds back to Siena. Enjoy it as you swing lazily through the foothills and scrape a pedal every now and then. Push up your visor and really take in the sights, smells, and sounds. This is your last day so you need to breathe in and enjoy each moment.

Volterra is one of the oldest inhabited cities in Italy. Originally founded around 900 BC by the Etruscans, it eventually was taken over by the Romans and used as a defensive position. As a result there are several noteworthy archaeological ruins here such as the Etruscan gateway, Roman amphitheater, etc. The most appealing feature of Volterra is that it doesn't reek of tourist-trapism. It's very genuine and actually a little grimy, but I like that!

*Each summer a popular Palio (horse race) is held in Siena, Italy. All the districts or* Contrada *in town that participate display their flags in support of their team.*
*Photo by Patsy Scott.*

From Volterra continue east on SR68 then take the SP47 north to San Gimignano. Though San Gimignano is a must-see, just be prepared for crowds of tourists. The city is one of the best-preserved hill towns in Tuscany and markets it like nobody's business! The towers are visible from several miles away making the town easy to locate. Originally a major trading center of its own, like so many cities that were decimated by the plague,

### Day 7 – Pisa to Siena   160 km/100 miles

From Pisa go south on SR206 to Cecina.
Arrive Cecina. Go east on SR68 to Volterra.
Arrive Volterra. Continue on SR68 and SP47 to San Gimignano.
Arrive San Gimignano. Go south on SP1, SP36 and then east on SR68 to Colle di Val d'Elsa.
Arrive Colle di Val d'Elsa. Head south on SR2 to Siena.
Arriva Siena!

San Gimignano never fully recovered and eventually aligned itself with Florence. Actually, if you really want to enjoy this city, spend the night here because in the evening most of the tourists head back to Florence and the town comes into its own. You may even see some locals wandering around! Otherwise, fight the crowds and take in a few hours of this Romeo and Juliet-like setting.

From San Gimignano swing south on SP1 and SP36, then take SR68 to Colle di Val d'Elsa. This is another old town worthy of a short stop. Or you may decide to just continue on SR2 and head south back to Siena. Another stop along the way is the small village of Monteriggioni. This is a beautiful

*The hill towns of Tuscany are surrounded by some of the nicest scenery in Italy.*
*Photo by Patsy Scott.*

*The Baptistery inside the Siena Cathedral, which was built in the 14th century, is dedicated to John the Baptist, and contains a baptismal font decorated with sculptures by Donatello and other artists of the time. Photo by Mark Allred.*

hamlet with several of its towers rising like phoenixes above the surrounding olive groves. Siena is just a few miles down the road and waiting for you to end this trip where you started—sitting on the *campos* enjoying your favorite drink!

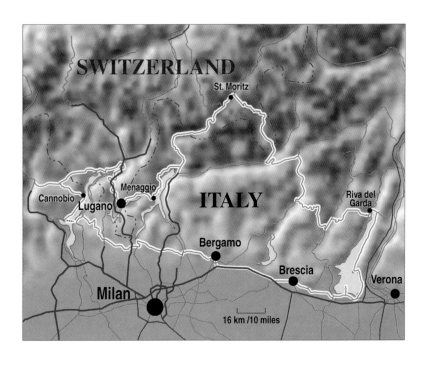

# Lake Country and the Italian Alps

**Distance:** *819 km/512 miles*
**Suggested Time Frame:** *4–6 Days*
**Highlights:** *Motorcycle through some of the most scenic locations in all of Europe—the lake district of northern Italy and the southern Swiss Alps. Visit Lake Maggiore, Lake Como, and Lake Garda in a grand loop that takes you up to St. Moritz, Switzerland, and back over the Bernina Pass. Azure lakes, snowcapped mountains, medieval towns, and smooth black asphalt all combine to create an unforgettable adventure across this heavenly piece of Europe.*

*This photo encompasses all that I love about Europe—snowcapped Alps, old quaint towns, and of course, a motorcycle on which to enjoy all these sights! Photo by Ron Ayres.*

*After the bikes are parked, spend some time strolling around town shopping for a place to eat. Most restaurants have their menus displayed out front making it easy to peruse entrees and prices. Sorry no hamburgers on this menu! Photo by Laurie Scott.*

The lake district of northern Italy is one of the most beautiful areas in all of Europe. I still remember the first time our family drove by this area about 35 years ago and the scenery struck me like a lightening bolt. I couldn't take my eyes off the lakes and the surrounding snow-capped mountains. Thank

*Just imagine yourself on this motorcycle driving down an alpine pass to Lake Lugano! Have you bought your ticket? Photo by Ron Ayres.*

goodness my dad was driving and I could keep my eyes glued to the window. Even after returning several times on a motorcycle, I am still amazed at the natural beauty of the region. Although a very popular summer destination for Europeans, the lakes are well suited for the tourist and have ample facilities to meet your needs. Don't be scared off by its popularity. There is a reason for it!

Our journey starts in Bergamo, a quintessential Italian city not far from the major metropolitan hub of Milan and right next to some of the best motorcycle roads in Europe. We wander up to the magnificent lake district, cruise inland through the Italian Alps, then hook back into the lakes at Locarno, Switzerland. After following the northern shores of Lake Maggiore and Lake Como, we head north to southern Switzerland and St. Moritz through some gorgeous alpine passes before swinging back to the northern tip of Lake Garda. From here we follow the eastern shore of the lake and eventually back to Bergamo, the Florence of northern Italy.

# Day 1   Bergamo to Cannobio

Bergamo is a relatively small, yet vibrant city just a short distance from Milan. The old city is loaded with tight cobblestone lanes, medieval ramparts, and its own fort. This is a perfect place to unwind from your jet lag and introduce yourself to the sights and smells of northern Italy. Spend at least a day here exploring the cafes, churches, and museums before heading up to the Lake District and the snow-capped Alps. From Bergamo follow the SP342 to Calco and continue on to Como. This is a sweet, gentle road that weaves through the countryside and some old sleepy villages. Eventually the road ends up in the city of Como, which lies on the south end of the lake and is another charmer. The old town is pedestrian friendly, so park your bike at one of several parking garages, then wander around town a bit. Once again, medieval walls, an old town square, and cathedrals combined with a lake front promenade make this a perfect place to take a morning stroll.

Continue on SP342 to Varese, and then I would recommend taking a detour to the Sacro Monte (Holy Mountain). Follow the signs north of town to Santa Maria del Monte, to the sanctuary, then wind back down

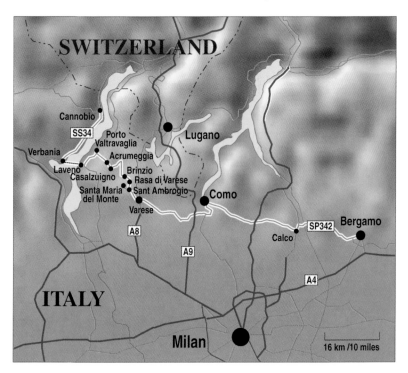

*Quaint harbor towns are a dime a dozen in the lake district of Italy. Just around the bend you'll find another gem. Photo by Joseph Nonno.*

toward Lago Maggiore through the quaint villages of Casalzuigno, Acrumeggia, Porto Valtravaglia, and then Laveno. This is a small twisty road and it's easy to get lost, but just keep a look out for these towns and you'll ultimately find your way. At Laveno take the ferry over to Verbania and finish up this journey by heading north on SS34 to Cannobio.

### Day 1 – Bergamo to Cannobio   130 km/81 miles

Start in Bergamo. Take the SP 342 to Calco and on to Como.

Arrive Como. Continue on SP342 to Varese.

Arrive Varese. From here follow the signs north of town to Sacro Monte.

Arrive Sacro Monte. Go back to Sant Ambrogio Olona and follow the small road to Rasa di Varese, Brinzio, then on to Casalzuigno and Porto Valtravaglia. Go south on SS629 to Laveno.

Arrive Laveno. Take the ferry to Verbania then head north on SS34 to Cannobio.

Arrive Cannobio.

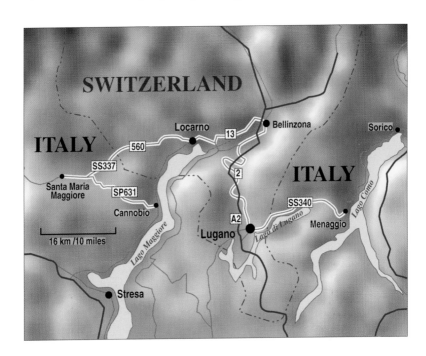

## Day 2  Cannobio to Menaggio

Cannobio sits right on the shoreline of Lago (lake) Maggiore, which is in both Italy and Switzerland and is 54 km (33.5 miles) long. Stresa is the tourist center for this lake, but I prefer Cannobio because it is a bit out of the way and there are some great motorcycle roads nearby. It is small and touristy, yet still retains a quaint charm that makes for an appealing layover on your first night. There is a comfortable and attractive campsite called Camping Rivera just north of town and right on the lake. You could spend several days here exploring just this one lake . . . and that is what many European families do! One vacation—one lake! There are castles, gardens, villas, and islands all within this very small area. The four to five days planned on a motorcycle can easily be stretched to 10 to 12 days for those of you who want to settle in and really enjoy the flavor of the Lake District.

Rather than follow the lake north from Cannobio, I prefer heading inland to Santa Maria Maggiore on the SP631. This road takes you through an alpine valley called the Val Cannobina and the Val Vigezzo. As the road climbs to this small village, the scenery changes from a temperate Mediterranean climate to a more alpine setting. This little village is well known in the area for being the training ground for many famous artists, which is

*The roads not only follow the shoreline but oftentimes climb above the towns for a scenic overlook. Photo by Joseph Nonno.*

### Day 2 – Cannobio to Menaggio   144 km/90 miles

From Cannobio go west on SP631 to Santa Maria Maggiore. Then take SS337 into Switzerland and follow the road, which changes to road 560, to Locarno.

Arrive Locarno and continue east on road 13 to Bellinzona.

Arrive Bellinzona. Take road 2 south to Lugano and then head east on SS340 into Italy and Menaggio.

reflected in the homes and the colorful decorations painted around their doors and windows.

The road heading from Santa Maria Maggiore to Locarno is another great ride on a bike. Take the SS337 into Switzerland—the road changes to road 560 and ends up in Locarno. This piece of asphalt is a bit less traveled since most tourists follow the lake route north to Locarno. As a result, it is often not as congested as it winds through some magnificent mountain scenery. Enjoy the twists and turns heading back down to the lake and if you feel like a break, stop at one of several refreshments houses along the way.

Locarno is situated on the northern tip of Lake Maggiore and is famous for the International Film Festival held there each year. Although touristy to the max, the old town is a delight to walk through and the Piazza Grande is perfect for a bite to eat at one of several swank cafes. If you want to stay longer, walk to the church of Madonna del Sasso, or take the cable car up the mountain—both offer up great views of the city and surrounding lake.

From Locarno it is just a short drive east on road 13 to Bellinzona. As

*Beautiful homes adorn the shoreline of the Lake District of Italy. Photo by Joseph Nonno.*

*Small towns and markets like these dot the shorelines of Lake Como and Lake Lugano. Photo by Joseph Nonno.*

you approach, the valleys become narrow and steep and confirm the notion that many years ago this was a valuable strategic location. Several castles were built here to protect passage into and out of the Alps. The largest is Castelgrande—today a UNESCO World Heritage Site. I would recommend visiting the castle and wandering around Bellinzona's old town before continuing on to Lugano.

From Bellizona take road 2 south to Lugano and the northern shore of Lago di Lugano, then head east on SS340 back into Italy and on to the small town of Menaggio. Lugano has a large financial district but still retains its old town feel. As you drive beside the lake, remember to be flexible—each town has its own appeal—find one that suits you.

If you get to Menaggio early, you can also continue on to the northern end of Lake Como where there are several campsites by Sorico. Though busy during the summer, the campgrounds usually can find a spot for that tired, solitary motorcyclist!

# Day 3  Menaggio to St. Moritz

Lake Como is the most popular lake in northern Italy and is the closest to Milan. The rich and famous have villas here and tourists bask in its native beauty. As you drive around the northern perimeter of the lake, be impulsive and stop whenever you like. As you pass through various small towns, or see a sign to some church or villa, be daring and pull off the road. Play tourist to the max as you drive by some of the most beautiful countryside in Italy.

From Menaggio go north on SS340d and follow this road through the small towns of Dongo and Gravedona. Continue up around to Sorico then

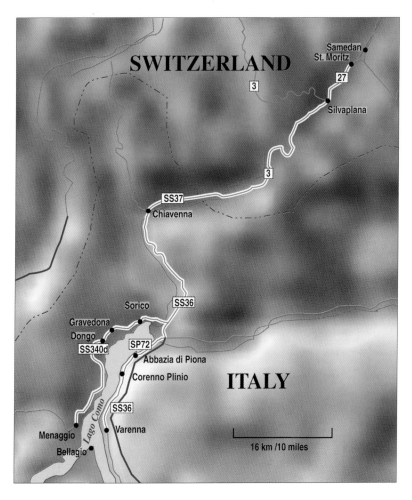

*The Alps in northern Italy are just as picturesque as the Alps in Switzerland and Bavaria. Photo by Ron Ayres.*

swing south on SS36 toward Varenna. The road crosses a marshland and several pools of water on its way south. If bird watching is your thing, keep an eye out for swans, cranes, and other waterbirds—just don't hit one! A bit farther down is a turnoff for Abbazia di Piona, an old abbey restored in the 19th century. Another charming stop is Corenno Plinio. This little village sits atop a rocky perch over the lake with its own medieval wall, towers, and

---

### Day 3 – Menaggio to St. Moritz   149 km/93 miles

From Menaggio go north on SS340d then swing south around the lake on SP72 to Varenna.

Arrive Varenna. Turn around and go north on SS36 to Chiavenna. Turn right (east) on SS37 into Switzerland and follow road 3 on to St. Moritz.

Arrive St. Moritz.

*Driving around the lakes you will see more mansions than you can count.*
*Photo by Joseph Nonno.*

old main square. Drop by the local church and enjoy the setting of this picturesque community. Continue south on SP72 to Varenna—another small town that caters to nothing but the aimless tourist. One of the reasons I loop down to Varenna is to give you the option to stay here and take the ferry south to Bellagio, one of the most well-known cities on the lake. I'm not much of a Bellagio fan, but many consider it one of the most beautiful spots on the lake. I probably hit it on a bad day (raining and overcast), but if you are interested, then spend the night in Varenna and catch the boat down. It makes for a very relaxing day trip.

Otherwise, head back up the lake into Switzerland for some cooler weather and a great piece of asphalt. Follow the SS36 all the way to Chiavenna, just south of the Swiss border. It's about 10 miles north of the lake and is at the foot of the pass to St. Moritz. I usually don't stop here because the road and scenery keep me pulling on the throttle. Turn right in Chiavenna on SS37, which turns into road 3 as you cross the Swiss border.

The road goes in and out of some tunnels as you climb through the scenic Val Bregaglia. Ahhhh . . . this is nice . . . first a beautiful lake now a great run up the Alps to St. Moritz . . . Europe at its very best!

Eventually you will end up in the celebrity center of southern Switzerland—St. Moritz. This city has been the host of two Olympics and numerous alpine skiing events. Basically, it's one big hotel and sports center and, to be quite honest, I prefer driving up the road about six clicks to the small town of Samedan. This town is more traditional and the setting is more Swiss. So drive on up the road a bit more, find yourself a *gasthaus,* settle in, and enjoy the cool, refreshing setting of the southern Swiss Alps.

*This hotel in Bellagio, Italy, has its own private dock. Photo by Joseph Nonno.*

# Day 4  St. Moritz to Riva del Garda

Today offers one of the best in motorcycle driving on this whole trip. At first the roads linger in the Alps, and then drop off dramatically to the northern-most edge of Lake Garda at Riva del Garda. Mountain passes through scenic valleys will seem endless and climax with a beautiful tour of another one of Italy's azure lakes. Start by heading southeast to Pontresina on road 29. Pontresina is a popular mountain resort and caters to alpine skiers in the winter and hikers in the summer. If you like this area, spend another day and enjoy this hikers paradise—home of one of the largest mountain climbing schools in the world. Glaciers, mountain peaks, and alpine valleys, combined

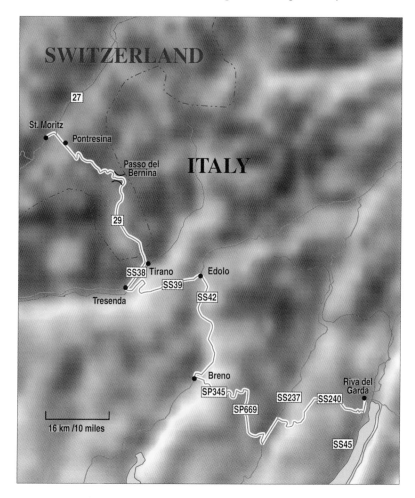

*Riding through the Alps of Northern Italy is pure nirvana! Photo by Ron Ayres.*

### Day 4 – St. Moritz to Riva del Garda   216 km/135 miles

From St. Moritz go southeast on road 29 through Passo del Bernina.
  Continue to the Italian border then follow SS38 to Tirano.

Arrive Tirano. Head to Tresenda on SS38 then go east on SS39 to Edolo.
  At Edolo go south on SS42 to Breno.

Arrive Breno. Go east on SP345, SP669, SS237, and SS240 to Lake
  Garda and Riva del Garda.

Arrive Riva del Garda.

*We take our time heading down an alpine pass to another lake. The more the merrier!*
*Photo by Ron Ayres.*

with hand carved benches for rest stops and refreshment stands for calorie restoration create a little bit of heaven all done in typical Swiss fashion.

From Pontresina the blacktop winds across the top of the Alps and over the Passo del Bernina. As you cross into Italy the road becomes SS38. Continue through Tirano to Tresenda. At Tresenda head east on SS39 to Edolo then veer south on SS42. As you drive through this area, the mountains appear massive and dominate the landscape. Eventually you will arrive in Breno, a small town with a castle and some old churches. Take a break for lunch as you prepare for the next leg of this trip. From Breno you will drive, in my opinion, on one of the most picturesque runs in Europe. The road starts as SP345 then changes to SP669. Then take SS237 to SS240 and drop down to Lake Garda. This is a small alpine road that cuts and weaves over passes and through rustic mountain scenery. Stay focused and enjoy the ride!

Eventually, you will end up in Riva del Garda, a quaint town with all the trappings of a typical 12th-century settlement. I would recommend staying at Camping Bavaria just east of town on the water, then head back to Riva del Garda and visit the main square, Piazza 3 Novembre, as you enjoy dinner overlooking another classic Italian beauty—Lago di Garda!

*This was our view from the balcony of a hotel on Lake Lugano. Not only is the scenery beautiful, but there were two great restaurants right out front of the lobby. Photo by Joseph Nonno.*

# Day 5   Riva del Garda to Bergamo

Start today's trip by heading east on SS240 from Riva del Garda, then follow the road south by the shoreline on SS249. One of the first towns is Malcesine about a quarter of the way down the east side of Lago di Garda. Malcesine is a popular summer resort with all the amenities. It's a small medieval village with a historic castle, narrow lanes, and cafes. There is a pleasant promenade, bathing spots, and ice cream shops as well. Be sure to try some *spremuta* (fresh fruit juice) or treat yourself to some gelato. If you want to spend some more time here, take the cable car up Monte Baldo for some terrific views.

After partaking of some *spremuta,* continue south on SS249. The drive takes you through the villages of Brenzone, Torri del Benaco, Punta San Vigilio and Garda. Brenzone is a cute spot that is not so touristy and quite charming. At Punta San Vigilio there is a beautiful villa built in the 16th century. Follow the tree-canopied avenue just off the main road and it will lead you right to it. Garda is similar to Malcesine—a darling town—but loaded with tourists. There are numerous outdoor cafes and if you don't mind squeezing around tables, stop and have some lunch.

From Garda, continue on SS249 south to Bardolino, Lazise, and Peschiera del Garda. Bardolino is known for its lively nightlife and has an old town castle worth a peek. As you approach the next town, Lazise, another well preserved castle looms on the horizon. There are old walls and

*With so many restaurants it sometimes is hard to choose, but you can't go wrong with Italian cuisine. Photo by Patsy Scott.*

traditional medieval streets dating back ten centuries. Peschiera del Garda is quite similar with walls and fortresses and churches converging to create another relic from the past. Either city is worth a visit and both are used by visitors as bases to explore the surrounding lake.

At Peshiera del Garda head west on SP11, then take the small road on the short peninsula to Sirmione. The road ends at the drawbridge where you can park. Cross the bridge and enjoy the pedestrian-only community of Sirmione. Wander the lanes, visit the castle, then top it all off with some gelato. It's a popular side trip, but worth the detour. This is Italy and Lago di Garda at its best.

From Sirmione, head west on SP11 and A4 toward Brescia and then back home to Bergamo. If you still haven't had a chance to wander around the old city, now is your chance. So settle in for a day or two, spend an evening strolling back through time, feast on some *casoncelli* (oversized stuffed ravioli) and enjoy *la dolce vita*.

### Day 5 – Riva del Garda to Bergamo    181 km/131 miles

From Riva del Garda go east on SS240 then south on SS249 along the lake. Follow SS249 on the east side of Lake Garda then veer west on SP11 to Sirmione.

Arrive Sirmione. Follow SP11 west to Bresica. At Brescia catch the A4 to Bergamo.

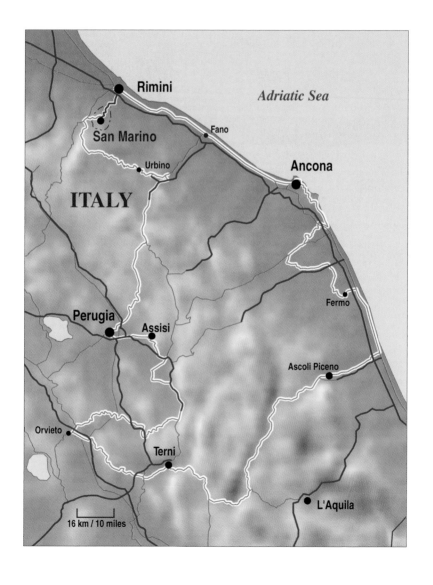

Rimini

*Adriatic Sea*

San Marino

Fano

Urbino

Ancona

ITALY

Fermo

Perugia

Assisi

Ascoli Piceno

Orvieto

Terni

L'Aquila

16 km / 10 miles

# Italy's Hidden Backroads: Umbria and Marches

**Distance:**  897 km/561 miles
**Suggested Time Frame:**  5–6 days
**Highlights:**  Great mountain riding through central Italy's Apennine Mountains all the way to the Adriatic Sea. Follow the eastern seaboard through the less visited Marches region and then swing back to historic Umbria. The hill towns and cities visited on this trek are not nearly as touristy as in Tuscany but just as magnificent. This is Italy at its best!

*The hill towns and vineyards of Umbria are just as magnificient as Tuscany and not nearly as crowded. Photo by Laurie Scott.*

*Colorful ceramic plates adorn the front of this Italian souvenir shop.*
*Photo by Patsy Scott.*

Interested in seeing the real Italy? Just below Tuscany are two remarkable provinces that probably have a tenth of the tourists that visit Florence alone. And to make it even better for motorcyclists, the Apennine Mountains run right through these two regions. Umbria is not far from Rome, but for some reason most tourists head north to Florence and Venice and miss this unique area just next door! Filled with hills, verdant farmlands, and sunflower fields, numerous hill towns adorn the countryside. Next to Umbria along the eastern coast is Marches, an even less visited area. Situated along the Adriatic Sea, this charming region hasn't changed for hundreds of years and represents, in my opinion, what Tuscany was to tourists 50 years ago.

This journey starts in Assisi, the home of St. Francis, a well-known pilgrimage town, and then heads north toward Urbino. Urbino is one of those renaissance relics with walls, palaces, churches, and backstreets that entice you to stay another day. From here continue on to San Leo, one of the most dramatic hill towns in all of Italy, before heading to the Adriatic Sea. This trip follows the coastline south to the Marches region and on to the towns of Macerata, Fermo, and Ascoli Piceno—three under-visited gems. Eventually, loop back on some great roads through the Apennines to Orvieto and Assisi. Great trip, great secrets!

*Outside cafes adorn every Italian town center. They are a relaxing place to unwind and enjoy a drink after a long (or short) ride. Photo by Joseph Nonno.*

# Day 1  Assisi to Urbino

Take it slow in Umbria. The roads are narrow. The terrain hilly and an occasional donkey may force you to ratchet it down a notch or two. No need to hurry on this journey. It starts in the pilgrimage town of Assisi, the home of its patron saint, St. Francis. Although somewhat touristy, the town is a charmer and not to be missed. If possible the best time to visit is in the evening when most of the tourists have left. There is a campground just north of town off the SS147, which is conveniently located just one kilometer from town. Please note that the roads are gravel leading into Camping Fontemaggio, so be careful steering your two-wheeler into a campsite. After

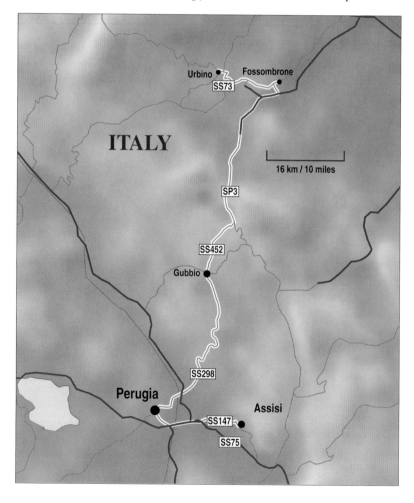

*The Piazza Grande in Gubbio offers a fine view of the Umbrian countryside.*
*Photo by Idéfix.*

setting up, meander into town via a traditional Italian country dirt road, and then visit the Basilica of St. Francis and the castle ruins of Rocca Medioevale. On a nice day the views from the castle are great.

From Assisi head west on SS147 then take SS75 to the city of Perugia. It's not too far away and is a larger city, but, heaven help us, it is the chocolate capital of this region. Known throughout Europe as the home of the Perugina chocolate kisses, these delectable treats are to die for. The city even hosts its own chocolate festival in October! I would suggest driving to the main piazza, buying a sack full of kisses, and then just walk around the narrow streets and on the wall surrounding the city while popping Perugina into your mouth every few steps . . . best walk I every had!

### Day 1 – Assisi to Urbino   189 km/118 miles
Starting in Assisi ride west on SS147 then take SS75 to Perugia.
Arrive Perugia. Head north on SS298 to Gubbio.
Arrive Gubbio. Continue north on SS452 and SP3 to Fossombrone.
Arrive Fossombrone. Take the SS73 to Urbino.
Arrive Urbino.

After stashing a few extra kisses into your saddlebags, go north on SS298 toward Gubbio. This narrow two-laner cuts through some beautiful countryside and fertile valleys, eventually ending up in the Umbrian hill town of Gubbio. Piazza Grande is the main square. It is surrounded by traditional medieval-style homes and structures that direct your view toward the spectacular scenery of the low-lying Umbrian landscape. I would recommend finding a nice restaurant on the square and having lunch while enjoying the locals walking by and the view below. Beautiful.

After Gubbio continue north on the very scenic SS452 and SP3 to Fossombrone, another old Roman fortress town. Make a brief stop here if you like, then continue on to Urbino on the SS73. As you approach, the sun

*Exploring requires parking your bike and wandering off the beaten path, so be sure to take a good pair of walking shoes. Photo by Mark Allred.*

*Fields of grain cover the Umbrian countryside. Photo by Joseph Nonno.*

may be setting, providing an almost surreal image as you approach the city. The parapets, rolling hills, and misty green farmland coalesce into a museum-like painting—no wonder so many great renaissance painters came from this area.

Urbino is a UNESCO World Heritage Site and requires several hours to explore. If possible, splurge a bit and try to find a place to stay in town. The local Tourist Information is right on the town's central square and they can help. Urbino was originally a Roman city, but its claim to fame occurred during the 15th century when it became a well-known noble court throughout this region and Europe. The city is also known for being the birthplace of the famous renaissance painter Raphael. A must-see is the Ducal Palace. It is huge and you can easily spend two to three hours here. Another point of interest is the Marche National Gallery, home to many famous renaissance paintings. After playing tourist, spend the evening at the Piazza della Republica unwinding, eating, sipping your favorite drink, or shopping at the many local cafes and shops surrounding the square.

# Day 2  Urbino to Fano

After a relaxing evening in Urbino, hop on your bike and head northwest on the SP9 to Macerata Feltria. Continue on this road all the way to San Leo. San Leo is a perfectly preserved hill town with a castle perched on a cliff overlooking the village. The road is tiny and precarious as it climbs to this little village . . . so be careful. The local churches and cafes make this an ideal stop for some hot chocolate and Italian pastries. Just don't get too cozy, you still have a few more miles to cover today.

From San Leo follow the signs to San Marino then take the SS72 east toward the coast and turn right on SS16 to Gradara. Actually you will have to cross over the freeway A14 to arrive here. Gradara is very small but has a castle where Dante's tragic *Divine Comedy* actually took place. It's quite a long, convoluted story so I won't spoil it. You can find out all about it when you visit the castle.

Continue down SS16 to Pesaro and Fano. Pesaro was heavily bombed during WWII and is now a seaside resort. It is the birthplace of the famous composer Rossini and a festival is held in his honor each summer. Fano was

*This village is typical of many small hill towns in central Italy with the church located near the town center surrounded by residences. Photo by Joseph Nonno.*

an old Roman outpost and has some original arches and walls still standing. This is also a beach resort with plenty of accommodations and campgrounds. Find yourself a nice one by the beach and spend a day swimming in the Adriatic Sea. Relax and enjoy!

### Day 2 – Urbino to Fano   120 km/75 miles

From Urbino take the SP9 northwest to Macerata Feltria. Continue on SP9 and SP6 to San Leo.

Arrive San Leo. Follow signage east to San Marino then take the SS72 east and the SS16 south to Gradara.

Arrive Gradara. Continue on the SS16 to Fano.

Arrive Fano.

# Day 3  Fano to Fermo

The Adriatic coast is absolutely gorgeous as it winds south from Fano to Fermo. Portions are low lying with sand, while others are hilly and rocky—either way you won't be disappointed. Start today by heading south from Fano on SS16 to Senigallia and on to Ancona. A port city of notable size, Ancona was once a strategic Roman harbor. There are several sites of interest here, such as an old Roman arch, but nothing worth a major detour.

As you leave Ancona on SP1 to Portonovo and Sirolo, the asphalt begins to wind gently along one of the nicest coastlines in Italy—the Riviera de Conero. Sharp cliffs, sheltered coves, and lonely Byzantine Churches are the

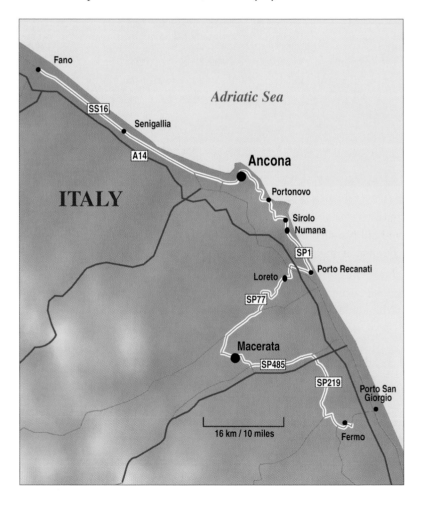

*The coastal areas of Italy are often dotted with small fishing villages and vineyards. Not a bad combination! Photo by Mark Allred.*

trademark of this short stretch of road. At Portonovo, an ancient church and old Napoleonic fortress guard the rugged shore, while farther south, the small hamlets of Sirolo and Numana are home to a medieval fortress and convent. Take your time driving through this area. Hike down to a sheltered cove, visit the local church, and truly bask in this relatively unknown part of Italy.

### Day 3 – Fano to Fermo   158 km/99 miles

From Fano continue south on SS16 to Senigallia and Ancona. At Ancona continue along the coast on SP1 to Portonovo and Sirolo.

Arrive Sirolo. Continue south along coast, then at Porto Recanati head west on SP77 to Loreto.

Arrive Loreto. Continue on SP77 to Macerata.

Arrive Macerata. Go south to SS485 then go east. Take the SP 219 south to Fermo.

Arrive Fermo.

Continue on SP1 south to Porto Recanati, and then turn inland to Loreto on SP77. Loreto is known for the Santuario della Santa Casa or Sanctuary of the Holy House. According to Catholic tradition, the Madonna's house was miraculously transplanted here in the 13th century. It is now protected and venerated in the Sanctuary. Many well know architects and artists worked on this building creating a truly remarkable setting and structure, so definitely take a break here to enjoy an abundance of early Italian renaissance art and history.

*Don't worry about eating too much pasta for lunch, the walk back to your hotel will help burn off the carbs. Photo by Joseph Nonno.*

*The Piazza della Madonna is flanked by the Basilica of the Santuario della Santa Casa and the Palazzo Comunale containing the works of famous Italian artists.*
*Photo by Massimo Roselli.*

From Loreto continue on the very scenic and windy SP77 to Macerata. The old town of Macerata is located above the more modern part of the city and is full of shops and narrow lanes. For those of you interested in opera, time your visit in July and August for the Sferisterio Opera Festival. The operas take place in a huge neoclassical arena built in the early 1800s. Very Italian! Go south from here on SS485, then east until you intersect the SP219. Continue south on SP219 to the ancient town of Fermo. Fermo sits on a hill overlooking the Adriatic Sea. The views are great and this little town is a nice spot to relax. You can either stay here or continue to the coast and Porto San Giorgio, a small fortress town. I prefer the old ambiance and traditional narrow terra cotta feel of Fermo. Unwind and enjoy some dinner as you relax watching the sunset overlooking the Marches countryside.

# Day 4  Fermo to Orvieto

The past few days have been rather leisurely, enjoying the Adriatic coastline. Today will cover quite a bit more distance through the more central and mountainous region of Italy. Start by taking the SP239 to the coast for one more look and reconnect with the SS16 going south. At Porto d'Ascoli veer inland on SP235 to Ascoli Piceno. Ascoli Piceno has two very nice town squares, the Piazza del Popolo and the Piazza Arringo. The Popolo is built with a natural marble travertine from the surrounding area. This square is the true historical center of town with the requisite cathedral, cloisters, and cafes lining the perimeter. Piazza Arringo is home to some of the finest religious art of this era at the Palazzo Communale gallery just beyond the cathedral. If you have the time, spend a few hours walking and exploring these very Italian town landmarks.

This stretch of road (the SS4) to Rieti is one of my favorites in Italy. It winds graciously through the spine of Italy on some great asphalt. The low-lying mountains and gorges make this a real fun drive. Although there are several small towns along the way, I usually just boogey straight on down to Rieti. If the road is not too busy, find your "zone" on this sweet piece of black tar. Eventually the road ends in the town of Rieti at the foot of the Sabini and Reatini mountains. Once a Roman stronghold, it was an

*Civita di Bagnoregio is set on a hill and can be reached by a walkway from neighboring Bagnoregio. Photo by Alessio Damato.*

outpost to protect the transfer of salt from the Adriatic to Rome on the Via Salaria (Salt Road).

From Rieti go north on SR79 then west at Terni on SS3 to Narni. The road north to Terni has some great sweepers as well as some sharp turns—another good run. Narni is jammed on a hill about 700 feet above sea level. It is perched over a small gorge by the Nera River. This small town is absolutely adorable. Usually not a whole lot of tourists, but in my opinion, the

### Day 4 – Fermo to Orvieto   281 km/176 miles

From Fermo take the SP239 east to the coast. Connect with SS16 and go south to Porto d'Ascoli. Go west on SP235 to Ascoli Piceno.
Arrive Ascoli Piceno. From Ascoli take the SS4 to Rieti.
Arrive Rieti. Head north on the SR79, then at Terni take the SS3 to Narni.
Arrive Narni. Head northwest on SS205 to Orvieto.
Arrive Orvieto.

*Quaint cobblestone streets like this one are commonplace in central Italy.*
*Photo by Joseph Nonno.*

small square, fountain, and cafes combine for a truly classic Italian setting. Definitely take a break here!

Continue from Narni by taking the SS205 to Orvieto. This road is a little smaller than the others, but once again, is a delight to ride through the scenic Umbrian countryside. Follow the asphalt across the A1 highway all the way to town. Orvieto sits about 1,000 feet above sea level on a clump of lava. There is parking at the base of the hill by the train station. A funicular or bus can take you up to the city. Hopefully, when you arrive it's close to evening time and most of the tourists have headed back to Rome. It's quiet and very peaceful at night as most visitors flock here during the day. Orvieto has much to offer—from a majestic *duomo* (cathedral) to an underground city covered with caves and tunnels. Go for a walk along the walls first, and then head into town for a night visiting the back streets and local shops. If you have the time, or want to spend another day here, take a side trip to the very small and remote hill village of Civita di Bagnoregio. It is only accessible via a pedestrian bridge from Bagnoregio and is just south of Orvieto. The town is definitely one of a kind and really not too far. Park your bike in Bagnoregio then hike to Civita from there.

*Italian gelato . . . nothing like the real thing. Diet starts after the trip. Photo by Patsy Scott.*

# Day 5  Orvieto to Assisi

To end this journey, we wind throught the hilly Umbrian landscape and visit four uniquely charming towns. This last day may cause you to think twice about driving back to Rome and leaving these secrets of Italy. Start by taking a great ride along the SS79bis. This road is another winding master-piece through Umbrian farmland and sunflower fields. The road ends in the town of Todi. Founded thousands of years ago, Todi has been built and re-built over the centuries. As a result, the town exudes an ambiance that can't be copied. Once you sit in the square, the clock will wind back and you will feel like you're on a movie set. The atmosphere and architecture combine to convince you to stay and enjoy this setting as long as possible. When you have the strength, pull yourself up from that sweet little cafe and hop back on your bike toward Spoleto. Take the SP382, SP420 and SS418 east from Todi.

Spoleto is another town that catches your eye from a distance. The arched bridge, castle, and traditional village blend seamlessly into the coun-tryside. Founded far before the Romans arrived, the town brims with

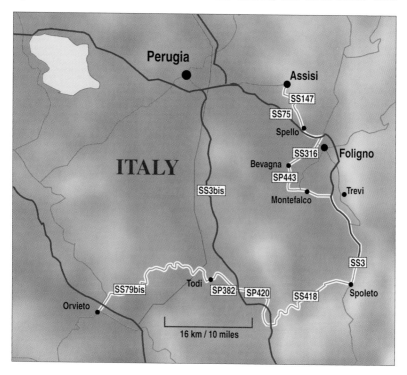

*Driving along the roads in central Italy is like having your own travel show. Spectacular views abound around almost every curve. Photo by Mark Allred.*

history and life. The old Roman theater, imposing cathedral, and traditional square speak volumes of history and culture. If you like this area, spend the night, take some walks across the bridge, and visit some churches and monasteries. You'll once again be transplanted back in time and not believe this is the 21st century.

Otherwise continue on SS3 north to Montefalco. This road climbs up to the village then twists and turns as it winds back down toward Spello. Montefalco is perched high enough to provide unobstructed views of the valley below. It's a great spot to grab an ice cream or drink before heading down the twisties on the other side of town. Follow the SP443 to Bevagna

---

### Day 5 – Orvieto to Assisi   149 km/93 miles

From Orvieto take the SS79bis to Todi.
Arrive Todi. Continue east on SP382, SP420 and SS418 to Spoleto.
Arrive Spoleto. Go north on SS3 then follow signs to Montefalco. Go
   north on SP443 to Bevagna. Continue on SS316 and SS75 to Spello.
Arrive Spello. Continue on SS75 the SS147 to Assisi.
Arrive Assisi.

and then the SS316 and SS75 to Spello. For a long time a Roman outpost, Spello still has many artifacts from that period. Parts of the wall, a gateway, and theater still exist from Roman times. The streets are steep and winding—giving you a good work-out as you drift from shop to shop along the cobbled lanes. The churches in town boast beautiful frescoes painted by famous renaissance artists as well.

*Even the simplest stone staircases are brought to life with summer flowers.*
*Photo by Joseph Nonno.*

*The rolling hills of Italy are covered with grain fields, vineyards, and cypress trees.*
*Photo by Joseph Nonno.*

From Spello you can head back up to Assisi on the SS75 and SS147 or if you have time, make a detour south to Trevi, another hill town perched high above the Umbrian plain. Either way you can't lose, but just remember . . . let's keep this little part of Umbria and Marches a secret. That makes it far more enjoyable for those of us who want to discover the real Italy!

# Spain

Spain is one of the most visited countries in Europe by Europeans, but one of the least visited by Americans. Most tourists from the U.S. head to Germany, France, and Italy and don't bother with the Iberian Peninsula. This is a big mistake. Spain offers some of the best motorcycling in some of the best locations on the continent. While the Alps are inundated with tourists, the Pyrénées Mountains are less crowded and, in many respects, just as beautiful. The blacktop takes you up valleys that are deliciously curvy and drenched with greenery and history. The Atlantic and Mediterranean coasts offer up resplendent doses of sun-soaked beaches and craggy shorelines similar to California's Highway 1 on the Pacific. The roads are usually quite decent, but the tolls can be a bit expensive—so be sure to follow the route outlined in this book and you'll be fine (and end up with more pocket change).

The best time of year to go is either early summer or early fall. The weather can be warm in mid-summer, especially on the Mediterranean coast. The Pyrénées and Atlantic coast are fine even during the summer months. Due to the warmer climate, many northern Europeans come here to catch up on the sunny weather resulting in numerous camping facilities up and down the coasts as well as in the Pyrénées Mountains. Just beware, the roads along the Mediterranean coast can be jammed during high season (July and August).

Spain is now part of the European Union so the euro is the standard currency. Credit and debit cards are commonplace making shopping a breeze. *Hypermarkets,* or super stores, are becoming more popular and are often found in many cities and towns. One final bit of advice, be sure to try the *churros con chocolate.* I'm a chocoholic and this is one treat I could savor breakfast, noon, and night. *Adiós* and *Olé!*

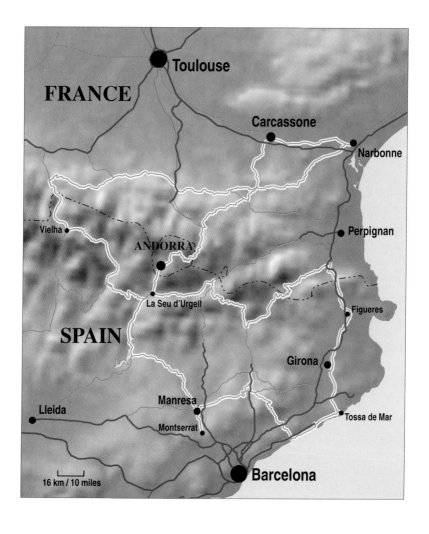

# Alpine Passes through Spanish Stone Hamlets and the Pyrénées Mountains

**Distance:** *1248 km/780 miles*
**Suggested Time Frame:** *6–8 Days*
**Highlights:** *Take a tour of the Costa Brava then swing inland to Catalonia and upwards through the Pyrénées. Stone hamlets, rich with culture, fly by the wayside as you swing your bike across mountain curves. Venture into southern France and the remarkable walled city of Carcassonne and then visit the poignant castle ruins of the Cathars in Languedoc. Race back through the tiny principality of Andorra high in the Pyrénées before returning once again to the quiet seaside resort (all with its own castle and walls) of Tossa de Mar.*

*The roads in the Pyrénées weave over mountain passes and through deep verdant valleys. Stone hamlets and arched bridges carry you back to an older, less visited Spain. Photo by Ruhrfisch.*

*There is always something happening on the waterfront in Barcelona.*
*Photo by Toby Ballentine.*

Several summers ago, I spent about three months traveling through Spain and the high Pyrénées Mountains. Not only was there much to see, but I fell in love with Tossa de Mar on the Costa Brava (which is where this journey starts and ends). As you travel inland from Tossa, the roads climb higher and higher. The Spanish Pyrénées Mountains are similar to the Alps of Switzerland and Italy. Forested verdant valleys, surrounded by rugged mountains and strewn with quaint stone hamlets each with its own character, fill the countryside. Roads like razors slice through the landscape beckoning any and all motorcycle enthusiasts with perfect photo opportunities unfolding around each bend. And the food is truly unique. It's like an eclectic mix of seafood and hearty farm cuisine with a few snails thrown in. Sounds pretty good, huh?

On another trip a few years back, our family rented a boat on the Canal du Midi and spent about 10 days traveling from Narbonne to Carcassonne in Southern France. The kids were young, the weather perfect, and the landscape spectacular. We moored our boat beside vineyards and under arched bridges and watched the locals play *boules* or lawn bowling under the chestnut trees. We even bought our own set and joined in the fun.

On this motorcycle trip, instead of motoring down a lazy canal, you'll be

*The ruins of the 11th-century Peyrepetuse castle lie high in the French Pyrénées. This fortress was originally used as a stronghold near the Spanish border.*
*Photo by Benh Lieu Song.*

riding on some crazy asphalt. This area of southern France was originally its own little country called Languedoc, with its own language. As a result, this region has its own history and culture. Desolate stone castle ruins lie high on mountain peaks, meticulously restored walled cities are ready and waiting to be visited, and great roads link them all together. Eventually this trip winds back into the Catalan Pyrénées and home to the Costa Brava and the town of Tossa de Mar.

## Day 1   Tossa de Mar to Montserrat

Tossa de Mar is one of the quieter towns along the Costa Brava coastline. It can be busy at times during the summer, but it's more family-centered than some of the other resorts on the coast. I prefer Tossa and the rough cobblestoned old town than the concrete hotel jungle of Lloret de Mar just down the road, but take your pick. The castle and walls make a perfect backdrop to a charming village as the clouds drift lazily overhead and the gentle waves lap up on the golden shore—so perfect in fact, that Hollywood filmed the classic *Pandora and the Flying Dutchman,* with Ava Gardner right here. There is even a statue of Ava on a hill overlooking the beach!

A nice campground, Camping Can Marti, is located just outside of town. It's close enough to walk to either the old town or even down to the beach (about 1 km). This is a great town to stroll through and enjoy a quiet seafood dinner while overlooking the small cove. Tossa de Mar can be easily explored in just one evening, but its charm will have you coming back for more.

From Tossa go south along the coast road G1-682 through Lloret, Blanes, and Malgrat de Mar. The closer you get to Barcelona, the more these towns resemble booming tourist resorts of concrete towers and discos. The

*Tossa de Mar is a classic Costa Brava beach town with not only a sandy shoreline but its own castle too! Photo by Jose Manuel.*

coastline, however, has its own natural rugged beauty—beaches, coves, and cliffs on your left and rugged mountains on your right. If you want to visit Barcelona, continue on N11. Barcelona is a very large, yet culture-rich city. For purposes of this journey, Barcelona is skipped, though if you have the time it is well worth a visit.

### Day 1 – Tossa de Mar to Montserrat   162 km/101 miles

Start in Tossa de Mar and follow the G1-682 to Blanes. At Malgrat de Mar connect with N11 to Arenys de Mar. Take the C61 north to Arenys de Munt and continue to C35.

Turn left on C-35 then right on BV-5301 all the way to Tona.

Arrive Tona. Turn right on C17 to Vic.

Arrive Vic. Go south and turn left on N141c at Malla. Continue on N141 to Manresa.

Arrive Manresa, go south on C55 to Montserrat.

Arrive Montserrat.

*Ahh, the convenience of a "park and eat" diner. Drive right up to the curb, walk a few steps, sit down, and enjoy the food and the local townsfolk. Photo by Toby Ballentine.*

At Arenys de Mar take the C61 inland to Arenys de Munt. Continue up to C35 where you turn left, then turn right onto BV-5301. Ride this beauty of a road to Montseny and Tona. This area is called the "greenbelt of Barcelona" and is home to rugged hills and forested terrain. Several streams feed this area providing an unusual array of landscapes, but the best part is how sweetly the black asphalt winds up through the nature park along tight sweeping curves. Eventually, the road connects with C17 at Tona. Turn right and head up to Vic, the capital of this region.

Vic was originally a religious center and has a fascinating downtown area at Placa Major. There are various and sundry churches and old relics in the old town. Outside cafes and tapas bars border the medieval corridors inviting you to stay a bit longer and do a little people watching. If Vic appeals to you, then by all means stay, and if you do, be sure to visit the small village of Rupit. Accessible by suspension bridge, this little town is like stepping back into 17th-century Catalonia.

After getting your fill of Vic, head south again on C17, then veer right on N141c at Malla. This road is another short little wonder that ultimately connects with N141 on to Manresa. I'm trying to get you to Montserrat by the end of the day, so head south on C55 and soon you will see some weird looking mountains and the famous Benedictine Monestir de Montserrat.

The monastery was built in 1025 in honor of the Black Madonna supposedly brought by St. Peter to this area. Destroyed and then rebuilt over the last 1,000 years, the monastery is now a holy shrine and visited by thousands of pilgrims each year. The setting is dramatic and makes for a good layover before heading back to Manresa and the Pyrénées on Day 2.

*Our visit to the Montserrat Monastery was made special by hearing a local choir rehearsing inside. Photo by Toby Ballentine.*

# Day 2  Montserrat to Vielha

From Montserrat head back on C55 to Manresa. The town is centered around the main basilica and the view coming off the bridge is quite impressive. If you like, spend a minute walking around or just drive casually across the bridge and enjoy the sight from your motorcycle seat. There will be more than enough opportunities to stop today. Continue on C55 as it

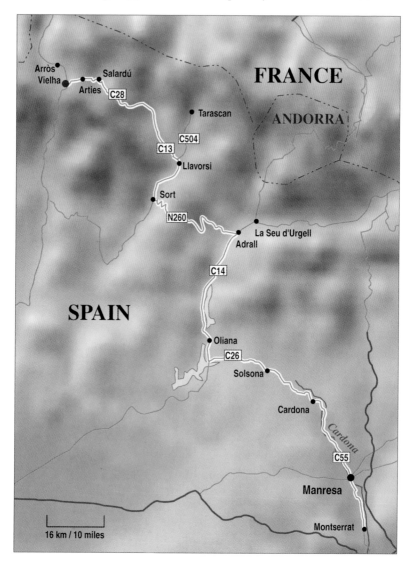

Arròs
Vielha
Salardú
Arties  C28
Tarascan
FRANCE
ANDORRA
C504
C13
Llavorsi
Sort
N260
La Seu d'Urgell
Adrall
C14
SPAIN
Oliana
C26
Solsona
Cardona
Cardona
C55
Manresa
16 km / 10 miles
Montserrat

*The cable car ride up to the monastery at Montserrat provides a panoramic view of the surrounding countryside. Photo by Toby Ballentine.*

## Day 2 – Montserrat to Vielha   242 km/151 miles

From Montserrat head back to Manresa on C55. Continue on C55 to Solsona. The road turns into C26 and connects with C14. Turn right on C14 to Oliana and Adrall.

Arrive Adrall. Turn left on N260 to Sort.

Arrive Sort. Turn right and at Llavorsi veer left on C13/C28 to Vielha.

Arrive Vielha.

meanders beside the Cardona River. Just beyond a curve in the road the Cardona Castle looms above its namesake village. The castle and town are very representative of the local Romanesque architecture. As you continue up the road, the traditional town of Solsona appears, once again reflecting the typical stone and Romanesque style of this area. Enjoy this road and the surrounding scenery and architecture. It's a bit off the beaten track from Barcelona making it a great run on your bike.

After Solsona, the road turns into C26 and eventually T's into C14. Turn right (north) and drive through Oliana. The road climbs deeper into the Pyrénées, past a beautiful lake and continues north into green mountain valleys lined with streams and lakes. At the small town of Adrall, turn left off C14 to N260. The road continues to wind and twist and then connects with C13 at Sort. Turn right (north) to Llavorsi. As you drive farther and farther north, valleys become even more verdant and typical stone hamlets border the road.

*Stone churches like this one in Arties are a common sight while traveling through the Pyrénées of eastern Spain. If it's a warm summer day, park your bike, and take a look inside. The stone walls keep the interior nice and cool! Photo by AchilleT.*

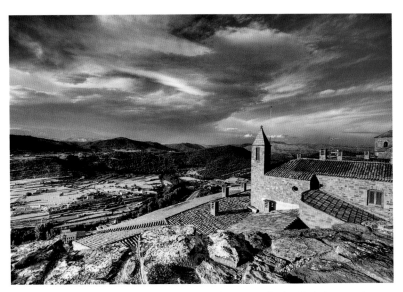

*The late afternoon view from the castle at Cardona is overlaid with dark menacing clouds. Paradors (luxury hotels) have been built in many monasteries, palaces, and castles, including this one, throughout Spain. Photo by Ville Miettinen.*

If you are interested in a little detour, veer right on C504 up the Vall de Cardós. You will pass Lladros and Lladore before arriving at Tarascan. This is a beautiful stretch of road that ends at a crystal-clear blue glacial lake. This is not on my designated route, but makes for a real treat. You can camp and hike from the village of Tarascan.

Otherwise, continue on C13/C28 all the way to Vielha. You'll pass through the small towns of Salardú and Arties. This whole area is rich in not only its scenery, but also its heritage. Churches, town squares, and bell towers hewn from stone provide bucket-brimming charm while mountain peaks provide heavenly backdrops. The road twists dramatically, making it hard to focus on the scenery, but hopefully you're riding two-up, so your better half can take the pictures.

Eventually, you will arrive in Vielha. This is the main town at the junction. It's a good place to stay because with its "tourist destination" status, all the necessary amenities are provided. However, if you really want to try a night out in the country, continue up the road a bit to Arròs, a delightfully typical small hamlet, and poke around for a pension. Rooms are available in these small towns at relatively inexpensive prices. Don't worry that you don't speak the language; the locals are very hospitable. So be a little daring, you will be making friends for life!

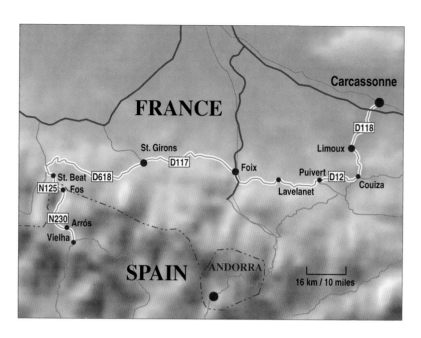

# Day 3/4  Vielha to Carcassonne

Pulling yourself away from the Spanish Alps will not be easy, but today you head into southern France to visit a couple of marvelous medieval towns—Foix and Carcassonne. Exploring these communities may take longer than a day, so be a bit flexible and bend your schedule if needed. A few years back, our family navigated a houseboat up the Canal du Midi and fell in love with this area. We easily spent a week slowly meandering up the canal from Narbonne to Carcassonne, stopping at small villages along the way. I came back with a great appreciation for the people and heritage of Languedoc, France.

This motorcycle trip follows a similar route as our houseboat, except on black asphalt and two wheels rather than on a keel in water. Start by leaving either Vielha or Arrós on N230 (which turns into N125 in France). Just past St. Beat, turn right on D618 toward St. Girons, another charming French village perfect to stop at for some croissants and hot chocolate. Continue on D117 to Foix.

Foix is one of the lesser known small, yet stunning cities of southern France. As you approach on D117, the imposing chateau rises on the horizon. For many years this town was fought over by the English, French, and Spanish due to its close proximity to the border. Even during WWII, Foix

*The Château de Foix was originally built in the 7th century and played an important role during the crusades against the Cathars. Photo by Ulysse 034.*

### Day 3/4 – Vielha to Carcassonne   243 km/152 miles

From Vielha take N230 north into France. Road changes to N125 and
  continue to Fos and St. Beat. A few miles past St. Beat turn right on
  D618 to St. Girons.
Arrive St. Girons. Take the D117 to Foix.
Arrive Foix and continue on D117 to Puivert, then stay straight on D12
  to Couiza.
Arrive Couiza and turn left (north) on D118 to Carcassonne.
Arrive Carcassonne.

was a waypoint on *le chemin de la Liberte,* or path of Liberty, for pilots, Jews, and refugees attempting to escape into Spain. The trail still exists for those interested in re-hiking it, but do so at your own risk! If you want to stay here, there is a nice campground situated next to a small lake called Camping du Lac, that is only about a mile outside of town.

From Foix continue on D117 to Lavelanet and then continue to Puivert where you stay straight onto D12 to Couiza then head north on D118 through Limoux to Carcassonne. Old town Limoux is worth a peek, but the true jewel is La Cité or Carcassonne. Though Carcassonne is the epitome of a "travel destination" and can be quite crowded, it is not to be missed. Originally built in the 13th century, the city was restored in 1853 and is now a very real example of a true walled fortress town—complete with walls, turrets, and tourists. La Cité has an ambiance that is not easily forgotten so put on your Harley-Davidson T-shirt and enjoy the shops, cafes, and narrow cobblestone lanes of this magnificent little city.

*Before black asphalt, water filled canals were the highways of Europe. This is the Canal du Midi that links the Mediterranean to the Atlantic and is now used primarily by tourists. Photo by Yellés Arif.*

*Carcassonne is a one-of-a-kind city in southern France. Rebuilt based on its original layout, the walls and parapets surround a classic medieval town built during the time of the Crusades. Photo by Colocho.*

There is a great little campsite just outside of town that is called Campeole la Cité. At night when the floodlights reflect off the walls and city, you'll be glad you came and glad you bought this book (considering all the money you are saving for this great view)!

# Day 5/6  Carcassonne to La Seu d'Urgell

Today our journey wanders through more of the Languedoc region of France and back into Spain. Once its own country between the 10th and 12th century, Languedoc has been influenced by the Romans, Spanish, Moors, and French. An ancient Christian sect, the Cathars, once lived in this country, but were ruthlessly eradicated by the Catholics due to their supposed heretical beliefs. Like many other relatively small areas in Europe, there once existed a country within what is now another country with its own rich culture, customs, and language. Makes for some interesting history.

Start by leaving Carcassonne on D6113 to Narbonne. Narbonne was another city our family visited while cruising the Canal du Midi and we all fell in love with it. The River Aude runs through the center of town and, in my opinion, the cathedral is one of the most spectacular in this area. While in

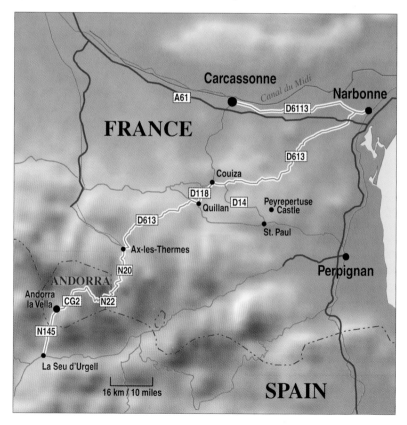

*Construction began in the 13th century for the Narbonne Cathedral and still remains unfinished. The interior's grandeur and size literally took my breath away the first time I visited! Photo by Benh Lieu Song.*

town poke your head in one of the tourist shops and glance at one of the books about the Cathars. Ruined castles on craggy peaks is their legacy. If you are interested, pick up a copy and on the way back to Spain drop by one of the most famous, the Peyrepertuse Castle. It's a little bit of a detour and

---

### Day 5/6 – Carcassonne to La Seu d'Urgell   282 km/176 miles

From Carcassonne take the D6113 to Narbonne.

Arrive Narbonne. Head southwest on D613 back to Couiza. From Couiza continue on D118. At Quillan take the D163 to Ax-les-Thermes.

Arrive Ax-les-Thermes and go south on N20/E9 the take N22 and CG2 to Andorra la Vella. Once out of Andorra the road changes to N145 on its way to La Seu d'Urgell.

Arrive La Seu d'Urgell.

you do need to hike up to the ruins, but it is well worth it.

From Narbonne, head southwest on D613 back toward Couiza. If interested in visiting Peyrepertuse castle, turn left on D14 to St. Paul then follow the signs to Peyrepertuse Castle, then climb on foot from the carpark to the castle. You will be amazed. How did they build these structures without any cranes or tractors?! If you are anxious to get back to the twisty mountain

*Seeing the ruins of the Peyrepertuse Castle is well worth it, but it's the drive up that's a real peg-scraping good time! Photo by Adam Baker.*

*This is the Casa de la Vall or seat of the General Council in Andorra located in the old town of Andorra La Vella, the only real city in this small principality. Photo by Karoly Lorentey.*

roads, then stay on D613 to Couiza. Take D118 to Quillan then D613 to Ax-les-Thermes. The road begins to gyrate as you are now re-entering the Pyrénées. From here link up with N20/E9, N22 and CG2 into the tiny principality of Andorra.

Andorra lies in the midst of the Pyrénées and as such is a ski destination for many Europeans. Andorra's semi-independence allows it to be a tax haven with an abundance of duty-free shopping and cheap gas—so fill up! The road winds through this small country of less than 80,000 people in no time. I think the entire country is only 30 kilometers wide. So buy a souvenir, and then continue down to Spain on N145 to La Seu d'Urgell. This small town lies in a wooded valley and at one time was the seat of government for Andorra. It's now a quiet, relaxing little charmer perfect for a layover. Traditional pensions and ski chalets abound in the area providing easy overnight lodging.

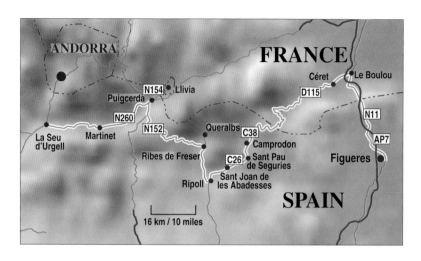

# Day 7  La Seu d'Urgell to Figueres

Get ready for some serious mountain riding today. The roads from La Seu d'Urgell to Céret are peg-scraping wonders and take you through the heart of the Catalan Pyrénées. So, after visiting the Romanesque cathedral in La Seu d'Urgell and wandering around a bit, pack up your stuff and head east on N260 toward Puigcerdà. The road follows the Riu Segre Valley through the Serra de Cadi Mountains. Stone villages pop up here and there as you cut across the mountain range. Various side roads tempt you to visit even more hamlets and you need to ask yourself just one question—do you have the time?

Eventually the road weaves into Puigcerdà just south of the French border. This is a popular tourist and ski destination. Stop here for lunch or if you want to explore the countryside, head northeast on N154 for a brief detour to medieval Llivia (only about five miles outside of town). Llivia was formerly the Roman capital of this area and is home to castle ruins and the oldest pharmacy in Europe (now a small museum). From Puigcerdà go south on N152, another dandy of a road, toward Ribes de Freser. There are a number of ski resorts along this route and the scenery is spectacular. Rugged mountains and green wooded ski slopes remind me of the San Juan Mountains in Colorado. If you aren't too pressed for time, go north to Queralbs, a small, lesser-visited Catalan village.

From Ribes de Freser, go south on N152 to Ripoll. Ripoll really isn't much of a town, but the road heading northeast out of town, the C26, is a great run. It curves though some great scenery and towns in what is called

*Storm clouds gather behind a small stone church set in a verdant green valley high in the Costa Brava Pyrénées. Photo courtesy of Tourist Office of Spain in New York.*

the Vall Alto del Ter. The first town is Sant Joan de les Abadesses. As you approach, you'll see the bridge over the river and then the huge Abbey of Sant Joan. Enjoy a short visit or just continue on the road. The designation changes the farther you go, but it's still the same road. Another town worth a brief stop is Camprodon with its arched bridge, parish church, and town hall. The asphalt continues to twist and turn until Céret. After Céret connect with the N11 and head south until Figueres.

Figueres is known as being the hometown of Salvador Dali, the famous surrealist artist, and a museum containing many of his paintings and exhibitions is located here. Stay in town or pop a tent at Camping Pous about 1 to 2 clicks on A2 north of town, or head farther east on C260 to Cadaqués, Dali's summer retreat. Cadaqués is a beautiful whitewashed village on the Costa Brava.

## Day 7 – La Seu d'Urgell to Figueres   227 km/142 miles

From La Seu d'Urgell take the N260 east to Martinet and Puigcerdà.
Arrive Puigcerdà. Go south on N152 to Ribes de Freser.
Arrive Ribes de Freser and continue south to Ripoll. At Ripoll turn left
(east) on C26 to Sant Pau de Seguries. Follow C26/C38/C15 and D115
on to Céret and Le Boulou. Head south on N11 at Le Boulou to
Figueres.
Arrive Figueres.

# Day 8   Figueres to Tossa de Mar

Spend some time on the beach in Cadaqués, because it's only a short drive to Tossa with only one significant stop in between. From Figueres go south on N11 to Girona. This town is definitely worth a stop and a walk. Originally Girona was a waypoint on the Via Augusta, the Roman highway from Rome to Spain. Many of the old buildings still stand, so park your bike and get some morning exercise by walking across the numerous footbridges and narrow lanes as you explore downtown.

From Girona, follow the C65 back to the Costa Brava and the town of Sant Feliu. Head south along the coast road G1-682 to Tossa de Mar. As you drive back to this old resort town, the castle perched beside the cove draws you in like an invitation back home. When you arrive, take a break, collect your thoughts, enjoy one more Catalan meal, and then settle in for another day . . . or two . . . .or three . . .

*On one of our visits to Barcelona we saw this example of the bizarre yet striking architecture of Anotoni Gaudi. Photo by Toby Ballentine.*

### Day 8 – Figueres to Tossa de Mar   93 km/58 miles

From Figueres continue south on N11 to Girona.

Arrive Girona and just south of town connect with C65 south toward Sant Feliu.

Arrive Sant Feliu and turn right on G1-682 to Tossa de Mar.

Arrive Tossa de Mar.

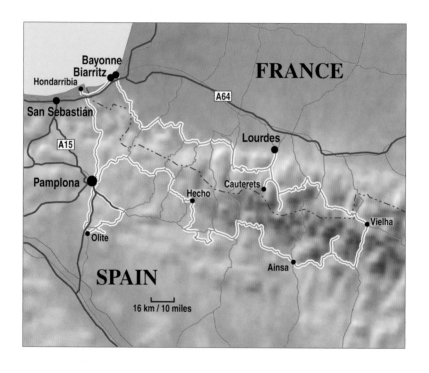

# Running with the Bulls through the Pyrénées Mountains

**Distance:** *1067 km/667 miles*
**Suggested Time Frame:** *5–6 Days*
**Highlights:** *Drive through the heart of Basque country and enjoy the culture, language, cuisine, and countryside of a country within a country that is rich with its own heritage. Start on the Atlantic coast, then cruise up to Pamplona, known for the original "Running of the Bulls," then bask in the small winding roads of the Pyrénées Mountains. Verdant valleys surrounded by granite slopes pull your eyes off the black asphalt, bewitching you with their beauty and charm. The trip eventually winds its way up to southern France and the "other" side of the mountains. What a deal—same mountain range and two different journeys all wrapped into one! Visit the pilgrimage mecca of Lourdes before returning back to the quaint seaside village of Hondarribia where this trip began.*

*Festivals like the Feast of Our Lady and San Sebastián fiesta in Tafalla are a great introduction to the culture-rich area of northeastern Spain. Photo courtesy of Tourist Office of Spain in New York.*

*This journey takes you right through the pristine Valle de Roncal and the villages of Isaba and Uztárroz. You are going to love it! Photo courtesy of Tourist Office of Spain in New York.*

Although I've never participated in the American tradition of bar-hopping (and certainly do not recommend it while motorcycling), there is a custom similar to it in Spain that I do recommend. I call it "pintxos hopping." In the Basque area of Spain, tapas are referred to as *pintxos*. For those of you unfamiliar with this tradition, tapas are the Spanish equivalent of our appetizers. In the States you usually stay in one location and order several types of appetizers; in Spain, the best way to enjoy this custom is to eat one or two at one bar, then move on to the next and the next and the next . . . it's great food and a great way to meet people. Just keep track of the number of toothpicks, since this is how each restaurant charges you for their tab. It's all done on the honor system. Originally tapas started in the Andalucia region of

Spain, but I prefer the tasty tidbits of the Basque region. They have their own unique flavor!

This trip will not only introduce you to the fine delicacies of the Basque country, but will show you the best roads Spain has to offer. Most of the journey is spent motorcycling in resplendent glacial valleys and over high mountain peaks. The Alps may be better known worldwide, but the Pyrénées are just as enjoyable. Start on the Atlantic coast from the small, delightful town of Hondarribia, swing up to Pamplona for the running of the bulls, and then follow endless mountain roads through numerous ancient stone villages. The journey eventually swings back through France and the northern edge of the Pyrénées with a stopover in the pilgrimage site of Lourdes before heading back to the Atlantic coast.

*The village of Aribe with its traditional stone arched bridge is typical of many communities in the Pyrénées. Photo courtesy of Tourist Office of Spain in New York.*

# Day 1   Hondarribia to Olite

This journey starts in the small town of Hondarribia nestled at the base of Mount Jaizkibela and close to the Atlantic shore. Hondarribia was founded in the 6th century and is composed of two sections, the walled city and the marina district. The walled portion is a Historic Artistic Monument. The tourist office is located in the old castle of Emperor Carlos V. A 15th-century gothic-style church adorns the downtown as well. The cobblestone center is lined with old homes and at the heart is a baroque-style town hall.

For a more festive environment, walk down to the District la Marina to

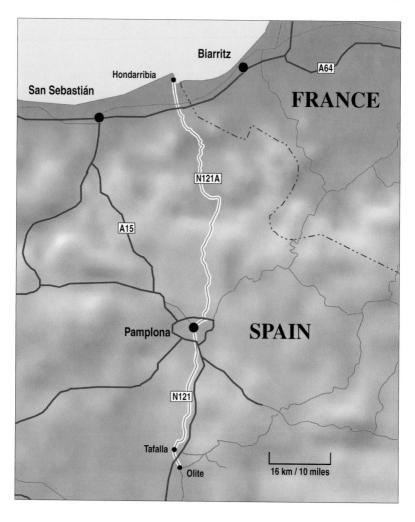

*Hondarribia is a bit touristy, but still is a charming place to start your trip through Basque country. Photo courtesy of Tourist Office of Spain in New York.*

see some beautifully colored homes or mosey down Calle San Pedro for more tapas. You could easily spend a couple of days here visiting the small nearby coastal cities of Irun, Zarautz or Mutriku. And for goodness sake, be a little daring and try one of the fish delicacies—different but absolutely delicious.

If you like this little getaway, plan a day trip to San Sebastián, one of the

### Day 1 – Hondarribia to Olite   128 km/80 miles

Start in Hondarribia. Take the N121A to Pamplona.
Arrive Pamplona. Continue south on N121 to Tafalla.
Arrive Tafalla. Continue on N121 to Olite.
Arrive Olite.

largest cities in Basque country. Not only can your wander around its old town and visit some pristine in-city beaches, but many believe this is the spot for the Basque's best cuisine. And if you want to try some *pintxos* hopping, visit the old town on the streets running parallel with the boulevard and you will see multitudes of bars. Makes for a great evening activity—not only do you get to see the real Basque culture, but actually taste it and feel it!

There are numerous places to stay in Hondarribia and the tourist office in the old castle will help you find someplace to your liking. A nice campground is Jaizkibel Camping located just one kilometer from old town Hondarribia.

Once you get your fill of this quaint area, load up your motorcycle and get ready to head for the hills. The N121A climbs inland to Pamplona, known for the "Running of the Bulls." You may be anxious to see Pamplona, but don't be in too much of a hurry. The N121A follows the Bidasoa River and then cuts through the lovely Baztán Valley. The road is a bit tortuous, but not to motorcycle enthusiasts. The black asphalt winds its way up from the coast with those teasing turns we have all come to love. Keep an eye on the road and let your pillion companion take in the sights— you can see the pictures later!

Pamplona was made famous by Ernest Hemingway and the festival of the San Fermin or the "Running of the Bulls." This festival takes place July 6–14 at 7 a.m. sharp. The bulls are let loose and follow a barricaded course to the bullring. If you are feeling daring, be my guest! Injuries occur every year, so participate at your own risk! For those who don't want to be chased by bulls, then I would recommend some simple sightseeing. There is a fortress and an exquisitely preserved downtown area near the tree-lined Plaza Castillo.

After getting your behind kicked by the bulls, head south on N121 to the old medieval walled city of Olite. This small town has its own palace with cone-shaped minarets and an old gothic church. The palace was rebuilt in 1937 and is now a Historic Artistic Site. Once the refuge for the medieval court of Carlos III, Olite is now just a sleepy town catering to tourists. Its old-time aura and tourist-friendly downtown make it a perfect spot to spend the night. There is a friendly tourist office in town that will help you find the perfect place to stay.

These twin-horned two-ton beasts are an integral part of Spanish culture and are the key participants in the Running of the Bulls in Pamplona and actual bullfights in local arenas. The matadors even have their own fan clubs and poster-waving groupies! Photos by Toby Ballentine and courtesy of Tourist Office of Spain in New York.

# Day 2   Olite to Hecho (Echo)

Today the roads will open up vistas that will astound you. The Navarrean Pyrénées contain numerous valleys *(valles)* that tempt you to divert off the suggested route and spend even more time exploring. Once again, your choice! If you have the time, not only will you find medieval hamlets tucked beneath towering granite slopes, but numerous areas to explore on foot as well. Outdoorsmen and hikers are at home in this neck of the woods. Although busy at times, the roads cut through rolling hills, forests, and snow-clad mountains for seemingly endless miles. Your wrist will become sore from constant motion, but you won't feel it until after the ride. The numerous twisties and scenic wonders will keep you transfixed before you start to feel the ache.

From Olite head northeast on NA5303. This is a narrow road that wanders through the high desert of the Navarra region. At San Martín de Unx connect with NA5310 to Ujué. Ujué is a hilltop village with extensive views of the surrounding area. The town is woven with small narrow cobblestone lanes and has a fortified church by the town square. I remember buying

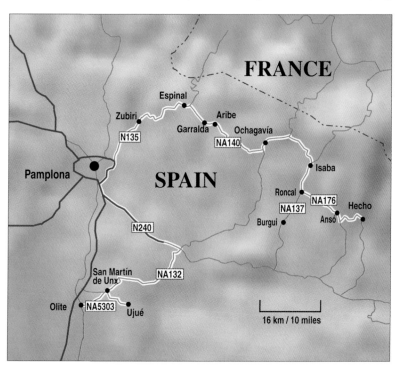

*In the summer, the Royal Palace in Olite serves as a backdrop to classical theater performances and medieval fairs. Photo courtesy of Tourist Office of Spain in New York.*

### Day 2 – Olite to Hecho   221 km/138 miles

From Olite head northeast on NA5303. At San Martín de Unx take NA5310 to Ujué.

Arrive Ujué. Head back on NA5310 and turn right on NA132. At the N240 junction turn left back to Pamplona.

Arrive Pamplona. From here take the N135 north to Espinal. Continue east on NA140 toward Garralda and Ariba.

Continue on NA140 to Ochagavía and Isaba. At Isaba turn right (south) to Roncal. Just south of Roncal turn left (east) on NA176.

Follow NA176 to Ansó and on to Hecho (Echo).

Arrive Hecho (Echo).

*The town of Isaba sits amid the green fields of the Valle de Roncal on a beautiful summer day. Photo courtesy of Tourist Office of Spain in New York.*

some cheese and bread at the local market and then taking a break at a picnic spot just outside of town. The morning was cool and clear and I felt like I had discovered the real Spain. After a brief respite in Ujué, head back on NA5310 and turn right on NA132. At the N240 veer back to Pamplona.

From Pamplona continue north on N135 and then after the town of Zubiri the road slithers like a snake. You'll love it. At the NA140 junction, head east toward Garralda. You will pass through the hamlet of Aribe and several other small typical villages before arriving in Ochagavia. Ochagavia lies beside a small river and is the epitome of a Pyrenean stone slate built town. Old stone structures beside the traditional Catholic church nestled by a stream spanned by an arched bridge all in the shadows of the Pyrénées mountains . . . and I could go on and on . . . just try to visualize it in your mind and you won't even be close to the charm you feel driving through these towns. If you like, stay at one of the local campgrounds and explore the Valle del Salazar. This valley winds south of Ochagavia and is dotted with even more interesting towns and bridges.

Otherwise continue east on the NA140 to Isaba. At Isaba head south on NA137 to Roncal. This area is called the Valle del Roncal and is yet another valley worthy of more time. The towns of Burgui, Roncal, and Isaba are popular bases for hikers and outdoorsmen. Just south of Roncal head east on NA176 to Ansó and then onto Hecho. This stretch of asphalt is a delight as it wanders across forested mountain slopes and stream-filled valleys. Ansó is another beauty and is best seen by parking your motorcycle in the car park below the town. Stroll up to town, grab some tapas, and then continue on NA176 to Hecho, a popular summer destination and rightly so. The town's homes are usually adorned with flowers and the narrow streets are lined with traditional cafes and bars making it a good stopover for the night. Drop by the tourist office for help finding a place to stay or camp at Camping Valle de Hecho just south of town. Spend an extra night here if you want to explore the surrounding area on foot.

*The "tora de fuego" is a common sight in many Spanish festivals. Sparklers are attached to a bull's horns and the spectators play dodge trying not to get burned. This is a tamer rendition of the custom. Photo courtesy of Tourist Office of Spain in New York.*

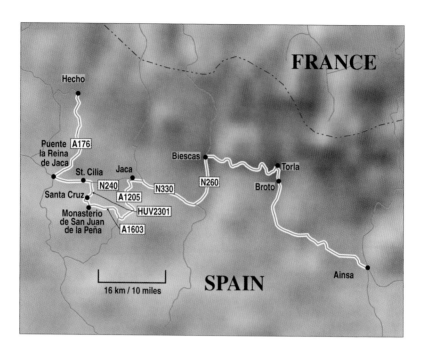

# Day 3  Hecho to Ainsa

Today, start your journey by driving south through the Valle de Hecho all the way down to the N240 junction. The valley is verdant and starts off narrow then slowly widens the farther south you go. A mixture of elm, pine, and beech trees envelope the valley and riverbed as you bike sways gently toward Puente la Reina. At Puenta la Reina head east on N240 toward Jaca. Not too far down the road, just after St. Cilia, go south on HUV2301 to the Monasterio de San Juan del la Peña. This is a nice detour to a uniquely located and built monastery. After Santa Cruz, the road winds endlessly up the Sierra de la Peña where the old monastery lies hidden beneath a natural rock outcropping. The original building was built in the 9th century and was supposedly a waypoint for the elusive Holy Grail. Now it is a tourist destination with great views of the snowcapped mountains to the north.

After a brief visit to the monastery, follow the road all the way around via A1205 to Jaca. Jaca was a major staging point for the pilgrimage to Santiago de Compostela where the Apostle James is buried. The cathedral and stone arched bridge trigger your imagination and help you visualize what it must have been like 1,000 years ago when hordes of pilgrims gathered here to start their journey. As you sit on your bike it is as if nothing has changed

*Puenta la Reina over the River Arga is a notable landmark on the pilgrimage route, the Way of St. James. Photo courtesy of Tourist Office of Spain in New York.*

## Day 3 – Hecho to Ainsa   139 km/87 miles

From Hecho head south on A176. At Puente la Reina de Jaca go east on N240 toward Jaca. A few kilometers past St. Cilia turn right (south) on HUV2301 to Monasterio de San Juan de la Peña.

Arrive Monasterio. The road changes to A1603 and A1205 as it loops back to Jaca.

Arrive Jaca. Continue east on N330 then veer north on N260 to Biescas. Follow N260 as it turns east toward Torla.

Arrive Torla. Continue south on N260 to Ainsa.

Arrive Ainsa.

except for the humming of your engine.

From Jaca continue east on N330 then head north on N260 toward Biescas, a quaint summer getaway with white-washed red-tiled homes. At Biescas follow the N260 on a sweet, twisting road to Torla, the entrance to the Parque Nacional de Ordesa. This park is at the heart of the Pyrénées and is a hiker's paradise. Numerous glacial-formed valleys overshadowed by granite curtains abound in the park. Lush forests give way to unblemished cliffs and snowcapped peaks. If you are interested in spending some time here, stay in Torla and plan your expeditions from there. There is a huge car park with various modes of transportation into this hiker's paradise.

From Torla continue south along the N260 through Broto and the Valle de Solana to Ainsa. This road weaves and wanders through more

*As you drive through the valleys in the Pyrénées, you can't help but notice how the local livestock blend in with the natural landscape. Photo courtesy of Tourist Office of Spain in New York.*

*Are you looking for the Holy Grail? Well, rumor has it that the chalice was once hidden here in the monastery at San Juan de la Peña. Photo by José Porras.*

magnificent countryside. Take your time as you approach yet another classic Spanish gem—the old town of Ainsa. Once the capital of the Kingdom of Sobrarbe, this small hilltop village is a Historic Artistic Site. Houses crammed together are adjacent to the requisite church and castle, all combining to create a blast to the medieval past. The best way to visit is by taking the old steps from the lower village and then climb up to the hilltop village on foot. You need the exercise after eating all those tapas! The views are commanding. There is a tourist office in town that will help you find a place to stay. One word of advice, this is a popular spot so you may want to call and make some reservations in advance. Good luck!

## Day 4  Ainsa to Cauterets

The next couple of days are, relatively speaking, long ones—both more than 150 miles per day. I know in the States that doesn't seem like much, but when traveling on these narrow winding roads through the Pyrénées, you will be beat by the end of the day. Let me restate that, you will be beat but also bewitched by the immense beauty of the terrain and of the mountains. Start by leaving Ainsa on the N260 east. This road weaves across rolling hills, ultimately winding its way up to some of the highest mountains in Spain. You will continue to pass through dozens of charming villages while following the black asphalt higher and higher. Although you have a big day, get up early and take a small detour up the Valle de la Benasque on A139. You are now in the Posets-Maladeta Nature Reserve, which is the home to some of the highest summits in northern Aragon. This is nature at its best and is reminiscent of the Tetons and Rocky Mountains in the U.S.

Continue your journey north on N230 toward Vielha. The mountains taper a bit, but the valley is green and lush. The tunnel takes you right through the mountain's mammoth granite before entering the township of Vielha. Drive north on N230, then head west on the very windy D618 into France and onto Bagnères-de-Luchon. Bagnères makes a great stop for lunch as its main street overflows with cafes and bars. So rest your weary

*Back in 1910 when the Col du Tourmalet was added to the Tour de France, cyclists pushed their bikes up the steep slope. Sure am glad I ride a motorcycle. Photo by Muneaki.*

behind and enjoy a bit of French cuisine before tackling the northern edge of the French Pyrénées. As soon as you are rejuvenated, follow the D618 to Arreau, then D918 to La Mongie, and follow the signs to the summit of Col du Tourmalet. This road is a killer and winds under several avalanche shelters before reaching the summit. Magnificent views await you and please . . . drive carefully!

At Luz-St.-Sauveur, head south to Gavarnie to see the Cirque de Gavarnie, a beautiful mountain amphitheater, or continue onto Cauterets. Just beware, the road to Gavarnie can become hopelessly congested in the summertime and the city is not too impressive! If you are running low on time, head north on D921, then south on D920 to Cauterets. This tourist destination is one of the more remote Pyrenean towns and was once the summer getaway for Victor Hugo. It is a little quieter than Gavarnie making it a better layover in my opinion. The Pyrénées National Park is close by for you to visit and there are numerous accommodations for the motorcycle-weary traveler. If you want to camp, try the pleasant campground Les Bergeronnetes, just north of town across the river.

## Day 4 – Ainsa to Cauterets   285 km/178 miles

From Ainsa continue east on N260 and then go north on N230 to Vielha. Continue past Vielha then turn left (west) on D618 into France and Bagnères-de-Luchon.

Arrive Bagnères-de-Luchon. Continue on D618 to Arreau. Keep going through town as the road changes to D918, and stay on the road until Luz-St.-Sauveur. Turn right on D921 and then go south on D920 to Cauterets.

Arrive Cauterets.

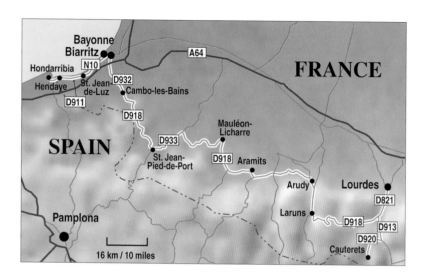

## Day 5 Cauterets to Hondarribia

From Cauterets head back on the same road D920 to Lourdes, the route number changes from D913 to D821. After a short morning drive, you will arrive at Lourdes—second only to Paris for the number of available hotel beds in all of France. Apparently on February 11, 1858, a 14-year-old girl had a vision of the Blessed Virgin Mary. After 18 such visits and some miraculous healings, the Roman Catholic Church listed Lourdes as an official pilgrimage site. Since 1860, more than 200 million people have visited this shrine, many looking for a miraculous healing themselves. The whole town is centered on this marketing phenomenon and is definitely what you would call a modern day pilgrimage center.

The road to Lourdes and then on to Laruns is a nice one (D918). The shimmering mountains and forested valleys line the black asphalt. On a clear day this run is smooth and peaceful, especially as you leave the mass of humanity at Lourdes. Continue to follow D918 to Arudy, Aramits and Mauléon-Licharre. At the D933 junction, turn left (south) to St. Jean-Pied-de-Port. This was once the capital of the area and another staging point for the pilgrimage to Santiago de Compostela in the middle ages. Now it is a rather unremarkable spot with a small old town and semi-imposing fortress.

From here, head northeast on D918 toward Bayonne and Biarritz. On your way you will drive through the town of Cambo-les-Bains, an old spa town. Continue on the D932 to Biarritz. Biarritz is a classic French seaside resort. The beaches are pristine and in the summer covered with bronze sun

*The Basilica of Lourdes is built beside the sacred spring for which Lourdes is most famous. This is one of the most visited shrines in all Christendom.*
*Photo by Roland Darré.*

worshippers. The Hotel du Palais was originally built by Napoleon III for his wife and is located at the heart of the city's most popular beaches.

From Biarritz follow the coastal roads of D911 and D912 through St. Jean-de-Luz and Hendaye. Stay on the coast and eventually return to Hondarribia. One little tidbit of historical trivia is that in Hendaye there is a small island in the estuary called Île des Faisans. This tiny locale has been the meeting place of several larger than life historical figures such as Louis XIV and Maria Teresa, and Hitler and Franco (during the Spanish Civil War). Finish the trip by arriving in Hondarribia, and treating yourself to some seafood delicacies or, if your legs aren't too sore, walking the town and enjoying the pleasant crowds at the local tapas bars.

### Day 5 – Cauterets to Hondarribia   294 km/184 miles

From Cauterets take D920, D913 and D821 north to Lourdes.
Arrive Lourdes. From here head south on D918 and follow the road as it winds back north and westward. At D933 turn left (south) to St. Jean-Pied-de-Port, then go northwest on D918 and D932 to Biarritz.
Arrive Biarritz. Follow the coastal roads D911 and D912 south to Hondarribia.
Arrive Hondarribia.

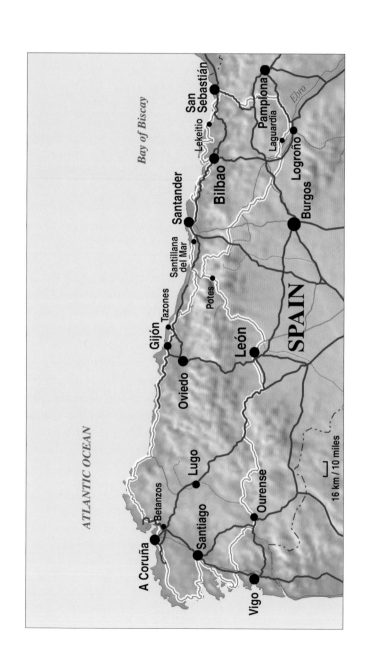

# The Cantabrian Mountains and the Pilgrimage Towns on Spain's Atlantic Coast

**Distance:** *2198 km/1374 miles*
**Time Frame:** *9–11 days*
**Highlights:** *Start on the coastal roads of northern Spain and then wind inland through the provinces of Navarre, Cantabria, Asturias, and Galicia. A combination of rugged coastal beauty and the mountains of Picos de Europa converge as you wander back in time to the medieval pilgrimage city of Santiago de Compostela. This is a part of Europe not overrun with foreign tourists; a place where motorcyclists can run free on roads truly less traveled on.*

*The scallop shell is the emblem of James, the Apostle, and marks the pilgrimage route of the Way of St. James all the way to Santiago de Compostela, his burial site. Photo courtesy of Tourist Office of Spain in New York.*

When my brother was stationed in Germany for the military, we spent an entire summer traveling and exploring Spain. The weather was terrible that year in central Europe, but in Spain it was perfect. We've been back a few times and have always enjoyed its distinct difference from central Europe. The northern coastal peninsula is not a high priority on the tourist radar screen and, hence, provides a less congested area for both you and your motorcycle.

This journey covers quite a bit more distance than the other trips in this book. The reason is that these separate legs blend well together and there is not a clean breaking point between the various daytrips. It starts and ends in

*If you llike shellfish, then you will definitely like the Atlantic coast of Spain. It's a never ending shell fest! Photo by Patsy Scott.*

*The towns of Northern Spain are loaded with arched bridges, meandering rivers, and stucco tiled structures. Photo courtesy of Tourist Office of Spain in New York.*

the charming coastal village of Santillana del Mar. Head east from here on the beautiful rugged coastline toward Bilbao and San Sebastián before cutting south into the heart of the wine-producing region of Logroño. The road then winds toward the Cantabrian Mountains and Spain's first national park, the Picos de Europa. Spin your wheels from here into Galicia, the home of *Gladiator's* Maximus, and then on to the spell binding old pilgrim city of Santiago de Compostela. End this journey how you began it by tackling the coastal road back to Santillana del Mar.

# Day 1 Santillana del Mar to Lekeitio

Located on the northern Atlantic coast, Santillana del Mar is the epitome of traditional Romanesque architecture and baroque mansions. Cobblestone lanes meander underneath wrought-iron balconies, red-tiled roofs, and stately palaces. Coats of arms are drawn on many façades identifying the homes of famous seafarers. Strolling through town pulls you back to a past that seems vibrant and real. Often missed by most tourists on their way to Bilbao or San Sebastián, this small community is not to be overlooked. There is a small campground just west of town called Camping Santillana, but I prefer staying in town at one of the local hostelries—a far better way to indulge in the local atmosphere. Spend some time here, find a good book, try a few restaurants, and unwind in a truly Spanish setting.

From Santillana head east on CA131 and A67 to Santander. Santander is quite a bit larger and livelier than Santillana and was once an exclusive summer tourist destination in the 19th century. The Gran Casino, sandy beaches, and elegant hotels are a bit pricey for my taste, so I usually drive through town, hook up with A8, then the N634 east, and jog north on CA148 to Santoña. If you are looking for a nice beach, there is one here called Berria. On a nice day, I guarantee you won't be disappointed with the views (both on and off the beach!)

*Santander was once a very popular seaside resort for Spanish Royalty. It still maintains a sense of elegance and charm. Photo courtesy of Tourist Office of Spain in New York.*

Head back on CA148 to N634 and mosey through the old coastal villages of Laredo, Castro-Urdiales and Getxo. This area was once a Roman stronghold and ruins from that era can still be seen in the vicinity. But if you

### Day 1 – Santillana del Mar to Lekeitio   243 km/152 miles

Head east on the coast road CA131 to the A67 and Santander.

Arrive Santander. Continue on A8 to N634 then connect with CA148 to Santoña. Head back to N634 and go to Laredo.

Arrive Laredo. Continue east on N634 through Castro-Urdiales to Bilbao.

Arrive Bilbao. Head to Getxo on the BI 634 then veer southeast on BI 2120 to Mungia, then northeast on BI 631 to Bermeo.

Arrive Bermeo. Follow BI 635 to Gernika-Lumo, then swing up to Gautegiz-Arteaga and follow the coast road to Lekeitio.

Arrive Lekeitio.

want to fast forward to the 20th century, then drive to Bilbao. This city is chuck full of modernistic architecture and art. There are various museums here, including the very famous Guggenheim. Filled with avant-garde art, this is a must-see for the art lover. To be quite honest, between the very sleek subway system, glass footbridges, and various museums, this very modern-looking city can easily enrapture you for a full day. So once again, your choice.

If you decide to move on, then stay on BI 634 to Getxo and at Plentzia veer southeast on BI 2120 to Mungia, then head northeast to Bermeo. Continue on the road BI 635 to Gernika-Lumo. Gernika-Lumo is best known for the aerial bombing attack in 1937. The Nazis in conjunction with the Nationalist troops of General Franco successfully launched a devastating attack on this small Basque town destroying about three quarters of the city. Its infamous notoriety was further reinforced when Pablo Picasso unveiled

*An older couple serenades me as I saunter through the old town square. Photo by Toby Ballentine.*

*The rough coastline of Cantabria reminds me of California's Highway 1. Photo courtesy of Tourist Office of Spain in New York.*

his painting, entitled *Guernica,* depicting this catastrophe at the 1937 World Fair. The painting is currently in Madrid and a tapestry of it is also hanging in the United Nations in New York.

After Gernika the road swings back up the coast to the small village of Elantxobe. The scenery here is splendid with the cliffs, ocean, and fishing fleet all combining to create a perfect setting. Eventually the road winds into Lekeitio. The town surrounds the mouth of a river with two sandy beaches nearby. Originally a fishing village, Lekeitio has grown into a fairly popular beach resort, but it still retains the flavor of a traditional Basque community. When you arrive, check out the tourist office for a place to stay or spend the night at the campground Endai, just outside of town.

# Day 2  Lekeitio to Laguardia

Today the ride will continue along the coast a bit farther, then veer south into the heart of Basque country and to the charming walled village of Laguardia. So begin, by pulling yourself away from Lekeitio and going east on BI 638 to Ondarroa. The road connects with N634 and continues along the coast through Zumaia, Getaria, and Zarautz. These small fishing villages are adorable and tempt you to stop and wander along their lantern-lit promenades and beaches. If you do feel like a morning hike, stop in Ondarroa and walk up to the church of Nuestra Señora de la Antigua. The views from the church are great. Hike back down, grab a cool drink, then continue on to Zumaia and Getaria. This is a very scenic run along the coast

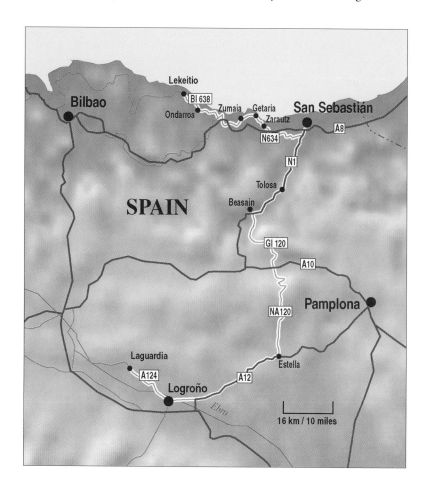

*Pristine, empty beaches dot the northern coast of Spain. Feel free to stop anytime.*
*Photo courtesy of Tourist Office of Spain in New York.*

and is known as the Cornisa Cantábrica in Spain. It has some of the most gorgeous coastal scenery you will see on this trip and reminds me of Highway 1 along the California coast.

The N634 connects with N1 near San Sebastián. San Sebastián is definitely worth seeing if you have the time. See Chapter 14 for more details. Just remember a visit to the city will add another day to your itinerary. The

### Day 2 – Lekeitio to Laguardia   235 km/147 miles

Follow the BI638 to Ondarroa. Eventually connect with N634 to Zumaia and Zarautz. At the N1 interchange go south to Tolosa.

Arrive Tolosa. Continue on N1. Near Beasain go south on GI120. Cross over the A10 and follow the NA120 to Estella. At Estella go west on A12 to Logroño.

Arrive Logroño. Take the A124 to Laguardia.

Arrive Laguardia.

N1 south to Tolosa is another real beauty. The sweeping turns and low lying foothills make both the scenery and the ride a delight. As you approach Beasain, go south on GI 120 (rather than the N1) and cut across the A10 all the way to Estella. You will love this ride. It's winding, but not overly so, and envelopes you in a rhythm together with the countryside. Great ride!

The city of Estella was once another way station for the influx of pilgrims heading toward Santiago de Compostela. As a result it grew into a monument filled 11th-century masterpiece. Although parking can be difficult (but not so bad on a motorcycle), the old quarter is home to palaces, churches, and a well-cared-for medieval town square. I would suggest parking your bike as close to town as possible, then walking around a bit. Maybe use this time to find a nice restaurant or grab some bread, cheese, and meat at a local grocer and sit around the square taking in the sights. There are also several attractions around Estella worth seeing, if you want to stay in town overnight. Visit the tourist office and they will be more than helpful in finding you a place to stay as well as showing you points of interest around the city.

*Riding horseback through Cantabria might take a bit longer to get to your destination . . . plus the cleanup is a mess. I think I'll stick with my motorcycle. Photo courtesy of Tourist Office of Spain in New York.*

*Paseo del Príncipe de Vergara, also known as El Espolón, stands in the center of the city of Logroño. Photo by Jynus.*

Personally, I prefer moving on to Logroño on A12 then heading northwest on A124 to Laguardia. The city of Logroño is rather large with a population of more than 100,000 right in the heart of the wine-growing area of Navarre. Surrounded by modern industry, the town at first appears distasteful, but at the center is a stereotypical old quarter with small squares, narrow lanes, and some really good restaurants. But if you don't have the time, move on to the real gem—Laguardia. With a population of only 1,500, this small village is one of the better preserved walled cities in Basque country. It features old mansions, narrow lanes that wander around hidden corners, and not a whole lot of traffic due to the many wine cellars located just a few meters below ground level. I would encourage you to stay in town if at all possible. Since it is rather small, calling in advance for a place to stay is recommended.

# Day 3  Laguardia to Potes

By European standards, we will cover a fair amount of mileage today. There aren't a whole lot of stops in between, so I would recommend getting up late (sleep in for a change) and then spend your afternoon and evening in Potes. This should give you enough time to explore the surrounding area a bit, too. From Laguardia take the A124 to Labastida, go south on N124, then catch the N232 west. The road cuts through the province of Cantabria in a fairly direct manner. Around Oña the blacktop starts to weave back and forth while driving through the towns of Valdenoceda and Soncillo. Just before Corconte turn left (west) on CA171 to Reinosa.

Reinosa lies in the lowlands just in front of the Cantabrian Mountains. There is a delightful market square surrounded by stone buildings in the center of town. You may want to drop by and make this your stopover for lunch. From Reinosa head west on CA183 then at Espinilla turn north on CA280 to Cabuérniga. The 280 is a sweet little ride that sweeps back and forth through green countryside. Turn left on CA182 and the road bends

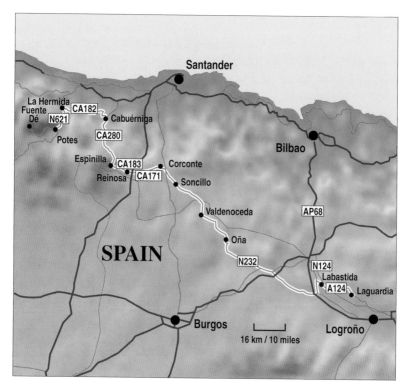

*The ride gets even better as you approach the Picos de Europa mountain range. Photo courtesy of Tourist Office of Spain in New York.*

even more quickly as you approach the mountains of Picos de Europa. At La Hermida go south on N621 to Potes.

### Day 3 – Laguardia to Potes   282 km/176 miles

From Laguardia follow the A124 toward Labastida. Turn left (south) to N124, then right (west) on N232. Follow N232 northwest to Corconte, then turn left (west) on CA171 to Reinosa.

Arrive Reinosa. Head northwest on CA183. At Espinilla go north on CA280 to Cabuérniga. At Cabuérniga take the CA182 to La Hermida, then go south on N621 to Potes

Arrive Potes.

Potes is surrounded by jagged mountains and is a typical Cantabrian village with stone houses, red-tiled roofs, and the obligatory medieval tower and town hall. The town now caters to tourists exploring the national park and makes a perfect layover for the night. Nearby are several points of interest worth a visit as well. The Monastery of Santo Toribio de Liébana, about two miles west of town, is known throughout the region for being the guardian of a piece of the True Cross brought back from Jerusalem. The other destination worth a visit is Fuente Dé at the end of the road heading west. Ultimately the road ends at the terminus for a cable car that climbs the mountain peak to the Aliva viewpoint. It's a great run on the bike getting to the terminus and the views from the cable car are breathtaking.

The Picos de Europa was the first national park in Spain and is noted for its deep gorges and canyons. Tourists from all over Europe come here to enjoy the hiking and beautiful natural setting. There is a nice campground

*Heading up to Fuente Dé you pass through the town of Espinama. Photo by JKD.*

*The Picos de Europa is like a miniature Switzerland, but far less visited and developed than its counterpart. Small century-old villages greet you without all the touristy fluff! Photo courtesy of Tourist Office of Spain in New York.*

about one km outside of Potes on the way to the Saint Toribio Monastery. It's called Camping La Viorna. The campsite is clean and well taken care off, and best of all, the views of the mountain peaks are just a tent flap away!

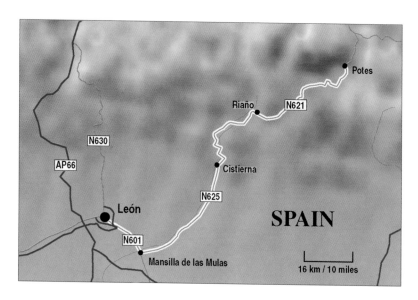

# Day 4  Potes to León

Today is a short trip, only about 96 miles. This will give you some time to sleep in or venture over to Picos de Europa for a morning hike. If you didn't make it to the cable car, you now have some extra time to catch up. I would highly recommend it. From Potes head south on N621 to Riaño and Cistierna. This road cuts through the Cantabrian Mountains and has some magnificent scenery. Just be sure to turn around every now and then to take a look at the peaks slowing sinking into the horizon (at least look in your rearview mirror). You need both perspectives to truly appreciate this run!

At Cistierna the road changes to N625. Follow it to Mansilla de las Mulas. Mansilla is a small walled village worth a brief stop, a little stretching, and some local hydration. Sit down and relax a bit around the main square and rejuvenate before heading on the N601 and N630 to León. León is another city that owes its growth and heritage to the pilgrims that flooded this area during the middle ages. Originally settled by the Romans to protect the nearby gold mines, the city is now a provincial capital and home to a magnificent cathedral and basilica. I would recommend staying in town. Find a nice restaurant for some dinner around the old quarter and enjoy the robust nightlife due to an abundance of college students.

*There is no escaping the dominant influence of the Catholic Church in Spain. Multitudes of small churches and large cathedrals cover the metropolitan areas and countryside. Photo by Toby Ballentine.*

## Day 4 – Potes to León   154 km/96 miles

From Potes follow N621 south to Riaño. Continue south, then at Cistierna the road changes to N625. Follow to Mansilla de las Mulas. Arrive Mansilla de las Mulas. Go north on N601 which joins N630 to León.

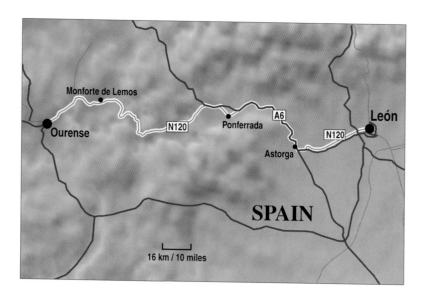

# Day 5 León to Ourense

For those of you who remember the movie *Gladiator*, today's run leaves León and eventually heads into the Galician region where the famed Maximus longs to return. The flashbacks are of him doing his trademark fingering of the soil from this locale (I know this is a useless piece of information, but interesting nonetheless). So, from León go west on N120 to Astorga. This is a relatively uneventful piece of asphalt, but the town of Astorga is worth a stop. Originally a Roman stronghold, it now houses a palace and a formidable cathedral. It is worth a stretch and a look-see before heading on.

From Astorga continue west on A6 to Ponferrada and the N120 again to Monforte de Lemos. The road starts to wind nicely from Astorga. The gentle sweeps continue from Ponferrada to Monforte. Both of these towns are old settlements and are just off the main road. The old town of Ponferrada is worth a peek and if you have the time, follow the signs to the town center and park in the underground garage just by the square. This quarter is closed to traffic making it very pedestrian friendly. There are numerous eateries. When leaving, please note that many streets are one way, making it a little hairy to get out of town.

As you approach Monforte de Lemos, the monastery rises on the hill ahead. If you are interested, the monastery and local Jesuit college are worth a gander. Otherwise, keep on truckin' to the rhythm of the sweeping curves

*Rough-hewn stone walls are a common sight in this part of Spain. Photo by Toby Ballentine.*

and continue on N120 to Ourense. Another town with a traditional old quarter, Ourense is not frequently visited by tourists. You get a good feel for a typical Galician town without the atmosphere being tainted by tourist buses. The beautiful Bishop's Palace is located in the old town near the Plaza Major and is now a museum. Old arched bridges and gothic cathedrals give this little city a pleasant demeanor and provide a nice introduction to Galicia.

### Day 5 – León to Ourense   270 km/169 miles

From León go west on N120 to Astorga.
Arrive Astorga. Continue on A6 to Ponferrada.
Arrive Ponferrada. Continue on A6 and N120 to Monforte de Lemos and Ourense.
Arrive Ourense.

# Day 6   Ourense to Santiago de Compostela

From Ourense take the A52 west, then jog north on the N541 to Pontevedra. The road sweeps nicely across the Galician countryside and the scenery becomes more verdant with each passing mile. Eventually the road leads into Pontevedra located right on the coast. This city also has a historic old quarter by the Plaza de España. Take a quick look if you like, then take PO308 even farther west to Sanxenxo and Portonovo. The road changes to PO318 and PO316 to O Grove. Turn around at O Grove then catch the PO550 north beside the Atlantic. The road hugs the coast and then swings up to Cambados. Sanxenxo and Portonovo are way too touristy for me, but O Grove is worth a stop if you like shellfish. Local bars specialize in treating tourists to fresh mussels, oysters, and scallops. Definitely drop by if you are a shellfish lover.

A bit farther north, the road runs through the town of Cambados. This is a more typical Galician town and not overly infected with tourists. It has a nice square, cathedral, and town hall (sounding familiar). From Cambados head north on PO548 to Padrón, arrival point of Apostle James and the site where he began his ministry on the Iberian Peninsula. The local cathedral has the supposed mooring stone for his boat on display.

From Padrón continue on the N550 to Santiago de Compostela. You now have arrived in the Spanish pilgrimage mecca for St. James the Apostle.

*The climax of the pilgrimage "Way of St. James" occurs when the pilgrim finally arrives at the cathedral in the city of Santiago de Compostela where St. James is supposedly buried. Photo courtesy of Tourist Office of Spain in New York.*

A huge cathedral has been built on the Plaza de España that is said to be the resting place of St. James. Apparently, the body of St. James was taken to Spain by two disciples after his death and then rediscovered in 813 AD. The rest is history and, soon thereafter, Santiago became a massive pilgrimage center during the middle ages. Today the old town is a World Heritage Site and is loaded with old monuments and relics from its religious and historic past. The old quarter is very pedestrian-friendly and a delight to spend an evening strolling around. So find a place to stay, then settle in a local cafe, and enjoy the sights, sounds, and people of this great city.

### Day 6 – Ourense to Santiago de Compostela   195 km/122 miles

From Ourense take the A52 west then connect north on N541 to Pontevedra.

Arrive Pontevedra. Take the PO308 then PO318 and PO316 west to O Grove. Turn around at O Grove then continue north on PO550 to Cambados.

Arrive Cambados. Take the PO548 to Padrón and connect with N550 to Santiago de Compostela.

Arrive Santiago de Compostela.

## Day 7 Santiago de Compostela to Betanzos

Although you could cut this trip by over a half by driving directly from Santiago to Betanzos, just remember—a motorcyclist tries to find the better road, not the shorter road. The better road on this trip takes you west and follows the coast in a sideways U-shaped route. Start by taking the AC543 to Noia, then go north on AC550 to Muros. At Corcubión, I would suggest a small detour to Fisterra. Noia and Muros are sleepy fishing villages on the coast with traditional old towns and waterfront colonnades. Cabo Fisterra or the "end of the world" is the most westerly part of Spain and was once considered the very edge of the known world. It is a beautiful scene with jagged rocks, foaming swells, and a traditional lighthouse. This entire run from Santiago to Fisterra is called the Rías Bajas and is an absolute delight to drive. It's far enough out of the way that the tourists are few and far between and the scenery is exceptional. The black top weaves beside jagged cliffs, verdant hills, and sandy beaches. No question about it, this is definitely the better road!

From Fisterra, take the AC552 to A Coruña and the AP9 to Betanzos. A Coruña is a large city next to a sizeable harbor. One interesting site is the Tower Hercules. This is the only working Roman lighthouse in the world and was originally built around 200 AD. The city itself has its fair share of old buildings, but otherwise is relatively modern. I would suggest just cruising on to Betanzos, find a place to stay, and spend the rest of the day here.

*The Way of St. James actually ends on the western coast of Spain in the small town of Fisterra. A symbolic bronze boot is dedicated to all the pilgrims who have completed this trek. Photos by Graham Stanley.*

Betanzos was originally one of the seven capitals of the Galician Kingdom and is now just a relic of its once glorious past. Stone walls, steep lanes, and of course, the requisite monastery and churches create the ideal environment in which to relax and unwind after a day of motorcycling.

### Day 7 – Santiago de Compostela to Betanzos  242 km/151 miles

From Santiago de Compostela take the AC 543 to Noia. From Noia go north on AC550 and follow the road to Muros. Weave around to Carnota and Corcubión.

Arrive Corcubión. Take the AC552 toward A Coruña then follow the AP9 to Betanzos

Arrive Betanzos.

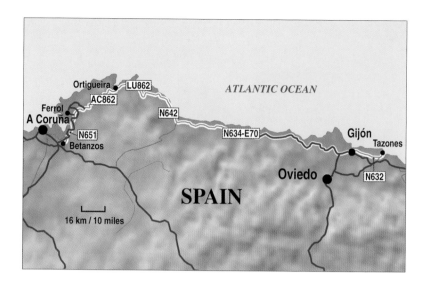

# Day 8  Betanzos to Tazones

I saved the longest run for today. It follows the coast and winds gently across rolling hills and coastal beaches. There are a few small villages along the way, but to be quite honest, none of particular note. You can spend most of your day on the blacktop enjoying the salty breeze and scraping your pegs. The

*Playa de las Catedrales, or Beach of the Cathedrals, on the northern shore of Galicia is one of the top beaches in Spain. Try to visit when the tide is out and the rock formations are spectacular. Photo courtesy of Tourist Office of Spain in New York.*

*The Costa Verde, or Green Coast, is just that—one of the most colorful I've ever seen. Photo courte*
*Tourist Office of Spain in New York.*

Costa Verde is fairly remote, but beautiful nonetheless. Eventually you will arrive in Gijón, a busy port city with all the expected artifacts, but by this time you're probably in the "cruising zone" and a little burned out on old squares, churches, and monasteries, so you may just want to head on to your final overnight stay in the small fishing village of Tazones.

This route starts by leaving Betanzos on N651 then AC862 north toward Ortigueira. Follow the LU862, N642, N634-E70 on the coast all the way to Gijón. Continue on N632, then follow the signs at the turnoff to Tazones.

## Day 8 – Betanzos to Tazones   336 km/210 miles

From Betanzos go north and connect with N651 and the AC862 toward Ortigueira. The road changes to LU862 along the coast then to N642. Continue east on N634-E70 to Gijón.

Arrive Gijón. Follow N632 east then take the small side road to Tazones. Arrive Tazones.

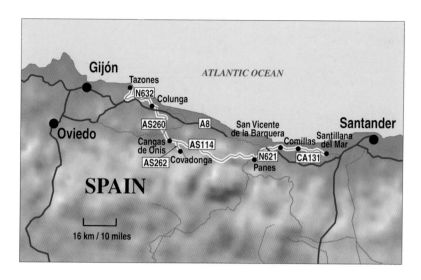

# Day 9  Tazones to Santillana del Mar

Today's trip cruises along the coast, cuts into the mountains by Picos de Europa, then heads back home to Santillana del Mar. From Tazones take the short road back to N632, then go east. Just after Colunga, turn south on AS260 to Cangas de Onís. This is a great little road and gets even better the closer you get to Covadonga. Cangas de Onís sits in a little valley by the rivers Sella and Güeña. There is a classic arched Roman bridge going over the gorge at the River Sella. Cangas de Onís was the original capital of Asturias and played an important role during the reconquest of Spain from the Moors.

Follow the AS114 east then take the AS262 south to Covadonga. This short jaunt takes you up a beautiful road to this historic mountain village. It was here that the Christians first withstood the Moors and the independent kingdom of Asturias was founded. From Covadonga head back to AS114 and go east to Panes, then north on N621 to San Vicente de la Barquera.

San Vicente de la Barquera is one of the most picturesque spots on the Cantrabrian coast. The bridges, castle, and church at Santa Maria are framed by colorful boats in the estuary and snowcapped mountains in the background. This is a great little town and one in which you could easily spend an entire afternoon. From here follow the coast road CA131 to Comillas and back to Santillana del Mar. It's been a long trip, but you have seen parts of Spain not frequented by the foreign tourist and eaten foods that will draw you back one day for more!

*The Picos de Europa mountain range creates a formidable backdrop to the small town of San Vicente de la Barquera on the Cantabrian coast. Photo courtesy of Tourist Office of Spain in New York.*

## Day 9 Tazones to Santillana del Mar   242 km/151 miles

From Tazones head back to N632, then go east. Connect with AS260 to Cangas de Onís.

Arrive Cangas de Onís. Go east on AS114, then south on AS262 to Covadonga.

Arrive Covadonga. From Covadonga go back on AS262, then head east on AS114 to Panes.

Arrive Panes. Head north on N621 to San Vicente de la Barquera.

Arrive San Vicente de la Barquera. Continue east on coast road CA131 to Santillana del Mar.

Arrive Santillana del Mar.

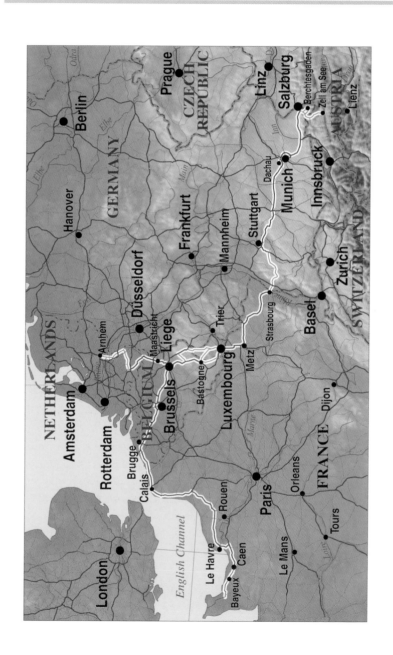

# The Band of Brothers Tour

**Distance:** *2467 km/1542 miles*
**Suggested Time Frame:** *10–14 days*
**Highlights:** *This trip focuses primarily on World War II sites and follows Easy Company of the 101st Airborne from the D-Day beaches all the way into Germany. Stops along the way include battles fought in Normandy (Brécourt Manor and Carentan), Holland (Nuenen), and the Battle of the Bulge in Bastogne, Belgium. The journey finishes up with some great rides through the Black Forest to Dachau, the infamous concentration camp, and then swings south into the Bavarian Alps. Visit Hitler's Eagles Nest and at the same time enjoy some of the best motorcycle rides in Europe. For you history buffs – this is a trip not to be missed.*

*Rows of crosses line the American Cemetery looking down on the D-Day beaches. Photo by John Ashley Hall.*

*This tank is located in the town square of Bastogne, Belgium. Photo by David Rogers.*

Just by way of introduction—I'm no Stephen Ambrose! I have read most of his books about WWII, but certainly do not claim to have his in-depth knowledge of the events and circumstances surrounding this hallowed group of men—the Band of Brothers. The book and miniseries are the re-source I've used to put together this tour. Most of the sites are well marked, while others may require asking the locals or inquiring at the Tourist Information for more detailed directions. This chapter will lead you to the major locales where Easy Company fought several of the battles during WWII. If you decide to take this trip, might I suggest you re-read the book, *Band of Brothers,* by Stephen Ambrose and also watch the 10-part miniseries. It will give you additional insight as this journey merely touches the surface. WWII was a major watershed event in our time, for that matter in all of history. You could literally spend months exploring the different historical sites and battlegrounds where thousands of veterans died to preserve our freedom. I still remember the first time driving my bike to the American Cemetery at Omaha Beach; upon seeing the thousands of crosses and stars my heart skipped a beat and I had to stop for a minute to catch my breath. My dad is a veteran of WWII and the overwhelming sanctity of the spot literally choked me up! As a nation and a people we just don't realize nor appreciate the sacrifices made on our behalf. May we never forget!

This chapter is broken into four separate sections as it follows the Band of Brothers. The first is "D-Day;" the second, "Operation Market Garden;" the third, "Battle of the Bulge;" and the fourth, "Across the Rhine into Germany." The journey will focus primarily on WWII sites, but I may throw in a small detour that's nearby and worth a visit. The sections will be linked, but, as mentioned earlier, based on your own research, there may be some personal diversions along the way. So get your highlighter out, pull out a map of Europe and let's follow the Band of Brothers as it parachutes into France and swings into Germany. This is a great trip—enjoy and good luck!

*A shower room, or* brausebad, *at Dachau where the Nazis gassed the Jews during World War II. Photo by John Ashley Hall.*

English Channel

D14 — Brécourt Manor — Pointe du Hoc — Omaha Beach — American Cemetery — Gold Beach — Juno Beach — Sword Beach — Le Havre — Honfleur — A29 — D913 — D514 — Arromanches — Carentan — Bayeux — N13 — Ouistreham — D513 — FRANCE — Pegasus Bridge — D37 — E46 — Caen

16 km / 10 miles

# D-DAY

For those of you who saw *Saving Private Ryan,* the D-Day beaches along the coast of France are a must-see stop. The allies, in the greatest amphibious assault in history, land on five beaches in Normandy beginning their push into occupied France and ultimately Germany. This area is chuck full of historical sites including the American Cemetery, pillboxes, memorials, Point-du-huc, Pegasus Bridge, Ste. Marie Église, and Arromanches, and are discussed in more detail in Chapter 1. For purposes of this trip, start in the small city of Bayeux just inland from the beaches. It's a great base from which to explore the surrounding WWII sites—plus there are some great restaurants here too.

For the Band of Brothers history buffs, there are two spots of particular note around Bayeux that should be visited. First is the rural town of Carentan, which was the original objective for the 101st Airborne and Easy Company. Due to the scattered landings of the airborne, various other engagements occurred while they were trying to regroup, but Carentan was still a primary objective. The town's capture is studied in military war colleges as the Battle of Bloody Gulch and several computer games, such as *Call of Duty* feature this particular battle. Carentan is about 27 miles from Bayeux. Head west on N13, then continue on N2013 to the town. There are various plaques honoring the 101st and the American GIs who came and liberated this city. In the miniseries, Carentan is the town where Lieutenant Winters, the acting commander of Easy Company, stands in the middle of the road leading into town, yelling at his troops to move out and

*This photo was taken by a friend while on a tour with Edward "Babe" Heffron and William "Wild Bill" Guarnere from the Band of Brothers. Guarnere lost his leg during the Battle of the Bulge. Photo by David Rogers.*

### Day 1 – Bayeux to Carentan and Brécourt Manor then back to Bayeux   102 km/64 miles

Head west on N13 then connect with N2103 to Carentan (south of N13).

Arrive Carentan. From here take the D913 north then turn left on D14 then left again to Brécourt Manor.

Arrive Brécourt Manor. Head back to Bayeux on the D913 and N13.

Arrive Bayeux.

*These pillboxes along the Normandy coast were used by the Germans to try to repulse the Allied landing force on D-Day. Photo by John Ashley Hall.*

eliminate the machine gun nest. He stands alone as bullets ricochet all around him and the troops just stare at him. Eventually, they join up, take out the machine gunner and help capture the town—quite an inspiring part of the film.

The other noteworthy engagement is at Brécourt Manor. In order to get here, take the D913 from Carentan north, and then turn left on D14 and left again on a small road to the manor. It's still occupied by the original family from the war. You can look at the hedgerow and field where the four German 105 mm howitzers were located. The guns were taken out by Easy Company under the leadership of Lieutenant Winters. Please note that the manor is only open to private tours, but a roadside visit is still worth the trip. The attack on Brécourt Manor is also in the miniseries and recounted in Ambrose's book. Both make great resource material before visiting the site.

As mentioned in my earlier chapter on D-Day, there is much to visit in this area. One of the best WWII museums I've been to is located in Caen and I would highly recommend a visit before continuing on to the next leg of this trip—Operation Market Garden.

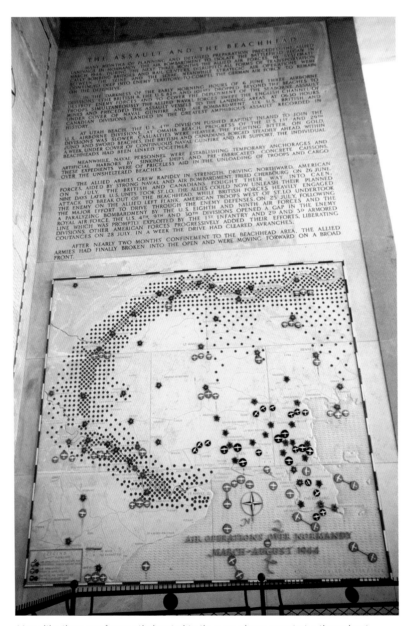

*Maps like these are frequently located in the several war cemeteries throughout Europe detailing specific battle strategies for that area. This one is showing the D-Day beach assault. Photo by David Rogers.*

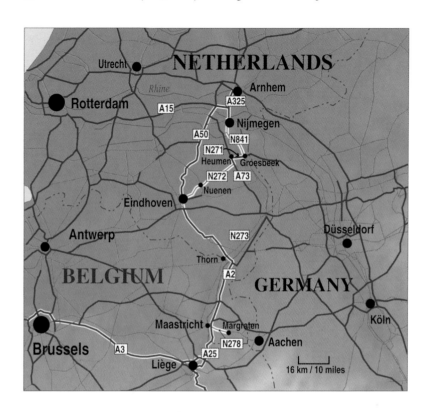

# Operation Market Garden

General "Ike" Eisenhower was without a doubt one of the greatest military leaders in recent history. Not only did he have a war to fight, but he had allies to appease. One of his most difficult responsibilities was keeping all the political and military leaders from the various allied nations headed in the right direction and not fighting amongst themselves. To Ike's credit, he not only showed his military prowess but also developed diplomatic skills that eventually lead him to the presidency of the United States. During WWII, Ike's perennial nemesis was Field Marshall Bernard Montgomery from Great Britain. They were continuously at odds due to Montgomery's fame from the Battle of El Alamein and his resultant untamed ego. In spite of these differences, General Eisenhower did acquiesce to Montgomery on a very daring plan to end the war early via Operation Market Garden.

Operation Market Garden was composed of two parts—Market: the airborne assault and Garden: the ground force attack. The largest airborne assault in history would land at various locations throughout the Netherlands in order to secure several bridges across the Maas and Rhine rivers. As those bridges were secured, the ground forces would advance, eventually to the city of Arnhem, cross the Rhine, outflank the Germans, and hopefully bring a quick end to the war. It was a daring and innovative plan, but due to poor planning, delays, and a disregard of intelligence information, the

## Day 2 – Bayeux to Brugge   480 km/300 miles

Leave Bayeux on the N13 which turns into the E46 direction Caen.
Arrive Caen. Continue on E46 toward Calais. Stay on the toll road all the way to Calais. Road changes numbers from D46 to A13 to A29 to A28 to A16 and then E40 in Belgium.
Take the N397 to Brugge (follow signage).
Arrive Brugge.

## Day 3 – Enjoy Brugge – Relax!

## Day 4 – Brugge to Maargarten   205 km/128 miles

Head back to E40 via N397 then continue east toward Gent and Brussels. The road changes to A10.
Arrive Brussels. Continue on A3 toward Liège.
Arrive Liège. Go north on A25 to Maastricht. The road changes to A2 in Holland.
Arrive Maastricht. Take the N278 east to Maargarten.
Arrive Maargarten.

## Day 5 – Maargarten to Arnhem   194 km/121 miles

From Maargarten go back to Maastricht on N278. Catch the A2 north to Eindhoven.
Arrive Eindhoven. Go east on Eisenhowerlaan and the A270 to Nuenen.
Arrive Nuenen. From here take the N272 northeast then catch the A73 toward Nijmegen. At Heumen take the N271 east to Groesbeek.
Arrive Groesbeek. Take the N841 north to N325. Follow to Nijmegen. At Nijmegen the road changes to A325. Follow to Arnhem.
Arrive Arnhem. Follow signs to Airborneplein.

## Day 6 – Stay in Arnhem and drive the Liberation Route

Get map at the Tourist Information.

## Day 7 – Arnhem to Bastogne   294 km/184 miles

From Arnhem go south on A325, then take the A15 toward Venlo. Catch the A50 to Eindhoven.
Arrive Eindhoven and connect back on the A2 south to Maastricht.
Arrive Maastricht. Continue south into Belgium on A25 (also E25) to the turnoff for Bastogne.
Arrive Bastogne.

operation ultimately failed. The battle has been memorialized in a couple of movies—in particular the classic with Robert Redford, *A Bridge Too Far*, and more recently in the *Band of Brothers* miniseries. Many lives were lost during this epic encounter and as a result there are various battle monuments in Holland dedicated to the sacrifices made by our veterans. This section will only highlight a few of the locations. Quite honestly, weeks could be spent visiting all the battle sites along the Market Garden corridor from southern Holland to Arnhem. One of the best resources available in exploring this region, if you are interested, is a book published by Major and Mrs. Holts Battlefield Series entitled *Operation Market Garden*. It includes a map detailing the entire operation. For purposes of this section, I will be taking you to the only American cemetery in the Netherlands at Maargraten, into Eindhoven and Nuenen where E-Company saw action, Groesbeek where the 82nd Airborne landed, and then Arnhem where the infamous "bridge too far" is located. I also include a brief stopover at Brugge in Belgium along the way (don't miss this town!).

All right, let's begin by leaving Bayeux via the N13 and E46 direction Caen. At Caen continue on E46 toward Calais. The freeway changes numbers several times but if you stay on course to Calais you'll be fine. This, by the way, is a great ride for a highway. The road does some long and lengthy S-curves through some beautiful, green countryside—definitely a good run on a bike. I'm trying to get you to Brugge, Belgium, tonight—it's about 300 miles—very doable if you get off to an early start and use the toll roads. If you're feeling tired, either Calais or Dunkerque make a good layover. From Calais stay on the toll road direction Dunkerque and Gent. Eventually you will see a turnoff on N397 to Brugge.

Although not a battlefield site during WWII (thank goodness), Brugge is one of the best-preserved medieval cities in all of Europe. Definitely worth the detour, it makes a great midway stop on the way to Holland before exploring the Market Garden Operation. During the 12th to 15th centuries, Brugge was a huge trade center and had one of the largest ports in the world. Those glory days are reflected in the historic and richly decorated downtown. Most of the buildings are still intact. With its own canal system, Brugge is considered by many to be the "Venice of the North." Spend an evening here and enjoy the charm and ambiance of this delightful town.

From Brugge, go back to the toll road E40 and head toward Gent and Brussels. Once again the road changes numbers, but just follow the signs to Liège and then go north to Maastricht. At Maastricht head east on N278 to Margraten. This small town is home to one of the most serene and beautiful (and rarely visited) American cemeteries in Europe. Often when I visit, my

*The Grand Place in Brussels, Belgium is loaded with guildhalls and medieval buildings (and tourists!). Photo by Mark Allred.*

bike is the only motorized vehicle in the lot. The cemetery evokes a reverent and calming peace as you walk beside the long rectangular pond that honors the names listed on the perimeter walls. There is also an indoor mosaic of the major Allied and Nazi offenses, deployments, and battles during the war. Spend some time here and, in particular, note and study the history behind Operation Market Garden. This is a good introduction to your trip up the corridor to Eindhoven, Nuenen, Groesbeek, and Arnhem. I would suggest spending the day in this area. There is a small town nearby called Valkenburg that has its own castle and narrow cobbled lanes. Or head back to Maastricht, it's a larger city but the downtown area is well preserved and a great place to wander. Try some the of the French onion soup—it's a delicacy here and is the best I've ever had.

The next stop is Eindhoven and the small town of Nuenen. On September 17, 1944, Easy Company parachuted into Son, a small town just north of Eindhoven. As seen in the miniseries, E-Company participated in the euphoric liberation of the city and were welcomed with open arms by the residents. The euphoria soon dissipated as reality struck in Easy's failed attempt to take the small village of Nuenen. Nuenen is actually the hometown of Van Gogh, the famous impressionistic artist, but became even better known when Easy Company was repulsed by the Nazis as shown in the miniseries. To get here, take the A2 north from Maastricht direction Eindhoven. Eindhoven was bombed during WWII and has since been rebuilt. There is a liberation monument with an eternal flame commemorating the 101st Airborne and British 30th Corps in the downtown area. It's interesting to note that Eindhoven was bombed by the Nazis in retribution a day after it was liberated.

After a quick look at the memorial, take Eisenhowerlaan and A270 east of town to Nuenen. Only six miles outside of Eindhoven, Nuenen was the site of a combined attack by E-Company and a British Tank Division. In the miniseries, this is the town where the British tank commander disregarded the sergeant's advice and proceeded into town without knocking out the German tanks. The tank group and E-Company were ultimately repulsed. This is also where Sergeant "Bull" is MIA, hides in the barn, and then later rejoins the company. The town is small but insightful. Be sure to visit the small memorial plaque from Easy Company dedicated to those killed in action.

The next leg of this trip heads to Groesbeek about 37 miles north of Nuenen toward Nijmegen. The 82nd Airborne landed near Groesbeek and

*The American Cemetery located in Maargarten, Holland, is dedicated to the soldiers who lost their lives in this area and participated in Operation Market Garden. It is off the beaten path and one of the most serene in Europe. Photo by Toby Ballentine.*

*The Hamm Cemetery is located just outside of Luxembourg City and is where General Patton is buried. His burial site is marked by a simple stone cross, identical to his fallen comrades. Photo by David Rogers.*

initially took the heights surrounding the area. This delayed the taking of the bridge by about 36 hours. The British further delayed the advance by not crossing the bridge for another 18 hours. In the movie *A Bridge Too Far*, the exasperated Americans can't believe their ears when the Brits refuse to cross the bridge, claiming they need to regroup before advancing any farther. The delays at this bridge have often been debated as to whether or not the men at Arnhem could have been saved if the mission had proceeded full speed ahead. Be sure to visit the National Liberation Museum in Groesbeek. It's located right on the original American drop zone area.

To get to Groesbeek from Nuenen take the N272 northeast then connect with A73 north direction Nijmegen. At Heumer go east on N271 through Molenhoek to Groesbeek. It's about 40 miles.

The last part of Operation Market Garden takes you to the city of Arnhem and "A Bridge Too Far." The actual bridge was destroyed by the Germans in October, 1944, but was replaced with a similar structure in 1948. In 1978 it was renamed the John Frost Bridge. John Frost was the British commander in charge of taking the bridge intact. In the ensuing battle only a small contingent was able to take control of part of the bridge.

They fought gallantly for four days waiting for reinforcements. Due to delays and miscommunication, the reinforcements never arrived and the bridge ultimately fell back into German hands. Lieutenant Colonel Frost and his men put up a valiant fight that was memorialized in Cornelius Ryan's book, *A Bridge Too Far,* and the subsequent movie. These heroic men almost pulled off the impossible and are true heroes of WWII. Arnhem is about 18 miles north of Groesbeek. Take the N841 north to N325. Follow the N325 to Nijmegen then continue to Arnhem. The road changes to A325. Follow the signs to Airborneplein (Airborne Square). This will ultimately end up next to Frost Bridge. Right by the bridge is a square dedicated to the men who fought here. There is a pillar and monument commemorating the battle. The last time I was at Arnhem, a veteran from the British forces was there—all decked out in his uniform—and I had a great talk with him.

One suggestion before continuing south to the Battle of the Bulge—spend a day or two in Arnhem. This was the focal point for Operation Market Garden and as a result several noteworthy historical sites are located nearby, i.e., drop zones, memorials, monuments, and the Arnhem Oosterbeek War Cemetery. If you decide to stay, go to the local tourist information (VVV) near the train station and ask about the Liberation Route. There are 23 marked spots of historical note in the surrounding area, which can make for a wonderful bike ride, especially if the weather cooperates.

After enjoying your own self-guided Liberation Route, head south from Arnhem to Bastogne where the 101st Airborne and E-Company fought valiantly against the Nazis in the Battle of the Bulge. Start by heading south from Arnhem on A325 for about five miles, then take A15 west toward Venlo. After about another five miles, go south on A50 back to Eindhoven. At Eindhoven follow the signs to Maastricht. The freeway will change numbers a few more times—just remember to head towards Maastricht and you'll be fine. If you're interested in a small diversion to a lovely white-washed Dutch village, then take the exit N273/N78 at Heel to Thorn. Don't go to Heel, but head the other way (stay west of the freeway) and follow the signs to Thorn. This is a darling little town and is often called the "white village" of Holland. The town has religious origins and the cathedral was used as an abbey for female Benedictines. The village itself is a delight to wander around with its cobbled lanes, town square, and cafes. It's off the beaten path a bit and, therefore, not so overrun with tourists—a perfect place to grab a cup of hot chocolate and *pannoek*e (Dutch crepe)!

After a short break in Thorn, hop back on A2 (E25) and follow the road south direction Maastricht, Liège, and Luxembourg all the way to

*Memorial to the U.S. troops who fought in Foy, Belgium, during the Battle of the Bulge. Photo by Toby Ballentine.*

Bastogne. When you arrive in Bastogne, go directly to the town square. There are several quaint hotels here and I would recommend staying the night as there is quite a lot to see. You can easily spend a day doing what I call the Foy, Malmedy, and Hamm loop. So find yourself a room, settle in, and enjoy dinner at a cute cafe in Bastogne before heading off for more of the Band of Brothers Tour tomorrow.

# The Battle of the Bulge

"NUTS" was one of the most famous lines ever uttered by an American General during the course of WWII. So said General McAuliffe to the German High Command during the Battle of the Bulge in Bastogne, Belgium. The Battle of the Bulge was a counteroffensive launched by the Nazi's during the winter of 1944, which turned into the bloodiest engagement fought by American troops at the time. About 19,000 troops were killed in action and about 50,000 were wounded. Adolf Hitler, trying to stem the flow of the Allied offensive into Germany, decided to attempt a surprise attack through the Ardennes Forest in Belgium to cut the Allies in half by driving a wedge to Antwerp, thus forcing General Ike to opt for a more manageable peace to end the war. General Eisenhower was indeed surprised, but thanks to the dogged determination of the troops around Bastogne (such as the 101st and E-company), and the quick response of General Patton, the German offensive was stopped in its tracks. Although Bastogne was liberated on December 26, 1944, this did not mark the end of the Battle of the Bulge. In the miniseries *Band of Brothers,* Episodes 6 and 7 dramatize the horrific battle and the agony of not only fighting the Nazis, but surviving freezing cold weather and rising above the mental and emotional duress caused by the daily stress of combat readiness. Serious engagements and skirmishes continued throughout the month of January and the battle did not officially end until January 25, 1945.

First thing in the morning, get up and take a walk around the small town square. In late 1944, the Germans attacked Bastogne and this is where General McAuliffe of the 101st Airborne held fast even after the Germans surrounded the town and demanded his surrender. There is a tank and a small memorial honoring his classic response at the edge of the square. There are also several museums in town, but I would recommend hopping on your bike and heading out to the Mardasson Memorial. It's just a few miles outside of town (follow the signs). The memorial is a star-shaped structure honoring the 76,000 American casualties during the battle. Be sure to climb to the top of the memorial for some great views of the surrounding area. There is also a very nice museum just next to the memorial and well worth your time. Many artifacts are on display as well as actual movie clips providing great background on the battle.

From the memorial, swing back to town, then take the N30 to Foy, direction Houffalize. Foy lies north of Bastogne and is overlooked by the Bois Jacques (Jacques Woods). The forest is up a slight rise toward Bastogne and is where E-Company spearheaded the attack to capture Foy. If you drive to the forest, you will still find remnant foxholes dug by the troops. There is also a small memorial in town commemorating the attack and subsequent liberation of Foy. The peaceful setting today lies in stark contrast to what

## Day 8 – Bastonge/Foy/Malmedy/Hamm/Bastogne Loop
### 270 km/169 miles

From Bastogne follow signs to Battle of Bulge Mardasson Memorial.
Arrive Mardasson Memorial. Head back to Bastogne and take the N30 to Foy.
Arrive Foy. Continue on N30 to Houffalize.
Arrive Houffalize. Connect with the E25 north then take the exit on N651 to Malmedy. Follow N651, N66 and N68 to Malmedy.
Arrive Malmedy. From here take the N62 south toward St. Vith. Continue on E421 to Luxembourg and Hamm.
Arrive Hamm. From Hamm head back north on E421. At Ettelbrück go west on N15 back to Bastogne.
Arrive Bastogne.

*This is the building occupied by General McAuliffe during the Battle of the Bulge. His famous response of "Nuts!" to the German High Command was supposedly said here. Photo by David Rogers.*

the Band of Brothers must have experienced more than 65 years ago.

Continue north to Houffalize. This is where General Patton and Montgomery met in their fight against the Nazis. Last time I was there, an abandoned German Panzer tank was on display. At Houffalize connect with E25 toward Liège then take the exit to Malmedy on N651. Follow the N651, N66 and N68. This is a beautiful run. The rolling hills of the Ardennes forest combined with some smooth rubberized blacktop create an unforgettable ride. You can barely feel the road while you swing back and forth through this beautiful region of Belgium. Eventually you will arrive in Malmedy, site of the notorious massacre of American soldiers by SS troops. On December 17, 1944 ninety unarmed POWs were executed just outside of town. At the crossroads you will see a sign directing you to a memorial site. There is a plaque and memorial dedicated to the soldiers who died here. At the Nuremberg trials after the war, the perpetrators were tried and convicted of this crime. Although sentenced to death in 1947, none were executed and eventually all were released by the mid-1950s.

From Malmedy take the N62 south to St. Vith, and then continue on to Luxembourg on E421. Just east of Luxembourg City is the small hamlet of

Hamm and another American Cemetery worth a visit. This is where General George Patton is buried. It's ironic that after surviving the combat zones of WWII, Patton died in an automobile accident in December 1945. His tomb is marked like all the others, no grandiose mausoleum, just a simple soldier's cross. Once again the reverence of this place can overwhelm you; what a debt of gratitude we owe these men.

From Hamm head back the same way (north to St. Vith), but this time at Ettelbrück turn left (west) on N15 toward Bastogne. There is a George Patton museum in Ettelbrück if you have time to visit, otherwise continue west on N15 back to your hotel. This entire loop is about 160 miles and not only does it visit some important WWII sites, but it is a great ride through some of the nicest countryside in the Ardennes Mountains. When the weather is right, this loop is one of my favorites in the Benelux Countries. Last time I went, the roads had recently been recapped with a smooth rubberized concrete. I felt like I was floating on asphalt! Hope you are as lucky as I was!

*This memorial to the Battle of the Bulge stands outside the museum in Bastogne, Belgium. Photo by Toby Ballentine.*

# Across the Rhine into Germany

The next part of this journey takes you to the borders of France and Germany to Haguenau and Strasbourg, then crosses the Black Forest (Schwarzwald) over to Dachau, one of the infamous Jewish concentration camps, before heading south to the Alps at Berchtesgaden and Zell am See. Although not exactly identical, this trip basically follows the same roadmap as the Band of Brothers. Some of these locations are discussed in previous chapters and, therefore, I may summarize a bit more briefly here. Regardless, this last leg of the Band of Brothers Tour is one heck of a motorcycle ride and not to be missed.

To start, leave Bastogne and head toward Luxembourg on the N4 toward Arlon. The N4 is a great road to start your morning and cuts through some nice scenery. Green, green, green! Just west of Luxembourg catch the A6, then the A31 south toward Thionville and Metz. Just north of Metz, loop east to the A4 direction Haguenau and Strasbourg. Stay on the A4 then take D1340 to Haguenau. This city is the place where the eighth episode, "The Last Patrol," takes place. The 101st Airborne remained here during the month of February, 1945. Most of the city was destroyed during the war, but the original gate is still standing and there is a historic museum downtown worth visiting if you are interested. Personally, after a brief visit, I would head south about 20 miles on the A4 to Strasbourg and spend the evening there. Strasbourg has one of the best city centers in all of Europe. Declared a UNESCO World Heritage Site, it is full of old timbered buildings, arched bridges, cobbled lanes, and a majestic cathedral making this town one of my favorites. Find yourself a quaint pension in old town Strasbourg and enjoy an evening getting lost in the heart of medieval Europe. Don't miss it!

After recharging in Strasbourg, get up and warm up that bike for another great run! Today you'll be taking a beautiful ride through the Black Forest before connecting up with the Autobahn to Dachau, a former Nazi concentration camp. When Easy Company entered Germany, they had the unfortunate experience of finding and liberating a slave labor camp near Landsberg. This event is dramatized in Episode 9 of the miniseries and leaves the men of E-Company thoroughly disgusted with the German war machine. The camp they liberated, Kaufering IV, was part of a network of slave labor camps affiliated with Dachau. These camps had huge underground installations used to manufacture fighter aircraft. The barracks were buried in the ground and covered with dirt so as to be camouflaged from Allied bombers. The mother camp, Dachau, is still in existence and open to

### Day 9 – Bastogne to Strasbourg   323 km/202 miles

From Bastogne go south on N4 to Arlon. Catch the A6 toward Luxembourg and the A31 south to Thionville and Metz. North of Metz take the A4 direction Strasbourg. Connect with the D1340 to Haguenau.
Arrive Haguenau. From here head back on D1340 to the A4 and Strasbourg.
Arrive Strasbourg.

### Day 10 – Strasbourg to Dachau   341 km/213 miles

From Strasbourg take the E52 then the B28 east to Freudenstadt.
Arrive Freudenstadt. Continue on B28 then connect with A81 north then the A8 east toward Munich. Before Munich take the B471 to Dachau.
Arrive Dachau.

### Day 11 – Dachau to Zell am See   258 km/161 miles

From Dachau go south on B304 to the A99 going east around Munich. Connect with A8 south to Berchtesgaden and Salzburg. Take the B20 exit off A8 to Berchtesgaden.
Arrive Berchtesgaden. Take the 305 west then B178 and B311 south into Austria and Zell am See.

the public as a memorial to the countless lives lost during this horrendous genocide of the Jews by the Nazis. It is definitely worth a visit and I would highly recommend making a trip to see it even though it is not the exact one discovered by the Band of Brothers.

The next and concluding leg of this trip, takes you south around Munich down to the Bavarian Alps and Berchtesgaden, and then ends in the small Tyrolean town of Zell am See. Berchtesgaden is where the Kehlsteinhaus, or Eagles Nest, is located. Built in 1938, it was given as a present to Adolf Hitler for his 50th birthday in 1939. Located on the ridge of the Kehlstein Mountain overlooking the Alps, it is only accessible via a spectacular 6.5-mile road and 400-foot elevator. Various Allied military regiments claim the bragging rights of first arriving at Kehlsteinhaus, but for purposes of this chapter we'll say it was the 101st Airborne and E-Company. The museum next to the Eagle's Nest restaurant does actually show a soldier with an airborne insignia on his sleeve—so let's leave it at that! When visiting be sure to take a peek in the fireplace where you will see a date engraved on the marble. It's hard to believe that Hitler was in this very room 65-plus years ago.

To get here take the B304 south from Dachau to the A99. The A99 loops around Munich and will connect with the A8 south to Salzburg. Just outside of Salzburg take the B20 south to Berchtesgaden. As you approach the Alps, the scenery transforms itself into majestic mountains cloaked with thick forests and running streams. The air is fresh and scented with pine and apple tart. This is without a doubt one of the most beautiful areas in all of Europe! I would recommend continuing on to Austria via the B305 from Berchtesgaden, then take the B178 and B305 south to Zell am See. Set up camp here at the very nice local campground or find a *zimmer frei* and spend a few days (or weeks) exploring the area. Between the Eagle's Nest in Berchtesgaden, the local museum by the Obersalzberg (you can actually visit the pillboxes and barracks drilled into the side of the mountain), the Dürrnberg Salt Mines in Hallein, and Salzburg, you could easily spend a week here. It's hard to imagine that this was the summer retreat for many of the world's most vicious war criminals. The Band of Brothers must have thought they had died and gone to heaven after experiencing the Battle of the Bulge and then arriving here. Likewise, when you arrive be prepared to leave your worldly belongings behind and settle in to this heavenly little piece of mother earth. And to add icing to the cake—there are so many great rides here you'll find it hard to get any sleep! All you have to do is point your bike in just about any direction and let the road lead you through some of the most remarkable Alpine scenery in the world. Quite honestly, last time I was here, two weeks was not enough!

*The Kehlsteinhaus or Eagle's Nest in Berchtesgaden, Germany, is the former summer retreat for Adolf Hitler. Photo by Laurie Taylor.*

So now you've done it. You have driven in the very path of E-Company all the way from the beaches of Normandy to Operation Market Garden in Holland and from the Battle of the Bulge in Belgium across the Rhine to the Alps of Germany. I hope you have not only enjoyed the motorcycle ride, but also gained a better appreciation for all the men and women who have served valiantly and sacrificed so much for our great country. I guarantee that this journey will not only open your eyes to the wonders of Europe, but touch your mind and heart in ways you won't soon forget. Remember, traveling isn't just about the destination, but getting there and learning along the way. My thanks go to E-Company and all the brave men and women who served during WWII. And, dad, a special thanks to you for your example and service during that time. May we not forget!

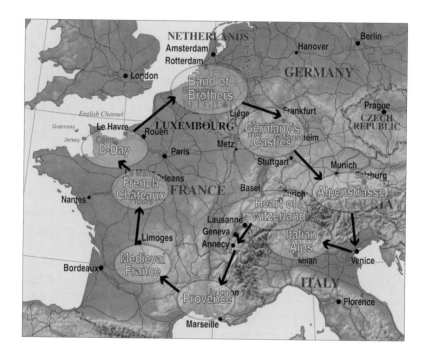

# The Grand Tour

So . . . how much time do you have? A week, two weeks, three weeks—or more? This last chapter intertwines several of the journeys discussed in my book into one Grand Tour. The trip covers several countries and about 4,000 miles. So pack light, don't forget the small tent, a map, and most important, a copy of this book! This particular chapter will outline the general direction you should go, suggest what journeys from this book to interlink, and make a few modifications along the way. Half the fun of traveling is exploring the unknown—an itinerary to me is merely an outline. As you read this chapter, open up your Michelin maps of each country I discuss, and then find a road that looks scenic and twisty that gets you there. Be daring. This is how I discovered Europe—by just having a general idea of a region or town, then getting on my bike and following the twistiest road possible to get there! You'll need at least one month to complete this Grand Loop of Europe but it will be a trip you will never forget. Oh, and I guarantee complications will arise, but that's the other half of the fun—just keep smiling and remember tomorrow is another day!

All right, here we go. I would recommend you start in Frankfurt. It's a major airline hub and you can usually get competitively priced tickets here from most major cities in the United States. You should have already arranged a rental outfit to have a bike ready and waiting (see the Introduction on bike rentals in Europe). Often the rental company will meet you at the airport, otherwise, catch the subway or tram to town, spend the night, then pick up the bike the next day. A bit of a hassle, but sometimes it's best to get a good nights rest before heading out on your trip. The reason I like Frankfurt is because the city is close to the Rhine and Mosel River Valleys. This area is absolutely gorgeous and a good introduction to riding in Europe.

From Frankfurt, head west through Wiesbaden and at Rüdesheim go north up the Rhine River. Then cut farther west over to the Mosel River and Cochem. Follow the Mosel River to Bernkastel and Trier, then swing south and east over to Heidelberg and Rothenburg. For some suggested routes and details see Chapter 6 "Germany's River Valleys and Castles Galore." You can easily spend three days exploring this area and may even want to spend an extra night in Rothenburg.

The next leg of this trip takes you south to Dachau, the Jewish concentration camp just north of Munich. It then continues south deep into the Bavarian Alps. I usually go straight to Füssen from Dachau and spend a night or two exploring King Ludwig's castles, then connect with the Alpenstrasse heading east to more fantastic scenery. Drop by the Linderhof, Oberammergau, and the Eagle's Nest while continuing on to Salzburg. This part of the trip is covered in Chapter 7 "The Famous Alpine Road and the Sound of Music Tour."

Follow the Alpine Road to Salzburg, spend some time here doing a little Sound of Music tour, then continue east to the Salzkammergut. This is the beautiful lake district of Austria. From here go south to Hallstatt, then west to Zell am See, a cute town nestled in the Tylorean Alps. End this leg of the trip by heading south to the Dolomites and Venice. See John Hermann's book, *Motorcycle Journeys through the Alps and Beyond* for sample routes through the Dolomites. Eventually, you should end up in Venice. Spend a couple of nights here to recharge and enjoy the food and ambiance as you tour the city from the seat of a gondola.

From Venice head west to the Lake District of Italy starting with Lake Garda then continue on to Como and Maggiore. At Lake Maggiore go north into Switzerland and St. Moritz. Chapter 11 "Lake Country and the Italian Alps" will help with routes and places to visit. Once in Switzerland you're in motorcycle heaven. Hopefully, the weather cooperates as you cruise to Interlaken and Lauterbrunnen. As mentioned in Chapter 8 "Heaven on Earth: Into the Heart of Switzerland," no matter which direction you head, the roads truly rock! Spend a few days in the Swiss Alps, driving, hiking, and exploring as you wind your way to Aigle in the southwest corner of Switzerland by Lake Geneva. From here you are a stone's throw from France and the charming town of Annecy. Though not mentioned in my other journeys, Annecy is one of the most delightful towns in all of France. It makes a great layover before continuing west into southern France.

You could easily spend an entire month in France. But for purposes of this Grand Tour, I would head west to Provence and Avignon (see Chapter 3 "A Week on Provence: Roman Ruins and Natural Wonders") and cruise around this area a bit before heading north to the Dordogne River Valley and the medieval towns of Sarlat and Beynac (see Chapter 2 "The Medieval Walled Villages of Central France.") From here cruise up to the chateaux of the Loire Valley (Chapter 4 "Chateaux Country along the Loire River"). If you have time to see just one Chateau, make it the Chenoceau with its majestic arches extending over the river. It's right next to the lovely town of

*The town of Annecy in southern France lights up like a jewel at night and is a gem not to be missed. Photo by Mark Allred.*

Amboise (great campground here).

From Amboise continue west to Saumur then over to Le Mont-St.-Michel and up to Bayeux and the D-Day beaches of Normandy. Spend a few nights here and if you are a history or WWII buff crack open Chapter 1 "World War II D-Day and Batleground Tour" and Chapter 16 "The Band of Brothers Tour" as you explore this area. Follow the "Band of Brothers Tour" up the coast of France over to Brugge, Belgium, then take a swing into Holland for "Operation Market Garden" if you have time. If you are running low on vacation, skip Holland and go straight to Bastogne from Brugge and the Battle of the Bulge war memorial. From here it's a quick little jaunt over to Frankfurt where you can return your bike and catch that flight home.

This Grand Tour is basically a huge circle loop through central Europe that crosses several borders and introduces you to a whole host of cultures. Not only will the scenery change dramatically, but the language, architecture, customs, and food will too! As I said earlier, you can cut and paste these trips into whatever fashion you so desire—just be sure you have enough time and are willing to make adjustments toward the end, if things are getting a little tight. Wouldn't want you to miss that plane ride back home! Be open, be flexible and make this a trip of a lifetime! *Bon Voyage!*

# Favorites

I can't tell you how many times I've had friends ask me what rides to recommend in Europe. They have called me, e-mailed me, and sometimes actually flown in to see me just to get my suggestions. I'm honored, but now all you have to do is buy this book! Now the question is—which ride should I go on? Which one is the best? Tough questions, but I am going to make a stab at it in a roundabout way. Different people have different criteria for what kind of ride they prefer. For some it's based on the number of twisties, for others it's the castles, and yet others the history and charm. So I've identified five categories and noted my favorite for each. Regardless, no matter where you travel in Europe you will not be disappointed.

## BEST SCENIC DRIVE

Although many think this should be the Alps, I actually prefer the Mosel River Valley near Frankfurt. The road winds gently beside a flowing river while traditional German towns and villages glide by. Castles perch periodically on craggy hilltops overlooking the valley. A truly heavenly run on a motorcycle. This drive is included in Chapter 6 "Germany's River Valleys and Castles Galore."

## BEST HISTORICAL DRIVE

You may not know this but central France is chock full of history. Chapter 2 "The Medieval Walled Villages of Central France" takes you through old towns that battled during the Hundred Years' War between England and France, then ventures into pre-historic caves before ending with a visit to the infamous WWII town of Oradour-sur-Glane. Oradour is where the Nazis massacred an entire town. The French never rebuilt the city but left the remains as memorial and reminder of the atrocities committed during WWII. This is a great all-around history lesson and the added bonus is the unbelievable scenery along the Dordogne and Lot Rivers.

## BEST TWISTIES ON THE PLANET

Hands down go to Switzerland. The roads through the Swiss Alps twist and turn relentlessly—first going up and then going down. You will need to

*Shouldn't this picture be of you? It's time to start planning that trip of a lifetime and decide which trip through Europe is your favorite. Bon Voyage! Photo by Ron Ayres.*

buy new pegs after you finish up this trip. Just be sure to bring a warm jacket because it's still cold in July at the top of those mountain passes. See Chapter 8 "Heaven on Earth: Into the Heart of Switzerland" for more details.

## BEST "OFF THE BEATEN TRACK" ROADS

Europe is known for being a premier tourist destination. But there are a few spots not as frequented by the suitcase-carrying vagabond. One of these places is in Italy—Umbria and Marches. Most tourists stay north by Florence and miss the charm of this delightful area just south of Tuscany. Imagine Italy in the 1950s and 60s before the throngs of tourists. You'll find it in Umbria and Marches. See Chapter 12 "Italy's Hidden Backroads: Umbria and Marches."

## BEST OVERALL JOURNEY

Personally I prefer the "Band of Brothers Tour" because I'm such a WWII history nut. Since my dad is a WWII veteran, these sites have a more personal meaning for me. In addition, this tour takes you across Europe from France to Holland to Belgium to Germany and Austria, so you get a nice overall view of the continent as well. That combined with the more recent history of WWII make it my favorite run.

# Index